Taxpayer Compliance

Volume 2: Social Science Perspectives

Law in Social Context Series

EDITORS:
Keith Hawkins, Oxford University, Centre for Socio-Legal Studies
John M. Thomas, State University of New York at Buffalo,
    School of Management

Taxpayer Compliance

Volume 2:
Social Science Perspectives

Jeffrey A. Roth and
John T. Scholz, Editors

Panel on Taxpayer Compliance Research
Committe on Research on Law Enforcement
  and the Administration of Justice
Commission on Behavioral and Social Sciences
  and Education
National Research Council

University of Pennsylvania Press
Philadelphia

Copyright © 1989 by the University of Pennsylvania Press
All rights reserved
Printed in the United States of America

Library of Congress Cataloging in Publication Data

Taxpayer compliance.

(Law in social context series)
Bibliography: p.
Includes index.
Contents: v. 1. An agenda for research—
v. 2. Social science perspectives.
1. Taxpayer compliance—United States. 2. Taxation—
Law and legislation—United States. I. Roth, Jeffrey A.,
1945–   . II. Scholz, John T. III. Witte, Ann D.
IV. Series.
HJ4652.T396   1989   336.2′91   88-36250
ISBN 0-8122-8182-9 (v. 1)
ISBN 0-8122-8150-0 (v. 2)
ISBN 0-8122-8187-X (set)

Contents

Introduction

How do citizens go about reporting their income to tax authorities? Why do some report all they have earned, while others cheat as much as they can and still others report more than is required? The lack of clear answers to these questions provided the primary impetus for this volume.

The IRS has a pragmatic interest in learning why some people comply with reporting requirements, while others fail to do so. The question has also intrigued scholars from many disciplines, as well as the community of practitioners who prepare tax returns and advise clients concerning tax matters. The Panel on Taxpayer Compliance Research was created in response to an IRS request to the National Academy of Sciences to critically review previous research on the factors that influence taxpayer compliance with reporting requirements. The panel was asked to state the conclusions that can be drawn from this literature, to identify the gaps in knowledge that future research may be able to fill, and to suggest how the needed research might be carried out. Its conclusions and recommendations appear in Volume 1: *An Agenda for Research*.

Our purposes in publishing this volume are twofold. First, we present papers that apply the perspectives of several social sciences to the study of taxpayer compliance, in order to broaden the range of factors and processes that may be considered as explanations for taxpaying behavior. Second, we hope to show social scientists who are not ordinarily interested in tax matters the fascinating range of theoretical concerns about human behavior that can be fruitfully studied in the context of taxpayer compliance.

The panel approached taxpayer compliance as a scholarly subject in its own right, one that has to borrow relevant theories and methods from a range of social science disciplines. To develop a more comprehensive basis for its research recommendations, the panel commissioned papers by specialists in a variety of scholarly fields, including economics, sociology, psychology, and political science. Although only a few of the authors had previously studied taxpayer compliance, they all had worked in areas within their disciplines that the panel considered relevant to taxpaying. All the authors were asked to illustrate what their specialty might contribute to the understanding of taxpayer compliance. The authors, the panel members, and invited experts from the tax practitioner, tax administrator, and social science communities participated in a three-day Symposium on Taxpayer Compliance Research, at which the papers were presented and discussed. Several rounds of review both before and after the symposium helped sharpen the particular perspective presented in each paper. Of the papers presented, two that focused entirely on methodological issues—one by Peter Schmidt and one by Robert Boruch—were included as appendices to Volume 1. Eight others were selected for inclusion in this volume.

Each paper in this volume attempts to extend the basic view of taxpayer compliance—as a product of self-interest, moral commitment, or both—in some way. In doing so, the authors take a variety of approaches: some review scholarly literatures that attempt to explain other behaviors, make conjectures about how those explanations might (or might not) apply to taxpayer compliance, and suggest research to test the accuracy of those conjectures. One presents a theoretical innovation that incorporates a commonly ignored compliance influence, assistance from tax practitioners, into an economic model of taxpayer compliance. Another discusses income visibility as an explanation of compliance behavior, drawing on an informal ethnographic inquiry.

All eight papers share two characteristics. They emphasize new approaches to understanding taxpayer compliance rather than the findings of previous research, and they present suggestions for future research grounded in their authors' perspectives.

This introduction provides an overview of the conceptual framework shared by the authors and elaborated in Volume 1. It then discusses each of the papers individually.

Framework for Compliance Research

The authors were asked to focus on federal income tax reporting requirements. They worked with a common definition of compliance: the timely filing of an accurate tax return. Under this definition, noncompliance can occur through failure to file a return, misreporting income, or misreporting allowable subtractions from taxable income or taxes due (exemptions, deductions, adjustments, tax credits).

This definition reflects no presumption about a taxpayer's intent because the panel believes that noncompliance can occur for many reasons other than deliberate evasion: for example, as a by-product of customary ways of doing business, through lack of diligence in record keeping, or because a taxpayer doesn't recognize the need to reexamine plausible but incorrect understandings of compliance requirements. In fact, noncompliance need not reduce the taxpayer's reported tax liability. The IRS has estimated that, of all the taxpayers who misreport itemized deductions according to its auditors, one-third fail to claim all to which they are entitled; among illegal nonfilers who have been detected, 40 percent had already prepaid all taxes due through withholding on income and many would have received refunds if they had filed.

The panel's definition of compliance recognizes that occasionally the compliance status of a return is ambiguous, in the sense that the correct application of the law to a particular situation has not yet been determined by the courts. Returns that fall within the bounds of such ambiguity were not considered to be noncompliant and were not a primary focus of the panel. Still, not all taxpayer claims of ambiguity are acceptable within this definition of compliance. Noncompliance occurs, for example, when a taxpayer simply fails to collect the information needed to resolve a question or disingenuously constructs a claim of ambiguous compliance requirements to support positions he or she wants to take.

The authors were asked to share the panel's presumption that self-interest and moral commitment explain part—but only part—of taxpaying behavior. Some taxpayers doubtless make compliance decisions strategically, by weighing the possible benefits from tax evasion against the risks of being detected. But the persistent finding that some taxpayers overreport their tax liability is hard to explain by motives of self-interest alone. Not surprisingly, taxpayers who claim to hold stronger moral commitments to taxpaying also claim to comply more fully—begging the question of why some taxpayers are more committed to obey than others. The authors in this volume were asked to enrich standard explanations such as these by looking both outward and inward—outward toward the environment that shapes compliance requirements, incentives, and values; and inward to the psychological processes through which people respond to complex, uncertain, and potentially value-laden situations.

The taxpaying environment contains people such as family, friends and relatives, social and commercial networks, cultural groups, and tax practitioners who communicate values and information about taxpaying. It also includes the amount and composition of the taxpayer's income and expenditures; in conjunction with legal definitions, these financial attributes determine what legal requirements the taxpayer must follow and also the costs of satisfying those requirements. Financial conditions also affect what opportunities are available for noncompliance, such as income not subject to withholding or information reporting, wealth that can be invested in illegal tax shelters, or an occupation that provides such readily overstated deductions as the business use of one's home or automobile. The taxpaying environment also reflects tax policy as stated in the Internal Revenue Code and tax administration as practiced by tax authorities. The papers in this volume by John Scholz, Robert Kidder and Craig McEwen, Robert Kagan, Steven Klepper and Daniel Nagin, Joel Slemrod, and Suzanne Scotchmer attempt to enhance our understanding of the taxpaying environment and its effects on compliance.

Why People Pay Taxes: Social Science Perspectives

John Scholz begins the volume with a general analysis of the political and institutional context that shapes the American tax environment, both through the tax laws and through the restraints placed on tax administration. Unlike the other papers in this volume, which deal directly with taxpayer behavior, this paper explores the dynamics of the U.S. political system, particularly in the past two decades, that have systematically placed regulatory and resource constraints on tax law enforcement.

   Scholz notes that taxpayer behavior cannot be understood without understanding tax laws and administrative procedures, which in turn reflect the broader institutional and political context of the income tax system. He also points to political features that help to determine the priorities that policy makers place on specific questions about taxpayer compliance behavior. For example, compliance research may confirm the conventional wisdom that a simpler tax law would substantially improve compliance. But acting on such a finding is problematic because of the diversity of the interest groups pressing policy makers to adopt their particular perceptions of a simple but fair tax system. Consequently, understanding taxpayers' behavior is helpful but not sufficient for improving the design and administration of tax laws. Scholz calls for research on the distributional effects of tax enforcement activity and on the reasons why compliance is especially poor among the self-employed and small businesses. He also calls for redirecting tax administration policy analysis, with less emphasis on measuring the revenue directly produced by enforcement activities and more on measuring the compliance effects of those activities. To gain an empirical understanding of these effects, Scholz recommends using randomized field experiments whenever possible.

Robert Kidder and Craig McEwen focus on the social context of the tax environment and social influences on taxpayer behavior. The authors introduce a typology of common situations in which socially structured incentives and motivations lead to compliant or noncompliant behavior. Each type is illustrated with interesting examples. The "socially induced" and "brokered" forms of noncompliance are of particular interest; the paper calls attention to the way in which the social structure of occupations and of tax practice can influence multiple factors in support of noncompliance, noting how little we know at present about social influences on compliance and emphasizing the importance of mapping out the social locations in which the different types of compliance and noncompliance predominate. The authors argue that particular attention should be focused on the occupational networks in which noncompliance is likely to be prevalent. They also propose that ethnographic techniques should be added to the existing repertoires of survey- and government record-based research to improve understanding of the operation of these networks and of other types of compliance and noncompliance.

Kidder and McEwen further point out that understanding the roles of tax professionals, both governmental and private, is essential in understanding taxpayer compliance. Government officials purport to determine for the taxpayer what is acceptable behavior, and private tax professionals are an important force in determining what both government officials and taxpayers are willing to accept as legal tax behavior. The authors suggest ethnographic observations, surveys, and analyses of official records for exploring the influence of tax professionals on taxpayer behavior. They discuss several policy implications in connection with the typology of noncompliance, including a caution against stringent enforcement policies based on an unduly narrow deterrence orientation; policies to reduce particular types of noncompliance may at the same time weaken some of the forces maintaining compliance.

Robert Kagan highlights the relationships among social structure, marketplace transactions, and individual incentives, focusing on the visibility of financial transactions as a key factor. Kagan defines visibility as the "frequency and ease with which [offenses] come to the attention of and can be prosecuted by enforcement officials." Visibility is primarily affected by reporting obligations imposed by law on payers of salaries, interest, and other forms of income and secondarily by the patterns of social and financial transactions that have developed in a given business or occupation. Both of these affect the quality of the "paper trail" left by transactions and therefore the individual's fear of being caught cheating.

After using IRS compliance data to illustrate the importance of visibility to compliance, Kagan amplifies on what these data show, using an informal ethnographic study of housepainters that indicates how various social and economic factors, such as the size of an enterprise and the nature of its customers, combine to affect transaction visibility and compliance rates. Kagan also discusses how social and economic trends (e.g., increased record keeping by third parties, growth of the service sector, societal affluence) are likely to affect compliance, sometimes making certain transactions more visible and sometimes driving more transactions into the less visible "underground economy." In conclusion, Kagan discusses the possibilities and limits of governmentally imposed reporting requirements as a compliance mechanism. He suggests that a concern with imposing excessive paperwork burdens must be balanced against the inequities arising from low compliance levels and the effect of those inequities on tax compliance.

Steven Klepper and Daniel Nagin survey research on criminal deterrence for its relevance to taxpayer compliance. One hypothesis of the deterrence literature has been prominent in taxpayer compliance research to date—that fear of punishment reduces illegal behavior. Klepper and Nagin review some of the difficulties in empirical tests of the deterrence hypothesis and point out the methodological problems of other research that indicates that compliance may be encouraged by commitments to morality and to society. They offer several reasons why deterrence models must be modified before being applied to taxpayer compliance. For example, tax laws, unlike many other laws, are enforced primarily through civil rather than criminal procedures. Furthermore, taxpayer compliance requires not simply refraining from prohibited acts, but also diligence in obtaining necessary information, keeping records, and carrying out computational instructions. While the narrow deterrence hypothesis—that fear of punishment discourages illegal activity—may have limited value in explaining and reducing taxpayer compliance, the broader notion that incentives can be used to encourage compliant behavior may be important in the context of taxpaying.

To test the importance of incentives in explaining and encouraging compliance, Klepper and Nagin call for empirical research focused on specific return items and tax enforcement activities. They note that even exploratory research at that level is rare. They suggest that lags in processing returns and notifying taxpayers of suspected deficiencies can be exploited as natural experiments to measure the effects of those notifications on future compliance. By comparing subsequent-year returns of randomly selected taxpayers who are audited for the IRS Taxpayer Compliance Measurement Program with the returns of other taxpayers, Klepper and Nagin suggest, the compliance effects of the audits could be estimated. They also call for research on how taxpayers' experiences with enforcement actions are shared and used by others to determine their own compliance behavior.

Joel Slemrod focuses on the other side of the incentive coin—taxpayers' costs in complying with tax laws. He first relates compliance costs to the characteristics of the tax law, such as its predictability, difficulty, and manipulability, and then reviews available estimates of the magnitudes of compliance costs for state, federal, and foreign tax systems. The paper also contains a discussion of extended microeconomic models that explicitly recognize the compliance incentive effects associated with the monetary and time costs of determining and reporting true tax liability, of structuring transactions to legally avoid excess tax liability, and of evading tax liability. A suggestion is made that there could be a substantial payoff from refining theoretical models to reflect taxpayers' uncertainty about true tax liability, about the probability of audit, and about penalties for noncompliance.

Slemrod calls for survey research on the complexity of tax laws and its relationship to compliance and for efforts to refine the measurement of tax law attributes, such as their difficulty and manipulability, which affect compliance costs. Because available data suggest that compliance costs may be especially salient to low-income taxpayers, he also calls for time-series analyses of how lower-income taxpayers have responded to the introduction of Forms 1040A and 1040EZ and to other innovations intended to simplify filing requirements. Finally, Slemrod proposes empirical research on the relationship between costs and compliance, using forthcoming IRS data on the compliance costs for specific return items.

Suzanne Scotchmer extends traditional microeconomic models of taxpayer compliance by recognizing that, because reporting requirements are complex and sometimes ambiguous, many taxpayers do not know their true taxable incomes when they file their tax returns. Uncertain taxpayers may simply make a best guess and risk either reporting more tax than necessary or being penalized for paying less than the legally required amount. Alternatively, uncertain taxpayers may pay a better-informed third party to prepare a return that reflects his or her best guess.

Scotchmer shows that if the third parties are not subject to penalties for advising their clients to underreport taxable income, then the returns they prepare will report less income on average than self-prepared returns. However, preparers who advise their clients to underreport are, of course, subject to legal penalties and may face severe penalties by their own professional associations. They must balance the risk of these penalties against market pressures to compete for clients by computing low tax liabilities for which there is a reasonable legal basis. Under these conditions, preparers will demand compensation for the risk of penalties. If they are compensated, it will not be optimal for them to try to eliminate all risk of penalties for underreporting. Therefore, Scotchmer concludes, while no preparer penalty could ever lead to perfect compliance by preparers' clients, the penalties do work as a screening device to eliminate the least competent preparers and those who most frequently advise their clients to underreport their legally taxable income.

John Carroll and Robert Cialdini shift attention to characteristics of the individual's tax schema and psychological processes that may affect compliance. Whereas the previously mentioned papers focus on environmental factors, these authors explore how taxpayers perceive their environment, make taxpaying decisions, develop habits, and change them in ways that are not necessarily explainable in terms of the objective circumstances that are sometimes presumed to affect their decisions.

The theoretical perspective of both papers is based on a recognition of the overwhelming complexity of potentially relevant information and decision criteria involved in even the relatively simple choices facing the taxpayer. These include the lack of clear information about the consequences of noncompliance, as well as multiple and often conflicting personal and social norms and expectations. Simplifying heuristics or decision aids developed to deal with common decisions (e.g., do what is consistent with what you did in the past, do what the authorities tell you to do, do what will keep you out of trouble) may provide reasonable guides to action in normal situations but may lead to behavior very different from the predictions of theories that ignore them. By understanding the actual decision processes and common heuristics used by taxpayers, tax policy makers may be in a better position to counter the effects of heuristics that sometimes support noncompliance.

Carroll provides an extensive review of the decision-making literature developed in psychology and illustrates potential applications of established research findings to understanding tax decisions. He begins with the basic utility-maximizing model that underlies most microeconomic models of taxpayer compliance then reviews the rapidly growing literature known as "behavioral decision theory." This work, which includes prospect theory and judgment heuristics, has documented through empirical studies a number of ways in which individuals violate the assumptions of the most commonly used economic theory. Behavioral decision theory suggests how taxpaying decision processes may be affected by framing the objectives of the decision, editing available information to simplify decisions, adjusting decisions incrementally from an established anchor or reference point, and relying on representative stories that seem plausible rather than on statistical information about probabilities. Carroll also discusses research on the perceptions and decisions of criminals. This work suggests, among other things, that perceptions of the risks of legal penalties are frequently erroneous, that they may be formed after rather than before crimes are committed, that criminals apparently consider only the most immediate consequences of illegal behavior, and that criminals' major decisions are likely to concern how to minimize the risk of getting caught, not whether the risk is worthwhile.

Carroll then suggests that what he calls the cognitive approach to decision making may be particularly useful for understanding tax behavior. It emphasizes limitations of attention, memory, and computational capacity in coping with a complex environment. This approach makes no assumptions about utility-seeking behavior, but rather views the human mind as an information processing system that takes in information from the environment, transforms it, and constructs a response. The paper emphasizes the need to obtain actual descriptions of the decision processes applied by taxpayers when preparing their tax returns and focuses on the issues of taxpayer competence and repertoires of tax decision skills, on the hierarchy of simplified decision rules (e.g., those associated with the decision to consider the possibility of tax evasion behavior versus those associated with the planning of a particular act of tax evasion), and on the environmental factors that activate different levels of decisions. Throughout the review Carroll provides examples of taxpaying behavior relevant to the points being made. He concludes that deterrence research is discouraging for those concerned with reducing noncompliance, and suggests that focusing research on the interactions between competence, motivation, and opportunity may eventually provide a getter guide to policy. An illustrative program of research is outlined utilizing surveys, competency tests, process-tracing techniques, longitudinal studies, and field tests of interventions.

Cialdini examines the role of social cues that may affect individuals' willingness to comply with the demands of others. He has identified procedures commonly used by compliance professionals—individuals in fields such as advertising, negotiation, recruitment, and sales, whose success depends on obtaining others' compliance. He has developed several general principles of influence to explain how these procedures work and reviews them here. The most relevant principle to tax compliance, Cialdini suggests, may be the principle of commitment/consistency: "after committing oneself to a position, one should be more willing to comply with requests for behaviors that are consistent with that position. To the extent that a commitment is active, effortless, public, and viewed as internally motivated, the desire for consistency will enhance the likelihood of behavior consistent with the commitment."

Cialdini elaborates a three-stage process that illustrates how the commitment/consistency principle might be employed to enhance compliance: (1) identify widely accepted norms potentially relevant to taxpaying; (2) focus attention on existing commitments to these norms; and (3) point out the inconsistency between these commitments and taxpayer noncompliance. He also discusses other principles and applications, involving reciprocity (e.g., the IRS provides an unexpected service to which the taxpayer feels an obligation to respond), social validation (e.g., the influence of peers, which may generally support noncompliance), authority (e.g., improving the credibility of the tax law and the IRS to increase people's willingness to follow authority), scarcity (e.g., creating a scarce opportunity to avoid a higher penalty by correcting a deficiency quickly), and friendship/liking (e.g., creating a personal bond between the IRS staff member and the taxpayer). Cialdini argues for more research on social influences on compliance decisions and for considering the possibilities of employing procedures widely used in other areas to enhance compliance. Given the lack of direct research and experience in the tax domain and the potential ethical concerns involved, however, caution would be appropriate in developing research and policy agendas.

Conclusion

As a whole, this set of papers is addressed to citizens and policy makers concerned with broadening their understanding of tax compliance as well as to interested scholars in the social sciences. For those concerned with compliance, the papers provide a challenge to narrow views of the compliance process and some innovative (and relatively untested) ideas for improving tax administration. For the social scientist with only marginal interest in tax matters, the papers illustrate the considerable opportunity for testing theories about human behavior on the cutting edge of various disciplines in the empirically rich domain of taxpayer compliance. The panel hopes that this collection motivates tax administrators, practitioners, and scholars alike to turn their combined attention to an area that is at once a major national problem and a fascinating challenge to those who seek to understand human behavior.

John T. Scholz

1. Compliance Research and the Political Context of Tax Administration

Enforcement agencies in democracies face a common set of political constraints against using government coercion to control the behavior of sovereign citizens. This chapter focuses on the constraints on enforcement of tax laws in the American political context. Unlike the other chapters in this volume, which suggest explanations for why citizens do or do not comply with the tax law, this chapter focuses on some of the basic characteristics of the political system that determine the nature of the interaction between citizen and government. Since one purpose of this volume is to encourage the development of knowledge to improve the tax system, an understanding of constraints affecting tax enforcement policies and the role of research in altering these constraints may encourage the development of more relevant knowledge. Acknowledging the serious constraints on enforcement policies and the restricted role of knowledge in altering these constraints may discourage utopian reformers of current enforcement policies, but the intent is to focus intellectual energies on problems likely to have an effect on the political system.

The first three sections in this chapter outline the political climate, the policy process, and the political culture that shape tax enforcement policies. In brief, I argue that the recent concern with increasing revenue without raising tax rates has sparked interest in compliance issues. The structure of the policy process is biased against enforcement techniques, however, partly because groups adversely affected by proposed enforcement techniques lobby against them while few groups lobby to support them, and partly because influential administrative and congressional policymakers are more concerned with other aspects of tax policy. Finally, the American

Department of Political Science, State University of New York, Stony Brook.

political culture harbors a basic distrust of enforcement authority, particularly in the tax arena, where enforcement activities directly affect all citizens. The fourth section considers the impact of compliance research in the context of these political constraints, and the conclusion suggests a few priorities for research activities intended to improve policy.

The existing literature on the politics of tax policy provides little information on enforcement issues.[1] Consequently, this analysis is based primarily on a brief review of enforcement issues in tax legislation during the previous decade; these issues are enumerated in the appendix. Selected reports, reviews, and congressional hearings on these issues were consulted to supplement interviews with past and present participants in policy deliberations, primarily from the Treasury Department and the Internal Revenue Service.

The Current Political Climate Favors Coercive Tax Enforcement Issues, but Limits IRS Resources Available for Enforcement

The changing political climate in Washington is a major force in determining the fate of tax enforcement issues. The major issues of interest to the president and Congress, the sequence of events, the attention of the press and public opinion, and the dominant concerns of elected officials from both parties establish a political climate in which enforcement proposals are evaluated.

In the early 1970s, the political climate was somewhat unfavorable for enforcement policies. Particularly after the Watergate crisis, attention focused on negative effects associated with tax enforcement. Congressional hearings investigated the IRS Special Services Staff for potential political abuse of investigatory authority,[2] and were concerned with providing adequate controls over invasive and questionable techniques used to gather information for criminal investigations.[3] They expressed grave concern about potential abuse of individual privacy if IRS computer capabilities were expanded for centralized retrieval and analysis of information about individual taxpayers.[4] Both Congress and the administration's Privacy Protection Study Commission were particularly concerned with preventing the disclosure of taxpayer information to unauthorized sources and limiting its use by other agencies.[5] The emphasis on the taxpayer's rather than the enforcement agency's problems was also evident in congressional hearings on the need for the IRS to simplify tax forms and reporting burdens[6] and provide direct services to aid taxpayers.[7]

Despite the attention to potentially negative aspects of coercive enforcement, the administrative capabilities of the IRS were not seriously damaged. While public distrust and concern with government abuse were real in the wake of the Vietnam War and the revelations of Watergate, congressional concerns about IRS enforcement actions prior to the Carter administration also reflected the desire of the Democratic-controlled Congress to discredit the Republican administration. But allegations of political misconduct were not publicly substantiated, and the number of IRS employees began to increase again after stabilizing in the first term of the Nixon administration (Figure 1). The 1976 Tax Reform Act added some constraints on enforcement (see Appendix), but also granted the IRS new powers to regulate tax professionals. Under the Carter administration, the IRS continued to grow, but at a slower pace that reflected Carter's concern with the size and intrusiveness of the federal government. The administration was mildly interested in enforcement issues, and proposed legislation to impose withholding on interest and dividends and on payments to independent contractors. But Congress was less concerned with enforcement, and affected interest groups were able to defeat these measures despite the president's Democratic majority in the Congress.

By 1982, the political climate had changed dramatically regarding enforcement issues. The drop in the inflation rate had reduced automatic revenue increases caused by "bracket creep," which had been a driving force behind tax legislation culminating in the major tax cuts of 1981. The size of the 1981 cuts, combined with the revenue effects of the lower inflation rate and economic recession, increased congressional concerns with growing federal budget deficits. At the same time, journalistic and scholarly reports about the "underground economy" and the "tax gap" had drawn attention to large amounts of unpaid tax liability. Since President Reagan remained committed to the scheduled tax reductions and opposed to new taxes, Congress, and particularly the Senate Finance Committee under the chairmanship of Robert Dole, sought to reduce deficits by approving the use of new enforcement techniques. Coercive enforcement issues allowed leaders to address both the budget deficit and concerns with the inequity of the tax system arising from outright tax evasion. At the same time, the emphasis on revenue issues reduced support for instructional and cooperative enforcement strategies associated with taxpayer services, which were viewed by the administration as revenue losers.

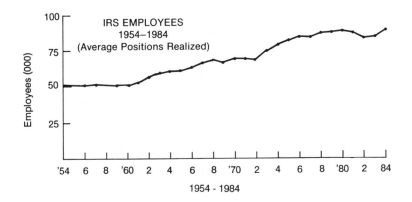

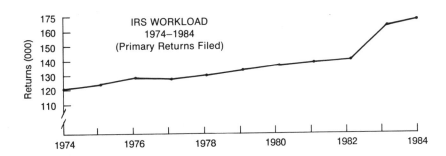

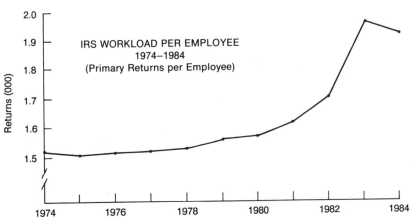

FIGURE I

The change in climate favoring coercive tax enforcement issues reflected a more general change in attitudes toward law and order issues. The rights of defendants had been a major concern during the previous decade, but the need for more effective law enforcement gained increasing attention, particularly in the decisions of the Supreme Court. The underground economy issue, although initially used by conservatives to blame the government for excessive regulation that drove economic activity underground, also focused attention on tax evasion as another rampant form of white collar crime. The result was a shift of concern that enhanced interest in effective enforcement techniques and reduced concern for their undesired consequences.

The Tax Equity and Fiscal Responsibility Act (TEFRA) of 1982 brought compliance issues to the forefront of tax policy; it included tough new measures as well as controversial enforcement provisions that tax administration officials had sought unsuccessfully for many years (see Appendix). The Deficit Reduction Act of 1984 also included several tax enforcement provisions. On the other hand, the dramatic repeal of two enforcement provisions in the year following enactment—withholding on dividend and interest in 1983, and contemporaneous record-keeping requirements for business use of automobiles in 1985—indicate the continued ability of interest groups to successfully oppose enforcement actions even when the prevailing climate favors tougher enforcement measures.

Although the Tax Reform Act of 1986 added only minor penalty provisions to enhance IRS enforcement powers, a major thrust behind many of the reforms was to eliminate provisions of the tax code that fostered noncompliance. Passive loss limitations on tax shelters, the 2 percent floor on miscellaneous deductions, the 7.5 percent floor on medical deductions, and increases in standard deductions all aimed at limiting the use of deductions and exemptions that had been subjected to considerable misuse. The revenue-enhancing effect of these limitations was more directly responsible for their passage, but the compliance effects were also discussed by legislators during consideration of the bill.

Ironically, budgetary support for enforcement continued to decline even as support for innovative enforcement techniques increased. The number of IRS employees had increased slowly during the Carter administration, but declined in the early years of the Reagan administration, reaching its lowest point in eight years during the year TEFRA was passed (Figure 1). Although the number of employees increased again in 1983 and 1984, the workload increased even faster because of the growth in the number of taxpayers and the increasing complexity of tax laws and the reporting situations of taxpayers. The increase in the number of returns processed per employee shown in Figure 1 reflects the upward trend of most other measures of workload as well. As a consequence, the percentage of returns audited annually has continued to fall. The difficulties in processing all returns with available manpower became apparent during the 1985 filing season.

The constraint on the IRS budget is particularly puzzling, given the general agreement that an increase in the number of IRS examiners will generate direct revenues substantially greater than their salary costs. If revenue concerns increase the attraction of enforcement issues for tax policies, why do they not lead to increased IRS budgets? The revenue argument made by the IRS has been explicitly rejected by the Carter and Reagan administrations; moreover, it has been employed with mixed results for at least thirty years. Two factors weaken the revenue argument, one related to other policy goals and the other to the institutional structure of budget decisions.

First, the revenue gain derived from increasing IRS examiners does not compensate for the negative impact of additional highly visible IRS employees on such concerns as the growth of government bureaucracy, the oppressiveness of the federal government presence, and the costs imposed on the private sector by increased IRS actions. Second, revenue arguments that appeal to tax policy decision makers responsible for meeting revenue targets are less effective in the specialized budgeting process in the Office of Management and Budget and in congressional appropriations committees, where the dominant concern has been in making "equitable" cuts for all agencies to reach spending targets set at a different level. The IRS has done just slightly better than other agencies in the current climate of government austerity, with manpower increases of 6.4 percent during the last decade, compared with 5.7 percent for total federal government civilian employment.[8] A strategy that cuts back on welfare and service agencies while giving the IRS more examiners to go after taxpayers appears to be politically troublesome.

In conclusion, in the current political climate it appears likely that enforcement measures will remain of interest to tax policy makers and that budget constraints may become even worse. Several compliance proposals were included in tax bills introduced in 1985 (U.S. Congress, 1985), and congressional interest has been growing in amnesty programs modeled on successful revenue-generating state programs. According to some legislative analysts, concerns with the deficit have extended the search for revenue-producing solutions to compliance problems whose revenue impact would have been considered inconsequential in the past.

The impact of current deficit concerns on the IRS budget is less certain, although it seems likely that current budget constraints will continue. Part of the problem is that Congress and the administration appear to have conflicting priorities for IRS budget increases. The administration has approved increases for targeted programs that produce direct revenue yields and that automate data systems in order to reduce the number of employees—the documented revenue-generating success of a 1983 initiative has led to a provision in the president's 1986 budget to increase the number of examination employees by 2,500 annually in 1987, 1988, and 1989, and funds spent on upgrading computer capabilities have tripled in recent years from the annual average of $33.5 million for the decade prior to 1982.

Congress, on the other hand, and particularly the Democratic-controlled House, tends to favor the traditional IRS argument for allocating increases to all IRS functions in order to support a broad strategy for maintaining voluntary compliance levels. But when Congress added more than a thousand positions to the 1986 budget to improve the IRS return-processing capability in order to avoid the problems that occurred during the 1985 filing season, the president disagreed and vetoed the bill. It appears likely that the pressure to reduce deficits under the recently passed budget reconciliation act at best will enhance interest only in enforcement programs with direct revenue yields and at worst will reduce IRS and other agency budgets proportionally. In either case, programs that cannot demonstrate the magnitude of their impact on total revenue collection are likely to lose positions to direct revenue producers.

The Policy Process is Biased Against Enforcement Issues

The importance of federal tax policy for individuals, corporations, and the government makes it one of the most active and important legislative arenas, involving all major policy-making institutions and most major lobbying groups on a continuing basis. In this section we will discuss the difficulty legislative proposals for enforcement authority face in gaining attention and support in this intensive policy arena. The argument in brief is that interest groups seldom support enforcement proposals and actively oppose such proposals that affect their members. Administrative and congressional leaders must take the initiative to overcome interest group opposition, but enforcement is only a minor part of tax reform issues these groups favor. The IRS is the primary originator, analyst, and advocate for enforcement issues, but it is only a minor player in the policy process. Consequently, enforcement issues have difficulty gaining legislative approval even when the political climate is potentially favorable.

INTEREST GROUPS OPPOSE ENFORCEMENT ISSUES

The bias against enforcement issues in the policy process arises primarily because interest groups oppose enforcement issues that affect them adversely, but seldom lobby in favor of enforcement issues that would reduce noncompliance by other groups. Opposition begins during the planning stage, when groups try to get enforcement measures eliminated from the administration bill before it is introduced in Congress. It continues during congressional consideration of the bill—even a casual reading of congressional hearings on controversial enforcement issues (e.g., withholding on independent contractors, on dividends and interest) reveals the typical situation in which an administrative official supports a measure against a number of affected groups that argue against it. Opposition continues even after legislation is signed into law—withholding on interest and dividends was passed in 1982 but repealed in 1983, contemporaneous record requirements for automobile deductions were passed in 1984 but repealed in 1985, and restaurant associations continue to work for repeal of the tip income reporting requirement passed in 1982.

Interest groups affect legislation by making policy makers aware of the arguments against enforcement proposals. In formal hearings and in private meetings, they appeal to political values (to be discussed in the following section), critique the arguments and analyses supporting the proposals, and provide more information and analyses opposing the proposals. They remind members of Congress of past and future campaign contributions—members of the tax-writing committees, and particularly the chairmen, receive considerably greater contributions than the average congressman. They organize grass-root campaigns for voters and influential community leaders to contact members of Congress in their districts (as financial institutions organized a massive mail campaign in 1983 to repeal withholding on interest and dividends.)

Why is it that groups seldom lobby in favor of measures to reduce noncompliance by others? Most likely, this behavior stems from the basic collective choice problem of tax policy that arises from the separation of taxing and spending decisions (Manley, 1970; Reese, 1980; J. Witte, 1985). Self-interest groups prefer to be "free riders," counting on political leaders to raise revenue sufficient for authorized spending while focusing the group's scarce lobbying resources only on measures directly affecting its tax payments. Each group opposes revenue-gaining tax proposals that would increase the group's tax payments and supports revenue-losing measures that would decrease them. Thus, controversial revenue-gaining measures in the administration's proposed legislation tend to be eliminated in Congress, while the revenue-losing measures tend to be accepted (Manley, 1970). It is not in the interest of any group to protect the common treasury, a thankless position that is left by default to administrative and congressional leaders. The strategy is aptly summarized by an adage attributed to Senator Long of the Senate Finance Committee: "Don't tax you, don't tax me, tax that fellow behind the tree."

Interest group opposition to enforcement issues, which are inherently revenue-raising, is a special case of this general phenomenon. In addition, many groups are vulnerable on a number of issues on which a tougher interpretation of existing statutes by the IRS could change questionable but currently accepted practices into a "compliance problem." Vulnerability further reduces the incentive of these groups to favor added authority and enforcement resources for the IRS that one day might be used against them. For such vulnerable groups, the strategy may be summarized as, "Don't pick on you, don't pick on me . . ."

Perhaps the greatest source of opposition is from established lobbying groups only indirectly affected by proposed enforcement measures. For example, financial institutions have lobbied against withholding on interest because of the direct costs they would bear and, more importantly, the losses in deposits they feared would result from withholding. A number of industries including real estate, insurance, and construction successfully opposed withholding provisions for payments to independent contractors because the benefit of unpaid taxes from the unreported income is reflected in lower labor costs. The restaurant industry less successfully opposed reporting of tip income by waiters for the same reason, just as automobile manufacturers unsuccessfully opposed restrictions on personal use of luxury business cars. Lobbying by those benefiting directly from noncompliance is less common because the benefits are generally too diffuse to overcome the problems of organizing and the moral position of defending noncompliance would weaken lobbying efforts, although the spontaneous grass-root demands for repeal of the contemporaneous record-keeping requirements for automobile expenses in 1985 indicates that such lobbying can occasionally be effective.

Enforcement proposals occasionally gain some lobbying support. In the current political climate, unaffected groups offer tacit support for enforcement measures to the extent that they reduce the pressure for tax increases or more unattractive sources of revenue. At times, one group will actively lobby for an enforcement proposal aimed at another group to gain more equal treatment; unions supported withholding on interest and dividends in 1982 to equalize the treatment of salaried and other forms of income. In the past five years, a few organizations have become more supportive of general enforcement measures. The Tax Section of the American Bar Association and the American Institute of Certified Public Accountants (AICPA) have initiated studies of compliance issues, and have cautiously supported proposals for improving enforcement capabilities. Such interest group support may improve the legislative chances of enforcement measures, but the inherent logic of interest group opposition will undoubtedly remain a major limitation on legislative initiatives to improve compliance through coercive enforcement.

Treasury and Congressional Leadership Can Counterbalance Interest Groups, But Are Only Marginally Interested in Enforcement

Interest group bias against enforcement proposals is obviously not always successful in preventing them from being enacted. But administrative and legislative leaders must be well prepared and willing to do battle in order to counteract interest group opposition. And enforcement issues are not generally exciting because the electoral incentives for members of Congress in particular are primarily to pass new legislation, not necessarily to see that the laws are enforced. But when congressional and administrative leaders do become interested in enforcement, they have means for overcoming interest group opposition.

The conventional wisdom about tax reform strategy is that reforms to remove special exemptions of certain groups must be balanced by rate reductions for larger groups who will support the bill as a whole. Thus groups must be targeted carefully to ensure majority support for the administration's proposed legislation. The 1982 and 1984 legislation suggests that the reduced rates are not as necessary if a broad coalition is sufficiently concerned with the deficit to support a tax bill that increases revenue without raising general rates. But the careful targeting of groups is still necessary to get majority support. (For political conditions under which taxes are likely to be raised, see Hansen, 1983.)

Revenue estimates and general revenue targets have become the major tool used by leadership to control the revenue reduction pressures from interest groups and their representatives on the congressional tax-writing committees. Revenue estimates associated with each item in the bill are used to shift the burden of change to interest groups opposing each item—for each item removed, the opponents are under pressure to find an alternative source of revenue (Reese, 1980). As long as congressional leaders and the president are committed to the overall revenue goals, this revenue reconciliation strategy can be used quite effectively.

For example, when restaurant lobbyists succeeded in getting the requirement to report tip income knocked out of the Senate version of TEFRA in 1982, the Finance Committee Chairman, Senator Dole, immediately got approval for a "one and one-half martini lunch" limitation on business deductions in order to raise the equivalent amount to meet the bill's revenue goal. The restaurant industry, caught off guard in the turbulent Senate session, quietly agreed afterward to accept the income-reporting measure if this even greater tax threat were eliminated. The change was made during the House-Senate Conference (Congressional Quarterly Almanac, 1982).

Tax policy leaders continuously get locked into such tests of strength with influential lobbies. Once a leader's reputation for controlling the tax process becomes involved, even very powerful lobbying campaigns may be opposed. At such times, the substantive issue becomes less important than who wins. Before it was passed in 1982, withholding on dividends and interest had been defeated at least twice (1962, 1979) because of the ability of financial institutions to mobilize grass-root pressure in opposition to withholding. But in 1982, this campaign failed as astute parliamentary leadership managed to preserve the measure in the final bill despite its unpopularity among rank and file members of Congress. Only in the following year, when financial institutions launched a massive mail campaign and leadership could no longer control the majority in each chamber that favored repeal of the motion, did the leadership give in, and even then they added more stringent reporting requirements in place of the repealed withholding requirements.

Congressional leadership, particularly the chairmen of the House Ways and Means and the Senate Finance Committees, share with Treasury the task of achieving revenue targets while balancing the many interests affected in a tax bill and deciding which groups to go after for revenue increases. But enforcement issues have relatively minor interest for tax policy leaders because of their small revenue impacts compared with other proposed changes in the tax code. For example, the information-reporting provisions that provided the biggest compliance items in the 1986 act were estimated by the Senate Finance Committee to eventually produce $648 million annually, whereas the simple elimination of the deduction for a working spouse produced $6 billion, and big ticket items like the repeal of corporate investment tax credit brought in over $32 billion.

Despite this relative insignificance, Treasury and Congress have become more interested in enforcement issues in recent years as the search has intensified for new methods of raising revenues without raising tax rates. They frequently disagree on priorities, however. Treasury proposed legislation on withholding during the Carter administration, but the lack of strong presidential backing led to defeat in a Congress fully controlled by the president's party. On the other hand, members of Congress initially paid more attention to the underground economy issue than did the administration, and played an active role in formulating the enforcement proposals in TEFRA.

The ability of Treasury and congressional leadership to craft complex tax legislation without undue reliance on interest groups can be attributed to the distinguished professional staff of the Joint Committee on Taxation (JCT) for Congress and the Treasury's Tax Legislative Counsel (TLC) for legislative drafting and the Office of Tax Analysis (OTA) for economic analysis (Manley, 1970; Reese, 1980; J. Witte, 1985). The ability to take initiative on enforcement matters is limited, however, by the under-developed capability to analyze revenue and compliance impacts of proposed enforcement legislation. During the 1982 planning of TEFRA, for example, the analysis and revenue projections for enforcement measures were initially generated by the IRS and adopted with skepticism by the JCT and OTA, who as a rule cut IRS estimates considerably before adopting them. When enforcement became a major issue, congressional leaders came directly to the IRS during initial planning (a very rare event), and a congressional liaison official was housed in the IRS to expedite analysis. Since then, neither the JCT nor OTA have developed either research methodologies or staff expertise to provide independent research on revenue impacts of enforcement proposals or compliance impacts of other tax measures. Compliance issues continue to be given low priority.

While leadership support is essential for defending enforcement provisions against opposition groups, individual members of Congress have occasionally played important roles in championing enforcement proposals, particularly when obvious tax abuses are documented and reported in the media. For example, Congressman Rosenthal took an active interest in supporting the Information Returns Program (IRP) that matched individual returns with information from other sources, and Rosenthal and others provided continuing support for the Taxpayer Services Program. Congressman Stark initiated efforts to crack down on the personal use of luxury cars owned by businesses partly in response to an outrageous advertisement encouraging the financing of personally used luxury cars through questionable tax write-offs. In general, however, members of Congress not in leadership positions have little incentive to become involved in supporting enforcement issues. Although a relatively large proportion of constituency mail they receive is related to IRS as compared with other agencies, letters generally complain about difficulties in correcting IRS mistakes or getting needed forms rather than about particular enforcement actions. Furthermore, the same free-rider problem that affects interest groups is transferred through electoral pressures to members of Congress, who are rewarded for the tax liabilities they reduce for constituents, not for enforcement measures that marginally raise the general revenues.

IRS is the Primary Advocate for Enforcement Issues, But Plays a Limited Policy Role

Tax policy makers in the administration generally consider enforcement issues to be the responsibility of the IRS. In response to problems encountered in the field, the IRS routinely develops suggested legislative proposals to strengthen enforcement. Operating divisions send their suggestions to the IRS Office of Legislative Liaison, where proposals are further analyzed for their legislative potential and forwarded to the Treasury Department for possible inclusion in the administration's annual legislative program.

But IRS proposals must compete for attention with current presidential interests and the standard Treasury Department interests in broadening the revenue base by reducing exemptions and deductions and improving economic efficiency through changes in the tax code (Reese, 1980). Proposals that do not aid the primary goals set for a particular administrative bill get little attention, particularly if they are likely to meet strong opposition for the small amount of revenue involved. Indeed, until the last few years the Treasury Department did not have an established review procedure for IRS legislative proposals.

The minor legislative role of the IRS reflects in part the centralization of legislative initiatives at the level of the cabinet and the president that has developed in the past several decades (Wayne, 1982). All formal statements to Congress from the IRS, as from all other agencies, must first be cleared through the Treasury Department and the OMB. Although enforcement issues have been encouraged and actively sought by the Treasury Department since TEFRA in 1982, accepted issues are those most relevant to the administration's current interests, not necessarily the most pressing enforcement problems as viewed by the IRS. For example, even when compliance issues became of interest in the planning of TEFRA, the initial IRS list containing proposals that the operating divisions had been pushing unsuccessfully in previous years was set aside, and a new list was developed that linked enforcement proposals more directly to increased revenue. The "tax gap" research and data resources that could provide estimates of potential revenue gains thus became more important than field experience for developing and supporting priorities among enforcement proposals for TEFRA.

Of course, if the administration ignores their legislative proposals, some government agencies take their case to Congress by proxy, working through lobbyists for groups who would benefit from the legislation. The IRS faces two handicaps that prevent such indirect representation on enforcement matters. First, IRS efforts since the 1950s to develop an apolitical, "professional" organization have minimized contacts with potential political allies. The resultant lack of a supportive constituency reduces the agency's legislative clout, although professionalism increases the willingness of Congress to grant broader enforcement authority and reduces partisan pressure to use enforcement resources for political purposes. Second, most potential allies would want less rather than more enforcement. Unlike agencies that perform services desired by their recipients, the revenue collection function is one service that most groups want weakened rather than strengthened, at least as it effects the group directly.

Enforcement resources and ongoing activities are also affected by the lack of a supportive constituency. The appropriations subcommittees in the House and Senate hear from active supporters for more drug enforcement and for continued subsidies to the Post Office, but few interest groups fight for higher IRS budgets. And when disputes with organized groups arise over IRS enforcement actions, organized groups with powerful lobbying capacities can threaten to introduce legislation intended to restrict IRS authority. Of course, politicization imposes risks for lobbyists as well if the administration supports the IRS, so there are incentives for the IRS and concerned groups to reach agreement on controversial enforcement matters. The IRS is well aware of the problems caused by its political isolation and has considered more active cooperation with professional groups like the ABA and AICPA who have demonstrated their concern with compliance problems. But the potential problems in seeking a more active political role for the IRS are also well known, and no consensus seems to have emerged within the IRS favoring political activism.

In summary, the legislative task from the IRS perspective is not simply to propose legislative solutions to the most pressing enforcement problems, but more generally to select and develop proposals supportable by careful analysis that also fit with the president's and Treasury Department's legislative agenda. IRS research on compliance has played an important part in the process of developing arguments to support enforcement proposals, although even a well-documented proposal will not even gain a place on the legislative agenda unless political conditions are right. Given the unpredictability of appropriate political conditions and the short time available to analyze issues once the time is right, the most appropriate role of compliance research may be to produce evidence about the magnitude of specific compliance problems and the effectiveness of alternative enforcement techniques that can be used on short notice when the issue becomes politically viable.

The American Political Culture Distrusts
Enforcement Authority

Throughout the history of the income tax system in America, the benefits of increased enforcement capabilities claimed by policy proponents have been challenged by opponents emphasizing the social costs associated with police powers (Hoeflich, 1983). Legislative debate on enforcement issues reveals the basic American dilemma over the use of coercive powers of government. As with the police and other enforcement agencies, IRS enforcement activities are recognized as essential to uphold necessary laws, but are also strictly limited by a deep-seated aversion to the use of police powers. This aversion imposes one more difficulty in gaining political approval of new techniques or additional enforcement resources. One policy maker summarized the basic tradeoff for tax enforcement issues in the following terms:

On the one hand, there is the need to prevent gross abuse which brings the tax law into disrepute by those who flaunt their evasion in front of others, conversationally and in practice, until the taxpayer morale is undermined and fraud becomes socially acceptable. On the other hand, there is the need to avoid excessive prying into personal affairs and elaborate record keeping in instances where abuse is not a threat or a fact (Smith, 1961:70).

To build an effective legislative coalition, interest groups who oppose enforcement proposals out of self-interest must attract the support of others with less direct stake in the issue by justifying their position in terms of public costs and benefits important in the American political culture. The importance of different values changes with the political climate and the particular policy issue, but most arguments favoring and opposing enforcement measures are based on the following set of factors.

The most obvious benefit of increased enforcement is derived from the added revenue collected both directly from evaders who are caught and indirectly from potential cheaters who are deterred by the increased threat of getting caught. By reducing noncompliance, revenue can be increased without increasing general or marginal tax rates.

The revenue issue is most persuasive when enforcement is targeted at major noncompliers, not at petty cheating by the average taxpayer. If we compare a system in which everyone cheated by the same percentage with a system in which no one cheated, the system with evaders could raise the same revenue as the system with honest taxpayers by adjusting the tax rate rather than by increasing enforcement. Marginal tax rates would be higher, but these rates are arbitrarily set by political processes anyway, and the costs and intrusiveness of more intensive enforcement would be avoided. In the 1982 TEFRA legislative debates, for example, the revenue increases expected from enforcement provisions were politically appealing because they were collected from sources where noncompliance was relatively high. Only dishonest taxpayers would have to pay more. The 1986 Tax Reform Act also justified the elimination of certain deductions in part because they were subjected to misuse. Thus equity, not revenue per se, provides the primary justification of enforcement in our current tax system.

Targeting areas of blatant noncompliance is also important to preserve the perception of fair enforcement that is considered important to maintain the relatively high levels of "voluntary tax compliance" achieved in the United States. Blatant noncompliance associated with high-income individuals or with socially disapproved practices make particularly attractive targets for enforcement legislation even when expected revenue gains are small. For example, enforcement initiatives attacking abusive tax shelters and luxury cars written off as business expenses passed Congress with less extensive evidence about revenue increases than other enforcement legislation.

Of course, tax policy debates have produced no general consensus on a "fair" allocation of the tax burden, as Eisenstein (1961) has discussed in detail. Furthermore, the tax policy process inevitably approves special tax provisions favorable to the influential groups of the moment (Surrey, 1957; J. Witte, 1985), leading to even greater ambivalence about the fairness of the code. Ambivalence about the tax code leads to ambivalence toward noncompliance as well. For example, conservatives have justified underground economy activities because they provide entrepreneurs with relief from excessive governmental intervention, while liberals have argued that the underground economy allows poorer taxpayers to evade taxes that the rich can avoid through legal loopholes (De Grazia, 1980). Nonetheless, fairness remains an important concern when targeting enforcement proposals at different populations; programs to uncover hidden income have greater appeal if targeted at criminals or high-income professionals than at moonlighting blue collar workers or mothers with part-time home-based selling jobs.

Arguments by opponents of enforcement proposals emphasize the negative aspects or social costs of enforcement, most of which reflect the strong American belief in individual freedom and aversion to coercive state powers that pervades our political culture. Of course, most groups would strongly approve of coercion for certain purposes. But the purposes that justify coercion differ among different groups. Furthermore, people do not trust the government to be fair, wise, and discerning in the use of coercive powers, in part because of conflicting pressures from politically influential groups about the appropriate uses of coercion. To avoid the mistaken or inappropriate use of coercion, some of the benefits of appropriate coercion are likely to be sacrificed even in the case of street crime. Particularly in the case of tax enforcement, in which mistaken coercion is most likely to affect politically active middle- and upper-income Americans, the tendency is even stronger to minimize the likelihood of abusive coercion, which is perceived as the worst potential outcome.[9]

As a result of this constraint on coercive powers, the enforcement philosophy in the IRS, as in most American enforcement agencies, emphasizes "voluntary compliance" by the average citizen, with coercive techniques to be employed sparingly and prosecution to be reserved for the few "bad apples" who blatantly disregard the law (Scholz, 1984). This constraint enhances the constitutional principle of checks and balances on the power of the primary institutions of government. Because the coercive power of government is limited, political elites in America are constrained to pass laws supported by the majority of affected citizens, particularly those bearing the costs imposed by the law. On an institutional level, political constraints on IRS budgets and discretionary authority to interpret and enforce the tax laws increase elected officials' controls over administrative discretion. And tax policy is one area in which Congress has demonstrated constant interest in preserving detailed controls over interpretations, even at the cost of enforcement efficiency.

The arguments against specific tax enforcement proposals take several forms: the intrusiveness of "big brother"; the need to protect honest taxpayers from erroneous, unreasonable, and arbitrary application of invasive enforcement techniques (and especially collection techniques); the individual's right to privacy; the need to avoid burdening taxpayers or third parties with unnecessary paperwork, reporting, and complex filing requirements. Each of these topics has been the primary subject of congressional hearings in the 1970s (listed above), and each is usually mentioned by at least some enforcement opponents in congressional debate. The persuasiveness of the opposition's argument is enhanced to the extent that the proposed technique affects both honest and dishonest taxpayers, particularly when the burden is placed disproportionately on a group that elicits political sympathies (e.g., the elderly, the poor, small businesses). Successful enforcement proposals require that techniques be focused on known compliance problems and not impose undue costs, harassment, or intrusive requirements on other taxpayers. The less focused the technique, the greater the problem must be to justify an intrusion. A few plausible horror stories about the unreasonable effects of a proposed enforcement measure on some innocent group can destroy the credibility even of a measure to correct a well-documented compliance problem.

The April 30, 1979, hearings of the House Ways and Means Committee on the proposal to require financial institutions to withhold taxes from dividend and interest payments provide a typical example of how arguments are used to oppose enforcement matters. Financial institutions opposed the measure in part because of the administrative burden they might face, but primarily because of the likely loss of deposits due to the payment of taxes from savings and investment accounts. They attempted to discredit government estimates of the amount of revenue withholding would raise.

And they argued that costs to financial institutions already weakened by the effects of escalating inflation would be quite high and that the withholding would reduce effective interest earned even by honest taxpaying investors, thereby reducing even further the rate of savings in America. The more powerful institutions also championed the politically more popular cause of weaker groups, arguing that the low-income elderly who depended on interest income and small financial companies that did not have automated record keeping would bear excessively difficult burdens. Hypothetical stories about the effects on the elderly were politically threatening enough that the Treasury Department proposed to exempt certain elderly persons despite the enforcement problem this would cause. The measure did not pass, most likely because even those in Congress sympathetic to withholding were more concerned at that time about the state of the economy and the stability of the savings and loan industry.

In sum, political consideration of proper tax enforcement levels reflects a complex tradeoff. Up to a certain point, increased enforcement activities focused on appropriate pockets of noncompliance are beneficial in reducing necessary marginal tax rates and in increasing the equity and taxpayer support of the tax system. Beyond that point, however, the costs, harassment, and intrusiveness inevitably associated with increased coercive enforcement outweigh the social gains and may in fact diminish support to the extent that revenue may be decreased rather than increased. Given the subjective nature of this tradeoff, the optimal level of enforcement changes not only with innovations in enforcement and evasion strategies, but also with public perceptions and the political climate in which evaluations are made.

The Impact of Compliance Research on Enforcement Policies

The brief survey undertaken for this paper offers no definitive conclusions about particular kinds of taxpayer compliance research most likely to influence enforcement policy. Indeed, the recent literature on the role of social science research in the policy process (see Lynn, 1979; Hammond, 1984) is generally skeptical about the possibility of designing a research program to produce specific policy results. What emerges from this literature is the impression that no discernible formula exists for ensuring that any given research program will have an impact on the legislative or administrative process. Research is recognized as playing a more unpredictable, indirect, latent, and cumulative role in defining policy issues, suggesting alternative approaches and focusing policy debates (Wildavsky, 1979; Hammond, 1984).

Derthick and Quirk's (1985) study of deregulation, a policy strongly influenced by "disinterested economic analysis," provides an analytic framework for the different kinds of policy influence that may be relevant to developing a research agenda. Their study integrates several different perspectives from the policy analysis literature into three different stages of research and analysis appropriate for corresponding phases of policy development. Each stage of research takes place in different organizational settings and poses different analytical problems. In the awareness stage, analysts document a particular problem and increase awareness of various policy alternatives, with little concern for short-term political feasibility. In the agenda-setting stage, analysis is introduced into the policy process as advice to political leaders potentially interested in initiating changes. Finally, the policy negotiation stage involves the development of specific proposals and arguments to appeal to different coalitions of interest required to enact legislation and change administrative procedures.

Research on the underground economy provides an instructive example of the awareness stage of research that eventually led to TEFRA. In the mid-1970s several studies by economists based on different indirect measurements found successively higher estimates of unrecorded economic transactions (Simon and A. Witte, 1981; Henry, 1983). In 1976, Henry estimated unreported income at $25 to $50 billion for 1973. A year later, Gutmann estimated that unrecorded transactions accounted for $176 billion over the official 1976 GNP estimates. In 1978, Feige presented a third approach which estimated the "irregular economy" at $369 billion in 1976 and $708 billion in 1978. Although journalistic articles about the irregular economy have appeared sporadically since the early 1970s, Guttman's estimates in particular attracted national attention from major newspapers, magazines, and television in 1978 (Henry, 1983), inspiring more investigative reporting of the underground economy by journalists. The combination of academic studies and broad media coverage of underground economy issues stirred congressional interest, particularly among some members of the tax, economic policy, and IRS oversight panels, which initiated the second stage of analysis.

Several factors that increased the influence of the underground economy studies during this first policy stage were also noted as important by Derthick and Quirk (1985). First, there was a growing consensus among researchers (economists in most cases) that a problem existed, and sophisticated methods were developed to measure the extent of the problem. Second, the problem could be explained in everyday language and was made plausible by journalistic and casual observations. The importance of sophisticated analysis to legitimate the journalistic observations and provide some estimate of the magnitude of the problem was noted by several observers, even though the methods used for the original estimates were later criticized by economists. Third, the problem was politically adaptable, in that liberals and conservatives alike could find ideological support in the underground economy issue, just as they could in the deregulation issue. One possible conclusion, then, is that compliance research to focus attention on a particular issue (e.g., the impact of normative appeals on compliance) need not be overly concerned with immediate policy relevance, but is more effective to the extent that different methods of study generally approved by the research community yield similar results, the results provide some notion of the magnitude of effects, and the analyses extend common sense explanations of compliance behavior. As Derthick and Quirk mention, the academic setting in which such research generally takes place, and the consequent indifference to political feasibility, is potentially advantageous in expanding the scope of issues under study that might become relevant as political conditions change.

The second or agenda-setting stage of analysis is more directly tied to policy-making institutions, as is illustrated by the further development of the underground economy issue. When Congress became interested in the underground economy issue, the Carter administration, in order to maintain the initiative on tax matters, created an IRS task force to estimate the tax loss associated with underreporting of tax income. Somewhat later, the Joint Economic Committee in Congress commissioned an independent study by nongovernmental researchers (Simon and A. Witte, 1980). Congressional hearings were postponed until the completion of the IRS study in 1979, and were generally critical of the study's low estimates of lost revenue and the conservative assumptions that excluded several areas of evasion from the study.[10] This criticism prompted the IRS to undertake a more extensive analysis of components of the "tax gap" (IRS, 1983), a project that developed the data bases and methods of analysis that played a direct role in initiating the list of revenue-enhancing enforcement measures proposed in TEFRA.

The link between research and policy is less dependent on the credibility of particular research methodologies or clarity of findings than on the credibility of appropriately placed research brokers, individuals familiar with both the research and policy-making worlds who can summarize the relevant implications of available studies for current issues of interest to decision makers (Lynn, 1979; Sundquist, 1978). Personal contacts and informal networks connecting researchers with key decision makers and their support staff provide an important conduit for research findings in an increasing number of policy areas (Heclo, 1978). Such networks already connect tax policy makers with research on the economic effects of the tax code, including members who are current and former tax policy makers, staff members of the OTA and JCT, and academic researchers in universities and policy-oriented research institutions. Informal networks to evaluate compliance issues for TEFRA developed rapidly around key individuals in the IRS, the Treasury Department, and the staff of the tax-writing committees, but no existing networks on compliance research could be tapped for broader academic research. Several developments may encourage more permanent networks and more prominent brokers to interpret taxpayer compliance research: major compliance conferences have been organized by the ABA and IRS, panels of compliance researchers have been scheduled at many professional organizations of scholars and practitioners (e.g., the National Tax Association-Tax Institute of America), research projects have been developed by the National Academy of Sciences, the American Bar Foundation, and the Arthur Young Foundation, and the IRS has expanded its efforts to involve academic researchers in its own research. Unfortunately, disciplinary boundaries continue to isolate the growing number of academic compliance researchers, and the main policy-making institutions (especially OTA, TLC, and JCT) remain outside these growing networks.

Finally, the policy negotiation stage, according to Derthick and Quirk, requires analytic capabilities that can evaluate proposals on multiple criteria relevant to different policy actors and can generate new results rapidly as negotiations change initial assumptions. The OTA, TLC, and JCT staffs perform such analysis routinely during mark-up sessions on tax bills, and have established a level of credibility that makes possible the complex legislative task of tax code alterations (Reese, 1980). When compliance legislation is being negotiated, an IRS legislative liaison official, working under a Treasury representative, would generally be the most knowledgeable analyst present, since the other staffs have little incentive to develop expertise in enforcement issues. The IRS Research Division, particularly since its reorganization in the early 1980s, has produced supporting evidence and studies for legislative initiatives that have been well received by policy makers. Although the OTA and JCT generally reduce IRS revenue impact estimates for enforcement proposals by adopting more conservative assumptions, IRS studies, particularly those associated with the Taxpayer Compliance Measurement Program (TCMP), have established considerable credibility despite the major problems of measurement and estimation affecting compliance issues.

In describing the role they play in the legislative process, IRS analysts note that the characteristics of successful research support for enforcement policy initiatives depend on the sympathy members of Congress may feel for the group or groups most likely to suffer. For example, concrete examples of outrageous evasion techniques were sufficient to justify concern with abusive tax shelters and with private use of business luxury automobiles, and the generally accepted deterrence hypothesis was the primary basis for raising penalties in TEFRA legislation despite the lack of information on the use or effectiveness of IRS-imposed penalties. Investigative journalism, detailed qualitative studies of particular compliance problems, and theoretical analysis of the effects of enforcement strategies done outside the IRS also provide support to analysts when there is little sympathy for the targeted group.

Such theoretical arguments and qualitative studies are less effective than quantitative estimates of the size of a particular compliance problem and concrete revenue projections related to proposed enforcement changes, particularly when such groups as small businesses, the elderly, and the poor are likely to be affected. Such quantitative studies (e.g., IRS studies of the extent of nonreporting of tip income, state income tax refunds, and income from sources filing information returns) utilize data sources such as information and tax return data, audit programs, TCMP data, and contracted surveys. Although time pressures impose quality standards different from academic research, the need to withstand criticism from opposing interests and maintain a reputation for solid research requires relatively high standards of IRS policy-related research. Academic researchers might be most useful in improving the standard design for this type of research and in establishing standards for alternative approaches (e.g., experimental studies) that would withstand scrutiny from opposing expert witnesses in the political arena. In addition, since Congress can seldom wait for appropriate studies and data bases to be completed once an item is under discussion, the development of potentially useful compliance data bases, appropriate methods for analyzing them, and a catalogue of well-analyzed compliance problems may increase the impact of empirical analysis on the policy process.

Many enforcement policy decisions do not require specific legislative changes and are limited more by internal organizational constraints than by the political context analyzed in this paper. But Congress, particularly the subcommittees on oversight of the tax panels, has occasionally taken an active interest in such administrative policy decisions. Research affecting these decisions is undertaken by the IRS and, to a lesser extent, the General Accounting Office (GAO), which maintains a large tax research staff with access to IRS data resources. The 1985 GAO *Annual Report on Tax Matters* lists 17 legislative recommendations developed in recent GAO studies to improve tax administration, three of which were passed by Congress in 1984. The report also lists twenty-two recommendations made to Treasury, the IRS, and the Tax Court in 1984 on subjects as diverse as the need to analyze compliance impacts of Taxpayer Assistance Programs before making cutbacks in positions and the problems related to the windfall profit tax. Thirteen study reports were completed during 1984, and eleven new projects were undertaken. GAO studies focus primarily on administrative procedures and generally produce narrowly focused and carefully documented studies with a few specific suggestions for improvement. They have encouraged the IRS to evaluate the compliance impact of different programs but have not themselves undertaken evaluative compliance studies that would impose research requirements different from their normal administrative studies. But compliance studies by the GAO might be a useful complement to IRS efforts, which can easily be questioned as self-serving; the GAO's independence and congressional support would enhance credibility to the extent that its studies corroborated IRS efforts.

Implications of the Federal Political Context for Taxpayer Compliance Research

Given the size of the tax compliance problem, both the limited amount of compliance research and the few sources of support are quite surprising. During the past five years, the IRS has played a very active role in broadening the scope of research and the size of the community concerned with tax compliance. But in the long run, the dominant role of the IRS and other government agencies in sponsoring compliance research does not seem compatible with the interests of the broader community. The professional organizations associated with tax matters, notably the American Bar Association's Tax Section and the accountants' Arthur Young Foundation, have taken a more active interest in research on tax compliance and enforcement. But to improve enforcement policies despite existing constraints, political leaders need to hear from the broader spectrum of representative interests who generally ignore enforcement issues. A research agenda focused on this broader set of interests is a necessary component to stimulate a continuing dialogue on enforcement policies. The following research issues discussed below represent suggestions at each stage of the policy process for policy-oriented research to support this dialogue.

POLICY AWARENESS STAGE

One of the least known aspects of enforcement strategies is who gains and loses during the enforcement process. Are particular groups more disadvantaged than others? What normative criteria are most appropriate for judging which groups should be most subjected to coercive policies? For such groups, what ratio of appropriate coercion of noncompliers to the inevitable mistaken harassment of compliers generally occurs, and what standard is appropriate? While these issues are loudly discussed by politically powerful groups, they are seldom raised for less organized groups. The issue of appropriate enforcement techniques for specific sets of compliance problems needs discussion and research support from private foundations and independent researchers not associated with the enforcement agency or with groups directly involved with enforcement processes.

AGENDA-SETTING STAGE

To focus existing debate on the most important compliance problems, basic research on alternative techniques to assess the nature and extent of particular compliance problems would be most useful. For example, the *Gross Tax Gap Estimates and Projections for 1973–1992* (IRS, 1988, Table I-1) indicate that about 35 percent of the unpaid income tax comes from the self-employed, or 41 percent if small businesses are included. Research that isolates and explains the most important pockets of noncompliance within this group could substantially enhance the understanding of compliance problems and focus enforcement policy debates on the most serious problems.

POLICY NEGOTIATION STAGE

To decide whether innovative enforcement policy alternatives should be adopted, extended, or halted, evaluation studies should become an integral part of all new administrative approaches to enforcement. The most important change to be made in current evaluations is that *compliance effects*, not just revenue produced during the enforcement process, should be the primary focus of evaluation, and the impact on the attitudes of affected taxpayers should be assessed.

This implies that field experiment designs capable of assessing such impacts need to be developed as an essential part of administrative practice. While this will necessarily be done primarily within the IRS and state revenue agencies, the development of appropriate techniques and the critical analysis of the data would be improved with the participation of independent researchers familiar with field experiments and policy evaluation in other arenas.

Ultimately, the ameliorative impact of compliance research on tax enforcement issues will depend on the development and institutionalization of a critical mass of scholars and foundations with a continuing interest in compliance issues. Such people and organizations can generate a respectable basis of analysis that policy makers cannot ignore, at least not in the long run.

Appendix: Major Compliance-Oriented Changes in Tax Laws, 1976–1985

Tax law changes affecting the following categories of enforcement issues during the 1976–1985 period are listed for each tax act:

1. Withholding at source;
2. Information reporting at source;
3. Record-keeping requirements;
4. Preparer responsibilities and liabilities;
5. Penalties;
6. Legal and administrative changes increasing investigatory and prosecutory abilities;
7. Elimination or reduction of deductions and exemptions that are easily abused and difficult to enforce.

Braces {} indicate that legislation restricted IRS enforcement authority. Otherwise, the listed items generally increased enforcement authority, although this classification is somewhat ambiguous for some items. Numbers in parentheses ( ) refer to the section of the indicated public law, not the Internal Revenue Code.

1976 TAX REFORM ACT

Restrictions on tax shelter schemes (201–214)

Tax treatment of foreign income (1013–1015)

Regulation of tax professionals (1203)

Withholding provisions (1207)

　　Gambling winnings

　　Fishing (excluding ten-man boats receiving proportion of catch)

Support test for dependents of separated or divorced parents (2139)

Public inspection of written determinants by IRS (1201)

Use of Social Security numbers (1211)

{Disclosure of tax returns and tax return information (1202)}

{Jeopardy of termination assessments (1204)}

{Administrative summons (1205)}

{Reporting and record keeping for tip income (2111)—clarifies that employers are only required to report tips reported by employees }

1978 REVENUE ACT

Changes in filing requirements and withholding (101–102) {tax counseling for the elderly (163)}

Tax shelter: modification of at-risk rules (201–204); partnership provisions (211–212)

Disclosure to the Justice Department in tax administration matters (503)

{Reporting requirements with respect to charge tips (501)—overturns revenue rule, states that only tips reported by employees are subject to withholding, and tips on charge receipts need not be assigned to a particular employee.}

{Employment tax status of independent contractors and employees (530)—provides "safe haven" tests temporarily, overturns IRS efforts to collect withholding taxes, and prohibits IRS from publishing rules declaring some ICs as employer}

1981 ECONOMIC RECOVERY ACT OF 1981

Tax straddles (501–509)

Prohibition of disclosure of methods for selection of tax returns for audits (701)

Changes in interest for over- and underpayments (711)

Penalty changes for false withholding information (721), valuation overstatement and negligence penalty (722), overstated deposit claims (724)

Changes in requirements relating to failure to file information returns (723)

1982 TAX EQUITY AND FISCAL RESPONSIBILITY ACT

Withholding on interest and dividends (301–308), including patronage dividends (304) and penalty (306) and clerical amendments (307), clarification that other taxes not to be deducted before withholding

Expanded income reporting, including

reporting of interest in line with withholding requirements (309)

registration of certain obligations (bearer bonds, etc.) (310), returns of brokers (311)

reporting of payments of remunerations for services and direct sales (312), relevant to independent contractor, especially for retail sales in homes issue

reporting of state and local income tax refunds (313)

reporting of tip income (314), including the assignment of 8 percent of gross sales to employer

Provisions to improve reporting generally, including

increased penalties for failure to file information return (315) and failure to furnish TIN (316)

mandatory withholding when TIN not furnished or inaccurate (317)

minimum penalty for extended failure to file (318)

information returns reportable on magnetic media (319)

Abusive tax shelters, penalties and requirements for promoters (320–322)

Increases in penalties (323–330)

substantial understatement (323)

documents understating liability (324)

fraud (325)

frivolous returns (326)

estimated tax (328)

criminal fines (329)

certain cash transactions (330)

Administrative summons (331–333)

third-party summons and third-party record-keeper limitations

Withholding on pensions and other retirement income (334–335)

Transactions outside United States or involving foreign persons

(336–343) summons, evidence, penalties, information requirements, withholding on nonresident aliens

Modification of interest provisions (compounded daily, set biannually) (344–346)

Sense of Congress increasing IRS budget (352)

Confidentiality and disclosure (356)

Disclosure for use in certain audits by GAO (358)

{Treatment of real estate agents and direct sellers for employment taxes (269)}

{Taxpayer safeguard amendments (restriction on liens, 347–350)}

1983 INTEREST AND DIVIDEND TAX COMPLIANCE ACT

{Withholding on interest and dividends was repealed, but backup withholding provisions and information-reporting provisions were made more stringent.}

1984 DEFICIT REDUCTION ACT

Partnerships (71–79)

Tax straddles (101–108)

Withholding

Withholding on dispositions of U.S. real estate involving foreigners (129)

Taxation on certain transfers of property outside the United States (131)

Tax shelters

   registration (141)

   list of investors required in some cases (142)

   penalties and injunctions (143)

   increased rates of interest on substantial underpayments (144)

Information reporting

   mortgage interest received in trade or business from individuals (145)

   cash transactions (146)

   IRAs (147)

   foreclosure and abandonment (148)

   furnishing TIN under backup withholding (152)

Substantiation of charitable contributions: modification of penalty (155)

Authorization to disregard appraisals of persons penalized for aiding in understating of tax liability (156)

Penalty for fraudulent withholding exemptions (159)

Application of penalty for frivolous proceedings to pending Tax Court
proceedings (160)

{repeal of 30% withholding requirement on interest received by
foreign persons on certain portfolio investments (127)}

1985 ACT

Repeal of contemporaneous record requirement, but depreciation and
investment credit limits on luxury cars reduced to make up for possible revenue loss and some form of substantiating records required.
Also keeps the provisions of records for other items.

1986 TAX REFORM ACT

(Note: Other tax changes indirectly affected compliance by reducing or
minimizing deduction items with low compliance level.)

Penalty increases
  failure to file information returns or statements
  failure to pay tax
  negligence and fraud
  substantial understatement of tax liability
Information reporting requirements
  real estate transactions
  social security numbers for dependents
Administrative provisions
  authority to abate interest due to IRS error or delays and suspend
    compounding of interest
  authority to rescind statutory notice of deficiency
  suspension of statute of limitations during prolonged dispute over
    third-party records

Notes

1. Although there are very few studies of the impact of the political process on
enforcement issues, the tax policy process has been analyzed in detail in several
excellent studies. Manley (1970) focuses primarily on the role of Congress, and
particularly the important House Ways and Means Committee. Reese (1980),
Rudder (1985) and a special symposium reported in the *National Tax Journal*
(September, 1979) update this account and add considerable detail on the role
of the Treasury. Pierce (1971) adds greater detail on the role of the presidential

institutions of the White House and the Office of Management and Budget, and relates tax policies more closely with spending policies. Greater detail on the general legislative role of the presidential institutions is given in Wayne's (1982) *The Legislative Presidency*. The most detailed historical account of the politics of tax legislation and the general characteristics of the legislative system is by John Witte (1985). An even broader historical account of the politics of taxation by Hansen (1983) focuses on major party realignments as sources of innovations in tax policy.

2. Hearings included the Subcommittee on Foundations of the Senate Finance Committee, 6/3/74, the Subcommittee on Administrative Practices and Procedures of the Senate Judiciary Committee, 7/31/74, the Subcommittee on Foundations of the Senate Finance Committee, 11/25/74, and the Subcommittee on Commerce, Consumer and Monetary Affairs of the House Committee on Governmental Operations, 6/24/75.

3. Hearings included the Subcommittee on Commerce, Consumer and Monetary Affairs of the House Committee on Governmental Operations, 6/20, 6/24, and 7/8/75.

4. Hearing of the Subcommittee on Governmental Information and Individual Rights of the House Committee on Government Operations, 3/13/75.

5. Congressional hearings included the Subcommittee on Administration of the Senate Finance Committee, 4/21/75, the Subcommittee on Oversight of the House Ways and Means Committee, 9/22/75, and the House Ways and Means Committee, 1/28/76. The president's Privacy Protection Study Commission held hearings on the IRS on 9/9/75 and 3/11/76.

6. Hearings included the Subcommittee on Oversight of the House Ways and Means Committee, 12/13 and 12/14/77 and 1/16/78, the Senate Special Committee on Aging, 2/24/78, and the Senate Select Committee on Small Business, 6/27/79.

7. Hearings included the Subcommittee of the Senate Appropriations Committee, 6/11, 6/12, and 6/25/74, Subcommittee on Oversight of the House Ways and Means Committee, 4/14/75, 5/21/76, and 7/27/77, the Subcommittee on Commerce, Consumer and Monetary Affairs of the House Committee on Governmental Operations, 12/15/75 and 3/22/78, and the Subcommittee on Administration of the Senate Finance Committee, 3/28/78).

8. IRS figures are for average positions realized from the *Annual Report, 1984,* Table 22. Figures for total civilian employment by the federal government are derived from the Office of Personnel Management, with the 1975 figure (2,741,000) reported in *Statistical Abstract,* 1985, and the 1984 figure (2,896,000) in *World Almanac,* 1985. These figures differ significantly from a 1983 IRS document on the budget process that indicated that the IRS did significantly better than other nonmilitary agencies under the Reagan administration because that report used estimated budget figures through fiscal 1983, not actual employment through 1984.

9. Gene Bardach developed this "minimax" strategy interpretation of the political culture of enforcement.

10. Hearings were held by the Subcommittee on Commerce, Consumer and Monetary Affairs of the House Committee on Government Operations, 9/9/79, the Subcommittee on Oversight of the House Ways and Means Committee, 9/10 and 10/11/79, and the Joint Economic Committee, 11/15/1979.

References

Brandon, R.B., Rowe, J., and Stanton, T.H.
   1976   *Tax Politics.* New York: Pantheon Books.
Cary, W.L.
   1955   Pressure groups and the Revenue Code: a requiem in honor of the departing uniformity of tax laws. *Harvard Law Review* 68(March): 745–780.
Congressional Quarterly Almanac
   1982   Washington, D.C.: CQ Press.
De Grazia, R.
   1980   Clandestine employment: a problem in our times. *International Labour Review* 119:544–583.
Derthick, M. and Quirk, P.J.
   1985   *The Politics of Deregulation.* Washington, D.C.: The Brookings Institution.
Eisenstein, L.
   1961   *The Ideologies of Taxation.* New York: Roland Press.
Hammond, P.B.
   1984   The Impact of Knowledge on Policymaking: Lessons from the Literature. Unpublished paper prepared for the Commission on Physical Sciences, Mathematics, and Resources of the National Research Council.
Hansen, S.B.
   1983   *The Politics of Taxation: Revenue Without Representation.* Praeger Special Studies/Praeger Scientific. New York: Praeger Publishers.
Heclo, H.
   1978   Policy networks in government. In Anthony King, ed., *The New American Political System.* Washington, D.C.: American Enterprise Institute.
Henry, J.S.
   1983   Noncompliance with U.S. tax law—evidence of size, growth, and composition. Pp. 15–112 in Phillip Sawicki, ed., *Income Tax Compliance: A Report of the ABA Section on Taxation, Invitational Conference on Tax Compliance.* Washington, D.C.: American Bar Association.
Hoeflich, M.H.
   1983   Withholding at source on non-wage income: a brief historical excursus. *Tax Notes* (May 23).
Internal Revenue Service
   1983   *Income Tax Compliance Research: Estimates for 1973–1981.* Office of Assis-

44   Political Context of Tax Administration

tant Commissioner (Planning, Finance and Research), Internal Revenue Service. Washington, D.C.: U.S. Department of the Treasury.

1984   *Annual Report 1984.* Commissioner of Internal Revenue. Internal Revenue Service, U.S. Department of the Treasury. Washington, D.C.: U.S. Government Printing Office.

Kuttner, R.

1980   *Revolt of the Haves: Tax Rebellions and Hard Times.* New York: Simon & Schuster.

LeDuc, J.A.

1983   The legislative response of the 97th Congress to tax shelter, the audit lottery, and other forms of intentional or reckless noncompliance. *Tax Notes* (January 31):363–392.

Lewis, A.

1982   *The Psychology of Taxation.* New York: St. Martin's Press.

Long, S.B.

1985   The Impact of Information on Law Enforcement. Paper presented at the annual meeting of the Law and Society Association, San Diego, Calif., June 7, 1985.

Lowery, D., and Siegelman, L.

1981   Understanding the tax revolt: eight explanations. *American Political Science Review* 75(4):963–974.

Lynn, L.E., Jr.

1979   *Studies in the Management of Social R&D: Selected Policy Areas.* Washington, D.C.: National Academy of Sciences

Manley, J.F.

1965   The House Committee on Ways and Means: conflict management in a congressional committee. *American Political Science Review* 59(December):927–939.

1970   *The Politics of Finance: The House Committee on Ways and Means.* Boston: Little, Brown.

National Tax Association

1979   Federal tax policy and the tax legislative process. Laurence N. Woodworth Memorial Symposium, National Tax Association, Tax Institute of America, Washington, D.C., May 14–15, 1979. *National Tax Journal* 32(3).

Pierce, L.C.

1971   *The Politics of Fiscal Policy Formulation.* Pacific Palisades, Calif.: Goodyear Publishing Company.

Privacy Protection Study Commission

1977   *The Citizen as Taxpayer.* Report of the Privacy Protection Study Commission, Appendix 2. Washington, D.C.: U.S. Government Printing Office.

Reese, T.J.

1980   *The Politics of Tax Reform.* Westport, Conn.: Quorum Books.

Reid, J.D., Jr.
1979   Tax revolts in historical perspective. *National Tax Journal* 32(2)(Supplement):67–74.
Rudder, C.E.
1985   Fiscal responsibility and the Revenue Committees. In Lawrence C. Dodd and Bruce I. Oppenheimer, eds., *Congress Reconsidered*. Washington, D.C.: CQ Press.

Scholz, J.T.
1984   Cooperation, deterrence, and the ecology of regulatory enforcement. *Law and Society Review* 18:179–224.
Sears, D.O. and Citrin, J.
1982   *Tax Revolt: Something for Nothing in California*. Cambridge, Mass.: Harvard University Press.
Simon, C.P. and Witte, A.D.
1980   The underground economy: estimates of GNP, structure and trends. In Joint Economic Committee, *Government Regulation: Achieving Social and Economic Balance,* Vol. 5. Washington, D.C.: U.S. Government Printing Office.
1981   The Underground Economy: What Is It and What Should We Do? Unpublished paper, March 1981, The Osprey Company, Tallahassee, Fla.
Smith, D.T.
1961   *Federal Tax Reform: The Issues and a Program*. New York: McGraw-Hill.
Sundquist, J.L.
1978   Research brokerage: the weak link. In Laurence E. Lynn, Jr., ed., *Knowledge and Policy: The Uncertain Connection*. Washington, D.C.: National Academy of Science.
Surrey, S.S.
1957   The Congress and the tax lobbyist: how special tax provisions get enacted. *Harvard Law Review* 70(May):1145–1182.

Tax Management, Inc.
1982   Tax Equity and Fiscal Responsibility Act; Subchapter S Revision Act; as amended by the Technical Corrections Act of 1982. The Bureau of National Affairs, Inc., Washington, D.C.
1984   Tax Management: The Tax Reform Act of 1984. The Bureau of National Affairs, Inc., Washington, D.C.

U.S. Comptroller General
1982   *Further Research into Noncompliance is Needed to Reduce Growing Tax Losses*. Report to Congress. Washington, D.C.: U.S. General Accounting Office.
1985   *1984 Annual Report on Tax Matters*. Washington, D.C.: U.S. General Accounting Office.

46   Political Context of Tax Administration

U.S. Congress
1982a *Background on Federal Income Tax Compliance and Description of S. 2198 (Taxpayer Compliance Improvement Act of 1982)*. Joint Committee on Taxation, U.S. Congress, March 19, 1982. Washington, D.C.: U.S. Government Printing Office.
1982b *Background on Classification of Employees and Independent Contractors for Tax Purposes and Description of S. 2369*. Joint Committee on Taxation, U.S. Congress, April 23, 1982. Washington, D.C.: U.S. Government Printing Office.
1983a *Background on Federal Income Tax Compliance*. Joint Committee on Taxation, U.S. Congress, June 21, 1983. Washington, D.C.: U.S. Government Printing Office.
1983b *Description of Issue Areas Relating to Efforts to Reduce Taxpayer Burdens*. Joint Committee on Taxation, U.S. Congress, May 18, 1983. Washington, D.C.: U.S. Government Printing Office.
1983c *Growth of the Underground Economy, 1950–1981: Some Evidence from the Current Population Survey*. Joint Committee, U.S. Congress, December 9, 1983. Washington, D.C.: U.S. Government Printing Office.
1985a *Tax Reform Proposals: Compliance and Tax Administration*. Joint Committee on Taxation, U.S. Congress, July 30, 1985. Washington, D.C.: U.S. Government Printing Office.
1985b *Analysis of Proposals Relating to Comprehensive Tax Reform*. Joint Committee on Taxation, U.S. Congress, February 26, 1985. Washington, D.C.: U.S. Government Printing Office.
Waggonner, J.D.
1979   Aspects of legislative persuasion: business. *National Tax Journal* 32(September):290–294.
Wayne, S.
1982   *The Legislative Presidency*.
Wildavsky, A.
1979   *Speaking Truth to Power*. Boston: Little, Brown.
Witte, J.
1985   *The Politics and Development of the Tax Laws*. Madison: University of Wisconsin Press.

Robert Kidder and Craig McEwen

2. Taxpaying Behavior in Social Context: A Tentative Typology of Tax Compliance and Noncompliance

From the vantage point of loss to the federal treasury, all noncompliance with federal tax laws is alike. Thus, a major argument for defining tax noncompliance as a problem is the estimated "tax gap" of over $80 billion. But from the perspectives both of social scientific understanding of taxpaying behavior and of policy efforts to maximize compliance, differences in kinds of noncompliance and in their causes and social locations are extremely significant. In the important experimental research on tax compliance by Schwartz and Orleans (1967), different types of appeals to taxpayers for compliance had different effects on different social categories of individuals. Self-interest and legal threat drove some taxpayers toward compliance, while moral appeals motivated others. Compliance and noncompliance could not be understood as unitary phenomena, nor could they effectively be influenced by a single policy or enforcement strategy. Similarly, in a study of legal compliance, McEwen and Maiman (1986) found that small claims defendants who paid or did not pay judgments against them appeared to behave as they did for reasons ranging from moral commitment to fear of punishment. Such findings as these remind us that adoption of too narrow a view of the complex behaviors involved in compliance and noncompliance with legal rules could lead to misguided research and theory and misdirected policy.

Unfortunately, just such a narrow view threatens to dominate efforts to understand taxpaying behavior. This view emphasizes noncompliance through careful calculation by individuals who see that the risks of violating

Robert Kidder, Department of Sociology, Temple University; Craig McEwen, Department of Sociology, Bowdoin College. The authors would like to thank Brian Perkins, CPA (Brunswick, Maine) for helpful advice about some of the examples used, and Barbara Yngvesson and two anonymous reviewers for constructive comments on earlier drafts.

tax rules are outweighed by the benefits of doing so (see, for example, Kinsey, 1987; Roth and Witte, 1985). In fact, with rare exceptions (e.g. Lewis, 1982) the tax compliance literature has neglected compliance variables other than economic benefit and potential loss through punishment. There has been an associated focus on the causes of noncompliance with only little concomitant attention to the interrelated phenomenon of compliance. As a consequence, definitions of noncompliance themselves often narrow the behavior in question to "intentional" violation, thus neglecting actions stemming from ignorance or mistake. In empirical research the treatment of noncompliance as a unitary dependent variable despite its many forms and causes has the effect of depressing relationships with independent variables. Adoption of a narrow definition and theoretical account of tax noncompliance thus has limiting consequences.

In this chapter we set out a broad but tentative typology of compliance and noncompliance, suggesting their interrelationships and the wide array of variables influencing taxpaying behavior. The typology serves largely as a heuristic device to call attention to the rich complexity of taxpaying behavior and the need for an ambitious research agenda focused not on noncompliance alone but on the nature and context of taxpaying behavior generally.

A Working Typology of Tax Compliance and Noncompliance

The most obvious conclusion of any review of the research literature on tax compliance and noncompliance is that we know very little about the taxpaying behavior of individuals. One of the special characteristics of tax laws in comparison to criminal laws is that they do not simply prohibit a particular conduct. Instead, they impose affirmative obligations to become informed about tax rules, to keep records, to report income and expenses, all in a timely fashion. In this sense tax laws must be incorporated into one's life in ways that conventional criminal prohibitions are not. But we know very little about how people incorporate them. How do people go about preparing tax returns? Who do they consult for information? How do they keep records? How significant an element is tax policy in their decision making about charitable contributions, record keeping, income-producing activity, and so on? Taxation plays a major role in the lives of tax professionals, administrators, and experts, but we would be foolish to assume it looms so large in the lives of others.

As a consequence, we do not have an adequate empirical base upon which to build a typology of tax compliance and noncompliance. However, the research and theoretical literature on these issues provides a wealth of hints about the variables that generate compliance. We have identified, from this literature, six variables or clusters of variables which may contribute to compliance or noncompliance with legal rules: coercion or its threat; self-interest; habit; legitimacy and fairness; informal social pressures; and level of knowledge about the rules. We will consider each of these variables briefly in turn in the context of a simple typology (see Table 1) of compliance that they yield if one assumes that a single variable will dominate any single instance of compliance or noncompliance.

No single taxpayer or avoider will fall cleanly within any of these ideal types. Every person will probably be subject to a mixture of all or most of the pressures suggested by the types. A more sophisticated typology would, therefore, involve the complex intersections of the six variables simultaneously. Ultimately, multivariate analysis should take the place of this simplified typology. We begin simply, however, in order to make clear the range of variables that need the attention of anyone seeking to understand compliance and noncompliance.

We do not wish to suggest that for us the highest research priority should be given to the psychological problem of identifying the balance of motives in individual taxpayers. Indeed, we believe that all of the variables—coercion, self-interest, habit, legitimacy, social pressures, and normative uncertainty—are socially structured; that is, they are unevenly but systematically distributed within and across different segments of soci-

TABLE 1   Compliance Variables and Working Typology of Tax Compliance and Noncompliance

Variables	Compliance type	Noncompliance type
Coercion	Defensive, Structured	
Self-interest	Self-serving	Asocial
Habit	Habitual	Habitual
Legitimacy/fairness	Loyal	Symbolic
Social pressures	Social, Brokered	Social, Brokered
Normative uncertainty/burden of compliance	Lazy	Procedural, Unknowing, Lazy

ety. It is that social structure and its relationship to taxpaying behavior that require priority on the research agenda.

A TYPOLOGY OF COMPLIANCE

Even given a concern with the problem of the tax gap and tax evasion, it would be a mistake to focus attention exclusively upon noncompliance. Empirical research must focus on compliance rather than taking it for granted in the preoccupation with the rarer and more problematic phenomenon of rule breaking. Theories must explain both compliance and noncompliance. Policy may be directed both toward encouraging and supporting compliance as well as discouraging noncompliance. We begin, therefore, with a typology of compliance.

Defensive compliance takes place with an eye toward the Internal Revenue Service and its enforcement and surveillance efforts. It is, in essence, "defensive taxpaying." For example, grudging every penny subtracted from her paycheck, Fran nonetheless reports all her income and takes only the appropriate deductions out of fear that she will be audited and found to be in violation of the tax code. She like others (Kinsey, 1984) overestimates the likelihood that the IRS will audit her tax returns.

Such behavior might be understood largely in terms of the deterrent capacity of the law. By imposing penalties for tax violations and creating a process of review that is viewed as troublesome and punitive itself (Feeley, 1979), the tax code induces some people to comply with its provisions. This view of tax compliance is developed with variations in the extensive literature on deterrence theory and much of the economic research about tax behavior (see, for example, Roth and Witte, 1985; Kinsey, 1985).

Given the knowledge that deterrence derives most of its power from perceptions of the likelihood of being caught in violation of the law, the IRS might experiment with efforts to increase that perception. For example, a large number of polite "warning letters" might be sent to taxpayers who are not audited but whose returns raise some suspicions of evasion. These could be sent to an experimental group and the following year's returns could be compared with those of a control group. Any efforts to lengthen the long arm of the tax law should also be monitored by a survey of attitudes of the same individuals to see if there are negative or positive attitudinal side effects.

Structured compliance is another response to the coercive element of law. It works not through the threat of punishment but rather through the elimination of or dramatic reduction in choice or opportunity to violate the law (Kagan, this volume, Chapter 3). For example, every month George receives his modest paycheck with federal and state taxes withheld. At the end of the year he gets a W-2 form from his employer indicating his total income and his tax payments. He simply copies those numbers on the short tax form and sends it in. His taxpaying has been taken out of his hands; he learns little about the tax code and tends to define and think about taxable income in terms limited to paychecks and withholding.

In fact, a majority of taxpayers do not itemize deductions but use the short form (Internal Revenue Service, 1984). It is reasonable to suppose that many of these filers engage in structured compliance. Clearly, structured compliance removes much of the opportunity for noncompliance, but it may also encourage evasion through ignorance and symbolic evasion—discussed below—by reducing the level of choice and participation of taxpayers.

Self-serving compliance occurs when an individual has the resources to invest in meticulous compliance with rules that serve to reduce his or her tax burden. The opportunities created by the tax code for minimizing taxes prompt some individuals to learn all they can about tax laws (or purchase advice and assistance) in order to use them to their own advantage. Thus, Gloria hires a tax lawyer and accountant to help her keep track of her income, investments, and expenses and to guide her economic choices so that they maximize her income or wealth while keeping her tax liability to a minimum. With the assistance of others then, Gloria enforces the tax code on herself because she sees that it is in her interest to do so.

In general, we know that some law-abiding behavior can be understood simply as a pursuit of self-interest. Driving on the right side of the road is not only habitual but safe in the United States. However, we might assume that because taxes are a burden on taxpayers it is in everyone's narrow interest to minimize tax compliance. Such an assumption misses a vital distinction. It is in everyone's narrow economic self-interest to minimize their tax liability. For some, however, that may mean maximizing compliance, while for others it may suggest noncompliance. Hypothetically, given a common interest in reducing tax liability and a tax code such as ours, individuals with greater resources are more likely to have the ability and incentive to comply closely with tax rules, while those with fewer resources are likely to have neither the resources nor incentives to do so. Self-interest encourages compliance by those with greater resources but not by those with fewer resources.

Habitual compliance builds over time as individuals develop a pattern of behavior to meet the demands imposed upon them by tax laws. These patterns may, of course, shift through the life course as the tax filing status changes with alterations in occupation, income, and marital situation. For Harriet, last year's tax return serves as a model for this year's and creates a certain continuity in her tax-reporting behavior, especially since she does the return herself. Over the years she has learned to file all her income and expenditure statements by category in appropriate boxes or folders. She has a fairly fixed sense of what is reportable income and deductible expense, reflected in the labels of her file folders, and that sense shapes her tax-reporting behavior far more than IRS publications do.

Unlike areas of law which prohibit particular behaviors, tax laws, like traffic laws, encourage or require "new" patterns of behavior. As Feest (1968) shows with respect to stop-sign behavior, surveillance even by citizens without enforcement powers improves compliance. In the tax area official surveillance is built into the system and reinforces habitual compliance. To the degree that taxpaying behavior becomes habitual, it would seem particularly important for policy makers to find ways to encourage first-time filers to do so carefully, knowledgeably, and conscientiously.

Loyal compliance occurs when people feel a moral obligation to pay their share of taxes and feel guilty about cheating on taxes. They too may be meticulous record keepers or rather sloppy. In either case, however, they tend to resolve doubts about their responsibility as taxpayers in favor of liability and may even overpay taxes somewhat. Larry, for example, works in a salaried clerical position, and his taxes are subtracted monthly from his check. He gives generously to his church and local charities, but when it comes time to file his tax return, he deducts only the few major contributions for which he has receipts. As he prepares his tax return, Larry takes satisfaction in being a good citizen who is paying his fair share of taxes and not trying to cut corners. As a consequence, he slightly overpays his taxes each year.

Such compliance as Larry's stems in part from a belief that tax obligations are appropriate demands of government that yield a reasonable return by way of services and protection for citizens. This sense of general obligation to abide by the rules of government as "part of the regular moral or social order within which (one) lives" (Boulding, 1970:510) is captured by the concept of legitimacy. People comply voluntarily because they believe that it is their obligation to do so. Although Alan Hyde (1983) has criticized the concept, legitimacy is viewed by most social scientists as one of the fundamental glues that holds societies together. Recently, McEwen and Maiman (1986) have provided some empirical support for the conclusion that legitimacy is important in explaining compliance with court orders.

Because taxation involves sacrifices directly on behalf of a government, levels of voluntary compliance with tax laws should be substantially influenced by the degree to which the government is viewed as legitimate. Levels of legitimacy may vary with social location (e.g., age, ethnicity, and social class) and over time. Given the fundamental importance ascribed to legitimacy by the social sciences, it is surprising that we do not know more about it (see, for example, Boulding, 1970; Abel, 1980; Lempert, 1980). The study of tax compliance and legitimacy should be especially fruitful in developing our understanding of both phenomena.

In addition to the general perceptions of the legitimacy of governments, individuals evaluate the fairness of particular rules. There is considerable evidence that the perception of fairness affects voluntary compliance with rules. Research in laboratory settings (e.g., Tyler, 1985) and in the field (McEwen and Maiman, 1986) shows greater likelihood of compliance with rules or rulings that people consider fair. This research suggests that taxpaying behavior may well be related to general perceptions of the fairness of the tax system as well as to perceptions of particular features of that system (for example, how tax money is expended; the fairness of particular deductions or procedures). People who perceive some unfairness in the tax system may either feel less obligated to complete compliance or may feel prompted to some level of noncompliance as a matter of visible or invisible protest (see discussion below of symbolic noncompliance).

Like sense of fairness, participation in the forging of rules and settlements to disputes appears to support legitimacy and voluntary compliance. In particular, consensually arrived at rules for behavior enlist in their support strongly held informal norms about keeping one's promise and being honest (Lempert, 1972; McEwen and Maiman, 1986). That is, the more involved people are in making rules and consenting to them, the stronger the sense of obligation they will feel to abide by those rules. Evidence for this comes from research about compliance with consensual agreements as compared to authoritatively imposed resolutions of legal disputes.

Two applications of these findings in the tax area appear plausible. First, we can hypothesize that people who feel less well represented in government decisions about taxes will be most likely to violate tax laws when an opportunity arises. Second, processes used to define and impose tax penalties may have significant effects both on immediate compliance and on long-term compliance. Taxpayers will be less likely to conform to rulings that are issued bureaucratically and impersonally than to those that are arrived at through a process of negotiation. In the long run, the cheaper bureaucratic imposition of tax liability may lead to an increased sense of alienation from the tax system and declining voluntary compliance (Strüm-pel, 1969). Experimental studies of different methods of imposing tax penalties might easily be designed and imposed, comparing both immediate and long-run effects of methods involving more or less participation (and education) of the taxpayer.

Social compliance results from the direct and indirect pressures and expectations of friends, family, and community. Although taxpaying is typically a private activity, it may be indirectly influenced by pressures for public conformity, partly through fear that the private will become public. In certain occupational subgroups, tax discussions and behavior may be much more public than in others.

It is certainly plausible to suppose that pressures for public compliance are more strongly felt in some communities and social networks than in others. For example, Carmine moves from her urban home to a small community and finds herself caught up in a wide range of civic and church activities. In this new location she finds herself thinking differently about her taxpaying and her responsibilities as a taxpayer. It is no longer simply an isolated individual act but part of her broader civic obligation. Through her close integration into powerful social networks, she approaches taxpaying as a social act with a concomitantly greater sense of obligation to abide by the rules.

The influence of social networks in shaping behavior is well documented, for example, in the extensive literature on the power of informal social control such as gossip and ostracism in small scale societies (see, for example, Nader and Todd, 1978). Some similar patterns are reported in a modern farming community in the United States where tort litigation is socially unacceptable (Engel, 1984). Both the direct pressures of social control and the indirect support of strongly held and locally reinforced values of patriotism, loyalty and civic spiritedness may reinforce other compliance variables—especially loyalty and calculation—in some areas. These observations lead to the hypothesis that rates of compliance will be higher in small, cohesive communities with traditional values than in other areas. To the degree that social location and cultural values support tax compliance, the IRS might choose systematically to promote those values in targeted public relations campaigns. The evidence from the Schwartz and Orleans (1967) study hints that such efforts might be promising at least for preserving current rates of voluntary compliance and that they might have the potential for marginal increases in compliance.

Brokered compliance occurs when one seeks advice and assistance in completing tax forms from professional or nonprofessional intermediaries. Sam, for example, takes his tax problems to an accountant who assists him in completing his tax return and at the same time insists that Sam report all his income and take only permissible deductions. Bound by ethical and legal standards, the accountant enforces the tax laws on Sam. By bringing his taxpaying behavior into the open, Sam exposes himself to direct personal pressures for compliance that are very powerful. As will be noted later, some of these informal pressures may be for noncompliance as well.

The concept and empirical examination of "impact filters" or "compliance brokers" should further our understanding of these informal pressures. By "filters" or "brokers" we mean individuals working in either official or unofficial capacity such as tax advisors, lawyers, or counselors who modify the interpretation and enforcement of laws. Muir (1968), for example, showed how a lawyer working for a board of education successfully convinced the board to comply with the Supreme Court's school prayer decision. The board had been intending to defy the court's order. Ross (1970) showed that organizational pressures on insurance claims adjustors led them to give more generous settlements to claimants than was strictly required by law. By doing so, the adjustors were able to keep their employers' companies out of complicated litigation. This research from other fields of law underlines the importance of understanding the kind and degree of effect that impact filters or compliance brokers have on taxpaying behavior. Because their guidance is most likely to be invoked by people not caught up in structured compliance, brokers should have a substantial influence on other kinds of compliance and noncompliance.

Finally, *lazy compliance* may be a relatively significant type or component of taxpaying behavior. By imposing obligations to learn complicated and changing rules, understand difficult forms, and keep detailed records, income tax reporting demands much of citizens. Many who fail to invest the time or energy into tax reporting may comply or overcomply out of "laziness." So it is with Harold, who for years has stared at the Internal Revenue Service's 1040 booklet and long form, convinced that he would be better off itemizing deductions, including his home mortgage, than by taking the standard deduction. Not a confident reader and a poor keeper of records, Harold regularly curses himself and takes the easy way out as the April 15 deadline nears by completing Form 1040A.

A TYPOLOGY OF NONCOMPLIANCE

Noncompliance may be viewed in terms of the same variables that help account for compliance. However, one cannot fully understand noncompliance by focusing exclusively on the factors affecting the decisions and behavior of taxpayers. Any account of rule violation must recognize not only the social circumstances and motives of violators but also the nature of the rule system and enforcement process that makes them deviant.

Tax rules are constantly defined and redefined through political decision making, agency rule making, court decisions, and the interpretations of rules by tax officials. Taxpaying behavior occurs in the context of this continuously renegotiated set of rules. A behavior that is compliant one year may be noncompliant the next. Noncompliance could be said, therefore, to be a product as much of the decisions of rule makers as of the actions of taxpayers. This observation recalls the lessons of the sociological study and public debate surrounding "crimes without victims" (e.g., Schur, 1965). Noncompliance can be increased by prohibiting previously acceptable conduct, and it can be decreased by making previously proscribed behavior permissible. At any single point in time, compliance and noncompliance are a result of the decisions of political, legal, and administrative actors *and* of the behavior of taxpayers. To understand noncompliance, one must investigate all elements of the complex interaction between taxpayers and tax enforcers (see Lewis, 1982:156).

Not only are tax rules, like others, the product of shifting political decisions, but the meanings of existent rules are sometimes ambiguous, at least for taxpayers. Even the IRS warns people that the advice of its personnel cannot be relied upon as the final word on tax rules. Tax forms and instructions require college-level reading ability for comprehension (Long, 1981). The tax code and accompanying administrative rules are voluminous and mastered only with substantial training and experience. An instructor at an IRS school claimed that agents could discover "errors in 99.9 percent of all tax returns, if they wanted to" (Long, 1981:205).

As a consequence of ambiguity, interpretations of some aspects of tax law may well be the product of routine accommodations worked out within networks of tax law advisors and tax administrators. In the context of an apparently shared professional socialization, tax professionals are likely to find ways to process large numbers of cases without extended contentious involvements. Like the "normal crimes" defined by the prosecutors and defense attorneys studied by Sudnow (1965), accountants and IRS officials are likely to develop "normal tax practices." These would result in interpretations of tax rules reflecting the particular working relationships in the "tax office work group," analogous to Eisenstein and Jacob's "courtroom work group" (1977), in local and regional offices. National networks of tax advisors and accountants as well as the central administration of the IRS may work against this tendency toward local work groups and standards, however. To understand the reported regional variations in tax compliance, this analysis suggests that one must examine the ways in which tax advising and administration are organized, not just the variations in taxpayer characteristics by region. Levels of compliance and variations among them are produced by an interaction between official decisions about the meanings of rules and private decisions about whether and how to pay taxes. Given the volume, complexity, and uncertain interpretation of some tax rules, a vital part of any future research agenda must be an examination of the processes that are at work in the definition of tax compliance and noncompliance.

The nature of the process by which tax law violation is defined provides the context for the typology and study of noncompliance. The fact that tax laws are at times burdensome and ambiguous enters into the typology itself. Noncompliance, like lazy compliance, should be understood in light of the special obligations for initiative and learning that are imposed by the tax code. Tax law violations are frequently sins of omission rather than sins of commission. These are noted in Table 1 beside the variable "normative uncertainty."

Procedural noncompliance results from failure to follow rules about when to file and which forms to file. Such violations do not necessarily result in understatements of tax liability but have to do with the procedures by which the taxpayer declares income and deductions. Take, for example, the case of Tessie, who draws a regular paycheck as a sales clerk but also earns a modest income by selling her weaving at craft stores and fairs throughout the year. She reports her additional income but fails to file the necessary quarterly reports of estimated income and makes no payments of estimated taxes. She owes a healthy tax bill at the end of the year plus some penalties for failure to file proper forms.

Official summaries of IRS's assessments of civil penalties indicate that roughly half of those penalties result from failures to initiate sufficient payment of estimated taxes. To abide by IRS rules regarding estimated taxes requires substantial investment of time and resources in bookkeeping, record maintenance, and attention to deadlines. In that sense, procedural compliance may be a luxury that relatively few can afford because it requires skill and resources that relatively few people have. The difficulties involved in achieving procedural compliance may be related to lazy and symbolic noncompliance described below.

Unknowing noncompliance involves underpayment of taxes through ignorance of complex, changing, and sometimes ambiguous rules. Ivan takes a deduction for the full purchase price of a home computer in 1984 after hearing from a teacher colleague that she had done so in the previous year. Ivan fails to examine changes in requirements for documentation of professional or business use of the computer. Amy regularly deducts as charitable contributions her many gifts to nonprofit groups actively engaged in lobbying on political issues, not recognizing that nonprofit does not mean charitable. Fred never reports as income the "fringe benefits" obtained from several vacation flights each year that he takes as a consequence of frequent flyer points accumulated through travel for his business firm. Although each of these taxpayers tries to minimize tax liability, none of them intends to break the tax laws. To the degree that particular kinds of unknowing evasion can be identified, it may also be possible to develop techniques to educate people about them or to structure compliance (e.g., reporting by airlines of frequent flyer benefits to IRS).

Lazy noncompliance is an extension of procedural noncompliance but involves the level of tax liability. It occurs when individuals discover that they cannot document legitimate expenses for business or health costs or fail to keep track of outside earnings for which there is no withholding. Walter has worked in restaurants for years and has never bothered to record systematically the tips that he receives in cash each night. Every quarter he underestimates his tip income. At the same time, he does not keep careful track of the cost of maintaining the tuxedo and accessories that he owns and uses for his work. Walter simply does not have the training, time, or inclination to do the filing and bookkeeping required to maintain such records. The problems of record keeping are compounded by cash flow difficulties that leave Walter without savings for payment of taxes on income not subject to withholding. The inability to save and to pay substantial chunks of taxes makes it even more likely that Walter's reports will understate his taxable income. Thus, the burden of income tax on Walter is twofold: it requires effort and skills to keep records and to save income for payment of taxes. He reduces these burdens through careless underreporting, which over the years may become habitual noncompliance.

Asocial noncompliance is the classic kind of evasion assumed by the appellation "tax cheater." Feeling little if any sense of obligation to pay a share of taxes, Peter arranges his contracting business so as to minimize his visibility to tax authorities and manages to avoid taxes altogether by accepting payment for his work in cash only, paying cash for supplies, and avoiding a written trail of his economic activity (Kagan, Chapter 3). His economic activity is planned with attention to tax laws and the likelihood of successful evasion. Like a con artist, he relies on the economic self-interest of customers outweighing their sense of civic responsibility.

The tax-avoiding contractor is only one example among many of those engaged in the underground economy (Witte, 1987; Feffer et al., 1983). Although a large proportion of untaxed income from the underground economy comes from illegal activity, a significant portion is earned legally. In some of these areas, efforts to license or regulate (as with day care or gambling or with the trades such as plumbing) may have the consequence of increasing the visibility of the activity and making it more subject to taxation. Research on the consequences of such nontax policies might yield valuable tax policy initiatives.

Symbolic noncompliance takes place to protest or compensate for perceived unfairness and inequities in tax laws. Tax protestors are a small and visible group who openly resist payment of taxes because of their distaste for the uses to which those monies are put. A potentially larger group of taxpayers are those whose incomes are subject to withholding and who have too few resources to take advantage of ways to reduce tax liability through IRAs, tax shelters, and so on. Many of these people probably exhibit structured compliance with regard to much of their tax liability. However, Ernest, feeling unfairly burdened with taxes, especially in a political climate in which such perceptions are reinforced at the highest levels of political office, chooses to underreport small amounts of income not subject to withholding and overstates charitable contributions and his energy-related tax credits in order to reduce taxes by a few dollars. This marginal cheating on taxes may amount to large sums when many taxpayers do it; yet it serves as a release for feelings that the system itself is inequitable or that taxes are being used for improper ends. Ironically it thus may be related to loyal compliance and structural compliance.

Social noncompliance develops in the context of a pattern of social or economic relationships in which tax avoidance is taken for granted or explicitly endorsed. Unlike asocial noncompliance, where the individual tax evader carefully creates the economic circumstances for tax invisibility and evasion, social noncompliance involves an ongoing set of economic and social arrangements over which the evader has no control. Drusilla's wages as a domestic, for example, are controlled by conceptions of "fair compensation" that depend in part on notions of "normal levels" of income underreporting shared both by upper-class employers and by domestics (Rollins, 1985). Employers pay household workers less for such things as overtime work than they might otherwise have to because they assume that extra pay will not be reported. "In kind" subsidies such as food and used clothing often count toward regular wages. Wages of warehouse or sales personnel may be set low to take account of the "inventory shrinkage" (employee theft) that everyone tacitly assumes to be part of the income of workers. Pressured to steal part of their wages, workers underreport "income" and "underpay" taxes. Or restaurant employees may get meals and leftover food as an untaxed fringe benefit that is part of the "employment package." In all these instances the tax avoidance of wage earners is interwoven with the expectations and economic practices of employers. Enforcement policies in such areas might usefully be directed at employers rather than individual employees who are caught in a system beyond their control.

Another variety of social noncompliance may exist among some occupational groups or informal social networks. Informal social pressures may be brought to bear on friends or coworkers to try a "new tax dodge": for example, to go on a winter ocean cruise billed as a "professional conference," to earn some extra income "under the table," or to try a bartering arrangement that can disguise taxable income. Professional and business conferences, trade magazines, and circulars as well as beer and cocktail parties may offer such bits of advice and informal social pressures to use them. The pressures for evasion may be more subtle and less powerful than those on workers in dependent economic circumstances, but they are important nonetheless.

These direct social and economic pressures for noncompliance occur within a larger and shifting context of culture and history. As Kai Erikson (1976) pointed out in his study of Appalachian cultural traditions, every culture is characterized by "axes of variation." These are sets of cultural pendulums that may swing back and forth throughout the history of the society. For the mountaineers of Buffalo Creek, for example, one such axis of variation was between independence and dependence, another between control and fatalism. Stable communities have their own set of such axes, or themes, and people within those communities will tend to organize their thinking, beliefs, and evaluations of others along these axes. As a result, the behavior of individuals within a particular community or society may support both the "thesis" of loyalty and law-abidingness and the "antithesis" of defiance and law violation. This vacillation is not just hypocrisy, a failure to live up to norms and values. Rather it is one of those underlying dimensions of thought, motivation, and evaluation which serve to organize a community while, at the same time, suggesting its vulnerability to change and influence.

In the United States there may be several axes of variation in culturally acceptable responses to the burdens imposed by taxes and the opportunities provided by government. Shifts in political leadership, in economic circumstances, in international affairs, and most relevant here, in tax policy may initiate a slide from one pole (of compliance) to another (of noncompliance) among people who are, "in good conscience," capable of both. It is certainly possible, for example, that development of a more strict and intrusive system of tax law enforcement could dampen the level of loyal compliance. The work of Lewis (1982), Strümpel (1969) and Schmölders (1970) provide both theoretical and empirical support for this hypothesis. Tax policies must not only take account of the possible side effects in a fluid cultural context, but they must also be responsive to cultural slides precipitated by historical events beyond the control of the IRS.

In particular, a longitudinal understanding of compliance patterns must incorporate the awareness that there may be shifts along axes of variation produced by the historical moment during which a particular cohort of actors entered the scene. In studying tax compliance, this could be a particularly important variable. Research has shown that worker cohorts entering the labor market at particular times in economic history are profoundly affected in all their future economic decisions (Easterlin, 1966; Blau and Duncan, 1967). Men entering the work force during the Depression, for example, experienced its profound effects on every subsequent career decision, making them excessively conservative with respect to risk taking in their careers for the rest of their lives (Elder, 1974).

Consider the potential for similar long-term effects on taxpaying practices and attitudes when cohorts of taxpayers experience such cyclical, periodic, or once-in-a-lifetime events as regional recession, depression, or deindustrialization. Consider, for example, the dying steel-producing sectors of Pennsylvania. One possible strategy for survival in such a situation is to take on "odd jobs" that pay poorly but can be hidden from taxation. The development of such a regional recession may create a temporary moral environment that says it is all right to "cheat" on taxes because the government has failed its basic obligation to provide economic security. Such events might create a whole cohort of persons who discover both the means and the justification for certain forms of tax cheating. This does not mean that "steel country" subculture is peculiarly inclined toward cheating. Ten years from now, noncompliance may be a thing of the past in that area, particularly if people who have lost jobs finally give up and move elsewhere. But in the new center of economic prosperity, networks of those in the cohort displaced by recession and forced to move may develop, and one ingredient of their network may be the passage of information about methods of tax evasion.

Combining the concept of cohort with axes of variation, the problem facing a nationwide research project on tax compliance would be to identify significant cohort experiences and then to test whether "cohort effects" vary according to predictable patterns established by nationwide axes of variation.

Brokered noncompliance takes place upon the advice of a knowledgable expert such as a tax accountant, lawyer, or bond dealer. Charity seeks tax advice when completing the long form for the first time. She is told that the charitable deductions and professional expenses that she has documented are quite low and that she could easily claim double that amount without any trouble from the IRS. The accountant then simply writes in the higher figure in the spaces provided on Schedule A of Form 1040. Ira learns from a bond dealer about a kind of investment where earnings are not reported to the IRS and is told that the return on this investment is particularly good since one "need not" pay taxes on it. Faced with expert advice that "everyone does it" and implicit pressure not to be stupid, taxpayers may drift uncomfortably into evasion. The impact filters or compliance brokers discussed earlier are central to such brokered evasion.

Habitual noncompliance, like habitual compliance, emerges over time as taxpayers establish a pattern of reporting income and deductions. Past tax forms provide beginning estimates in completing this year's tax form and give a sense as well of what one can "get away with." Thus, initial instances of brokered or lazy noncompliance may get fixed in place and become virtually automatic in succeeding years as habitual noncompliance develops. Walter the waiter, Ira the investor, and Charity the stingy donor all may get "locked in" to a pattern of noncompliance.

IMPLICATIONS OF A TYPOLOGICAL APPROACH

No neat typology can do justice to the complexity of compliance and noncompliance, especially in view of the paucity of empirical data about taxpaying behavior. Even modest reflection, however, leads to the conclusion that most people exhibit some mixture of these types of socially structured motives or incentives for compliance. Each of the compliance variables probably has some relevance in all cases of compliance and noncompliance, but their values vary. The typology calls attention to the likely predominance of one or another of these influences in particular cases while the variable analysis helps provide a clearer analytic framework for viewing the typology.

Such a typology as that outlined above can be especially useful in thinking through tax policies and enforcement strategies. It reminds us that attention might be given not just to increasing marginal compliance but also to preserving and reinforcing current levels of compliance. In addition, each proposed strategy must be evaluated not only for its potential to increase compliance in one area, but also for its potential effects in reducing compliance in other areas. Finally, by identifying particular types of compliance and noncompliance and their social correlates, it may be possible to target enforcement strategies to particular audiences, thus reducing the likelihood of unintended side effects of those strategies.

In particular, one might ask, for example, to what degree should enforcement efforts and rule making be directed at individual taxpayers or at the social networks and advisors that influence the taxpaying behavior of individuals? For example, spot checks of tax accountants and advisors by "undercover" IRS field personnel using standard factual information could identify particularly egregious patterns of tax avoidance advice.

To what degree can changes in the tax code itself eliminate ambiguity, increase structured compliance, and reduce the burden of organization and record keeping on taxpayers? If lazy noncompliance is common, then tax simplification may eliminate the problem for those who cannot keep clear records of deductions. A scheme of monthly billing on a credit card might help those with income not subject to withholding to keep current with payments and reduce cash flow problems. Unintentional evasion through ignorance suggests either changes in the tax code to eliminate poorly understood sections or efforts at publicity aimed at specific target groups about their tax responsibilities, or both.

How careful must policy makers be in balancing strict enforcement against voluntary compliance? Do increases in the former lead to a decline in the latter and, if so, with what net effect? A widespread pattern of loyal compliance may suggest public campaigns to emphasize the moral obligation to pay taxes and to clarify what benefits and protections those taxes bring. These efforts might be targeted at groups particularly likely to be responsive to them based on some understanding of the social location of attitudes and compliance patterns.

The treatment of compliance and noncompliance as types can thus lead to very specific ideas about policies and their effects and directs attention to the potential trade-offs of policy changes as they promote compliance among one group but depress it in another. What we do not know, however, is the relative importance (in terms of numbers and tax liability) of these various types of compliance and noncompliance and their social locations. A research agenda for the study of tax compliance must ultimately promise to provide this knowledge base.

A Tentative Research Agenda

A research agenda for the study of tax compliance and noncompliance must include a mix of basic research that expands our knowledge of taxpaying behavior and provides a context for policy decisions and mission-oriented work that focuses on particular policies and their expected or actual impact. It is our judgment that the state of knowledge in the field requires heavy emphasis initially on basic research primarily about taxpaying behavior and secondarily about tax-enforcing behavior. Before outlining these areas of basic research and several more specific research issues, we address some of the general strengths and weaknesses of potential data collection techniques.

DATA COLLECTION TECHNIQUES: METHODOLOGICAL OVERVIEW

Official data about noncompliance (through estimates of the "tax gap," data on noncompliance from the Taxpayer Compliance Measurement Program, and statistics on civil and criminal violations) are necessarily selective and unilateral. They identify some kinds of noncompliance and not others, some noncompliers and not others, in ways dependent on official values and enforcement organization as well as on the actual distribution of violation. Nor can official data about noncompliance distinguish very well among compliance and noncompliance types although they may be helpful in some approximations of those distinctions. Using official data exclusively to discover the social correlates of noncompliance runs some risk of circularity in that official expectations about noncompliance lead to a more careful search and identification of noncompliance among particular social categories. Finally, official data can only provide rough measures of the volume and character of undetected violations.

Interviews and self-administered questionnaires provide another potential source of information about tax compliance and noncompliance. Only through questioning can one practically gather data about taxpaying behavior and attitudes and the economic activities that provide the context for taxpaying. In-depth interviews appear to be underused for this sort of fundamental research.

The use of "self-reports" as a part of questionnaires allows particular focus on compliance or noncompliance with tax laws. In response to the problem of measuring undetected crime, criminologists have pioneered and refined self-report techniques, and these have been used sparingly in the tax area (Westat, Inc. 1980). The self-reports, even those specifically identifying kinds of actions such as underreporting income, typically do not indicate the kind, extent, or severity of the noncompliance. It is not enough simply to identify "compliers" and "noncompliers." Refined self-report instruments when combined with other data about economic context and attitudes could be especially helpful in refining a typology of compliance and noncompliance.

The experience in delinquency research suggests two methodological problems that need to be addressed in self-report research. First, random sampling of respondents in the general population means that very few serious tax cheats will be identified simply because they are rare. This problem might be overcome by developing creative ways of sampling special "high-risk" groups identified through examination of official data.

Second, the reliability and validity of self-report data need to be carefully monitored. A variety of comparisons working forward from and backward to official records have been used to examine the quality of self-reports of delinquency (Gold, 1970). Individual reports of attempted evasion need to be checked against official judgments about tax compliance based on filed returns. The difficulty of cross-checking while protecting confidentiality and gaining trust is significant but might be overcome.

A third source of data on tax compliance and noncompliance is that gained from *ethnographic techniques,* which combine field observation with interviewing of key informants. For research focused specifically on taxpaying behavior, ethnographic techniques may be inefficient because of the likelihood that little of the behavior observed will have much to do with taxpaying. On the other hand, ethnographies will be particularly rich sources of data about social noncompliance because they identify the organizational and social pressures in a particular occupational setting. Careful selection of research sites where noncompliance is thought to be especially common might have reasonably high payoff. The greatest utility of this technique would seem to lie in studies of tax advising and enforcing where most of the daily activity is salient.

Research Issues

Taxpaying behavior and attitudes.

An ambitious research program on "taxpaying behavior" should have very high priority in a research agenda. In essence, such a program should address a question such as the following: how do people learn, understand, and approach their taxpaying responsibilities in the context of their economic activity and social relationships? Answers to this question seem to us to be essential both for development of tax enforcement strategies and to build an inductively derived conceptual foundation for more focused research. Intensive interviews of random samples of individuals would provide the data to begin to answer this question.

Such interviews would include questions on the sources of taxpayers' socialization to and organization of taxpaying behavior. Specific taxpaying strategies might be presented to find out how much is known about them, where the information comes from, and to what extent specific networks have influenced the execution of those strategies. This survey would help to establish the relative significance of different sources of information and influence: occupational networks, brokers, mass media, and family, for example. It would also allow refinement of these categories by permitting for comparisons by class, age cohort, region, and other potentially influential variables.

One particular focus of such research might be tax socialization by families. It is probable that for certain classes of Americans, socialization to the tax system is predominantly controlled by parents or other elder members of extended families. We should expect differences in taxpaying attitudes between someone whose father always just filled out the "short form" and cursed quietly about "Uncle Sam's hand in my pocket" (structured or defensive compliance), on the one hand, and someone whose parents talked year round about how particular financial decisions were to be considered in light of tax advantages and disadvantages (self-serving compliance). People are likely to "inherit" attitudes toward tax payment. Moreover, to the extent that one is a member of even a moderately wealthy "family-as-financial-institution," one's taxpaying practices are likely to be shaped by family norms and imperatives rather than individual inclinations. The practices that develop in these kinds of networks may be particularly significant to the IRS since they may represent choices affecting sizable revenue potential, and they are more likely to be choices in the "gray" areas of tax law, where contests over interpretation can become very complex.

SOCIAL LOCATION OF COMPLIANCE AND NONCOMPLIANCE TYPES. Within the context of a general understanding of taxpayer socialization, attitudes, and behavior, we must learn more about the distribution and social location of the taxpayer types (or another formulation of them) described earlier. To do so is important not just for building our understanding of taxpaying, but also because it should advance thinking about tax policy and the trade-offs involved in policy decisions. For example, it makes a difference whether brokers such as accountants and tax lawyers generally reinforce compliance or whether they undermine it. It makes a difference to know how much loyal compliance there is in comparison to defensive compliance, especially among those whose compliance is not structured. It makes a difference whether a large or small proportion of people who underreport taxable income fail to perceive that their income is legitimately taxable (unknowing evasion); find the burden of bookkeeping and of saving to pay taxes that are not withheld too heavy (lazy evasion); or organize their economic activity quite consciously and carefully to avoid taxes (asocial noncompliance). It also should be important to know where to find particular kinds of compliance and noncompliance. To the degree that particular problems are localized to some degree in occupational, regional, age, or income groups, educational, public relations, and enforcement strategies might be targeted to the appropriate population.

Several research strategies might be employed to examine the relationships between social location and compliance variables. One would make use of tax return data (especially the TCMP data) to identify the social characteristics of overcompliers, compliers, and various kinds of noncompliers. It may even be possible to develop rough indicators of some compliance types from the ways income tax returns are completed.

Survey research could extend the study of available data by providing self-report measures of compliance and a battery of behavioral and attitudinal measures that could help identify how individuals understand their own taxpaying behavior. These data could be used to estimate the distribution of compliance and noncompliance types in the population and some of their social and personal correlates. Comparisons between findings from the TCMP data and survey data would be an important part of the analysis. In addition, some research should focus on individuals who have been found to be evading taxes. Because this sample is the product of an official decision-making process, it is unlikely to be perfectly representative of the population of violators. However, as the criminological literature demonstrates, much can be learned by studying life histories, perceptions, values, beliefs and social circumstances of offenders. Intensive studies of small samples of individuals guilty of different sorts of tax evasion would enrich our understanding of noncompliance types.

TAX COLLECTION BEHAVIOR.   As a consequence of their ambiguity, interpretations of some aspects of tax law may well vary a little or a great deal from office to office and over time through the "routine accommodations" discussed earlier. Some of this variation may be necessary to make the system run smoothly, but it may also have impact on the "tax gap." To the degree that the practices of IRS agents are subject to administrative control and change, tax practices may be a particularly important as well as sensitive area to explore through careful research.

This research might begin with a test of the hypothesis that regional variations in rates of noncompliance are related not only to variation in taxpayer characteristics across regions but also variations in official tax practices. Official data could be examined for regional variations in the ways specific subsections of tax returns are completed. Because informal accommodations between IRS officials and tax advisors are the focus of study here, it would be important to study returns prepared by tax advisors. For example, tax returns from the grain-belt states might show a particular pattern of deduction claims that might vary systematically from ways of using the same subsection among taxpayers in Florida's citrus belt. Levels of deductions for "business-related travel" might differ systematically from one region to another, because different informal norms may have arisen among local accountants as to what amount the IRS would "give" a taxpayer (that is, how much an individual could expect to "get away with" before being asked to produce proof).

Research on this topic must be sensitive to the possibility that *overall* indices of regional variation (e.g., per capita rates of tax payment, even if major variables such as class or educational level are controlled) may be insignificant because they mask regional variations in the *balance* between compliant and noncompliant behavior. That is, localized networks may ultimately produce approximately the same levels of tax payment, while arriving at those levels through different mixes of tax law interpretation and "practical" advice to taxpayer clients.

Ethnographic research of the sort done on plea bargaining (e.g., Buckle and Buckle, 1977; Mather, 1979) should complement examination of available data. In effect, researchers would sit in with IRS agents as they audit individuals and negotiate with tax accountants. The observers would be looking for: patterns in the informal training of IRS personnel within specific offices; standardized routines in identifying cases to audit; office "lore" about types of taxpayers and accountants; evidence of routinized, personalized relationships between office personnel and private accountants; definitions of the relevant "audiences" which influence both specific case decisions and broader local-office policy decisions. Several studies of this sort would help flesh out our understanding of the role of official discretion in defining compliance and noncompliance and contributing to or closing the "tax gap."

COMPLIANCE BROKERS. Tax attorneys, accountants, and tax preparers, as well as financial advisors, investment counselors, and bankers act as impact filters or compliance brokers. The extent and character of their influence on compliance and noncompliance is an important subject for empirical investigation.

That investigation might begin with a careful comparison of third-party prepared returns to a matched (on income, occupation, and so on) "control group" to see whether any substantial variations appear in kinds and amounts of deductions and ultimate tax liability.

Exploratory ethnographic research, followed by interviews of a wider sample of tax advisors should be the major source of data for understanding compliance brokers. In this case, it would involve participant researchers observing relations between local IRS officials, professional tax preparers, and the clients of tax preparers. One might simply spend time as an "assistant" in the office of a CPA. Another might take a temporary job with a large-volume preparing company such as H.&R. Block. Ultimately, observers would need to cultivate "informants" within the occupational communities they are studying and develop their understanding of that work through a combination of observation and questioning.

Since one potentially significant force in the creation and maintenance of such networks is the business schools where government and private accountants both receive professional training, ethnographic research in a few such schools might prove to be a necessary component of this procedure.

The research need not be statistically rigorous. Five or six locations would be sufficient to produce valuable results. The purpose is not to describe the entire landscape of network relationships and professional practice. Rather, this method provides an "insider's view" of the work of compliance brokers and an empirical foundation for more refined research about tax advisors.

A good model for this approach is H. Laurence Ross's study (1970) of insurance claims adjustors. In it, we see that generalizable results can be derived from intensive research on a very small percentage of cases and that this work can be done systematically, so that its results are not merely anecdotal.

Such research might be followed by systematic interviewing of a wider, more representative sample of compliance brokers. In addition, one might gather taxpayer-eye-view data about the behavior of these brokers. For example, several standard tax situations might be prepared and advice purchased from a variety of tax advisors about how to treat that tax situation. The success of such research, as of other research proposed here, depends, of course, on maintaining strict protections of the confidentiality of all research subjects.

ECONOMIC NETWORKS AND SOCIAL NONCOMPLIANCE.   Specific occupational categories appear to develop sets of expectations and information about tax compliance and noncompliance based on the specific characteristics of the occupation. Domestic workers, waiters and waitresses, and perhaps people in many other occupations become involved in social networks where noncompliance is encouraged or taken for granted. It is what we have called "social evasion," and for many, this may be more than a mere opportunity to evade. It may be evasion based on both social pressure (to support the "morality" of the evasion behavior of others in the network) and economic necessity because of a network-imposed economic calculus.

Ethnographic research can reveal the way in which these networks operate and the probable balances between revenue enhancement and reduction which their operations produce. The choice of networks to study should be determined by their probable significance for increased revenue. The home repair industry, for example, may involve widespread instances of evasion because of the possibilities for unrecorded transactions. The conduct of such ethnographies need not be terribly expensive. Some research support could be given, for example, to people conducting ethnographies for other reasons. This "piggybacking" could produce a wider range of examples for the development of a "portrait" of economic networks than would total support for a smaller number of ethnographies.

Meetings of professional or business organizations and newsletters and publications of occupational groups provide another potential source of information and focus of research about social compliance and noncompliance. Among academic professionals, for example, the *Chronicle of Higher Education* and *Academe* regularly present discussions of tax payment issues relevant to academics. Surveys of such specialized organs can lay bare many significant dimensions of tax payment issues that are problematic for a group and that therefore may be closest to the patterns of noncompliance characteristic of that group.

The purpose of surveying such literature would be to help identify targets of more systematic research. However, with careful controls, a survey of this literature might also serve as the foundation for the development of a definitive description of the American ecology of tax-relevant occupational networks. Such a description could, by itself, be used in developing models describing the relationship between occupational networks and taxpaying behavior.

LOYAL COMPLIANCE AND SYMBOLIC NONCOMPLIANCE. A particularly rich and important area for investigation involves the relationship between attitudes and beliefs of citizens and their taxpaying behavior. Some aspects of this study are already built into the research agenda already outlined. Two further suggestions are in order as well.

First, some of the most intriguing hints about these relationships came from longitudinal studies of taxpaying that suggest, for example, a bicentennial effect (Kinsey, 1984). This finding suggests that fruitful research might be done retrospectively (and perhaps comparatively across states) to see whether effects on tax revenues, the kind and extent of noncompliance, and voluntary contributions to the treasury vary in any systematic way with shifting political and public views. For example, did federal tax returns in states with the strongest local tax-cutting movements track differently than those in other states?

Secondly, prospectively it would be wise to prepare a longitudinal survey design that can follow tax attitudes and taxpaying behavior through any changes in the tax code that purport to increase fairness, equity, and simplicity.

Possibilities for quasi-experimental research are almost endless in this area. Inspired by the pioneering research of Schwartz and Orleans (1967) and utilizing the decentralization of tax offices, several sorts of experiments might be tried. For example, media campaigns and special mailings making particular appeals to taxpayers might be used for targeted areas and their impact on tax returns monitored. Special IRS efforts at general public education or education of specific occupational groups and at providing tax advice could be evaluated in a similar fashion. A special mailing (or several different kinds—making different appeals—allocated randomly) might instruct, warn, cajole self-employed workers or dentists or any group about their particular tax responsibilities and problems. Tax returns of recipients could be examined before and after the mailings to gauge their effects.

Conclusion

In sum, the study of tax compliance and noncompliance can develop most productively through an appreciation and recognition of the variety and social context of taxpaying behavior. To these ends we have proposed a rough typology of compliance and noncompliance and a research agenda. The former must remain provisional at best until a firmer empirical foundation for conceptualizing taxpayer behavior is developed.

References

Abel, R. L.
   1980   Redirecting social studies of law. *Law and Society Review* 14(3): 805–829.
Blau, P., and Duncan, O. D.
   1967   *The American Occupational Structure.* New York: John Wiley & Sons.
Boulding, K. E.
   1970   The impact of the draft on the legitimacy of the national state. Pp. 509–517 in S. Deutsch and J. Howard, eds., *Where It's At: Radical Perspectives in Sociology.* New York: Harper and Row.
Buckle, S. R. T., and Buckle, L. G.
   1977   *Bargaining for Justice: Case Disposition and Reform in the Criminal Courts.* New York: Praeger.
Easterlin, R.
   1966   Economic-demographic interactions among long swings in economic growth. *American Economic Review* 56(5): 1063–1104.
Eisenstein, J., and Jacob, H.
   1977   *Felony Justice.* Boston: Little, Brown.
Elder, G.
   1974   *Children of the Great Depression.* Chicago: University of Chicago Press.

Engel, D. M.
  1984 The oven birds' song: insiders, outsiders, and personal injuries in an American community. *Law and Society Review* 18: 551–582.
Erikson, K. T.
  1976 *Everything in Its Path*. New York: Simon & Schuster.
Feeley, M. M.
  1979 *The Process is the Punishment: Handling Cases in a Lower Criminal Court*. New York: Russell Sage Foundation.
Feest, J.
  1968 Compliance with legal Regulation: observations of stop sign behavior. *Law and Society Review* 2: 447–461.
Feffer, G. A., Timbie, R. E., Weiner, A. J., and Ernst, M. L.
  1983 RFP for individual income tax returns: proposed alternative ways for filing computer-prepared individual income tax returns. *Federal Register* 48(61): 13131–13135.

Gold, M.
  1970 *Delinquent Behavior in an American City*. Belmont, Calif.: Brooks/Cole Publishing.

Hyde, A.
  1983 The concept of legitimation in the sociology of law. *Wisconsin Law Review*, 379–426.

Internal Revenue Service
  1984 *Annual Report 1984*. Commissioner of Internal Revenue. Internal Revenue Service, U.S. Department of the Treasury. Washington, D.C.: U.S. Government Printing Office.

Kagan, R. A.
  1989 On the visibility of income tax violations. Chapter 3 in this volume.
Kinsey, K. A.
  1984 Survey Data on Tax Compliance: A Compendium and Review. American Bar Foundation Tax Compliance Working Paper 84-1, December 1984. American Bar Foundation, Chicago.
  1987 Theories and models of tax evasion. *Criminal Justice Abstracts* 18:403 (1987). Revision of American Bar Foundation Tax Compliance Working Paper 84-2, December 1984. American Bar Foundation, Chicago.

Lempert, R. O.
  1972 Norm-making in social exchange: a contract law model. *Law and Society Review* 7: 1–32.
  1980 Grievances and legitimacy: the beginnings and end of dispute settlement. *Law and Society Review* 15: 707–715.
Lewis, A.
  1982 *The Psychology of Taxation*. New York: St. Martin's Press.
Long, S. B.
  1981 Social control in the civil law: The case of income tax enforcement. Pp.

185–214 in H. L. Ross, ed., *Law and Deviance*. Beverly Hills, Calif.: Sage Publications.

Mather, L.
  1979   *Plea Bargaining or Trial? The Process of Criminal Case Disposition.* Lexington, Mass.: Lexington Books.

McEwen, C. A. and Maiman, R. J.
  1984   Mediation in small claims courts: achieving compliance through consent. *Law and Society Review,* 18(1): 11–49.
  1986   In search of legitimacy: toward an empirical response analysis. *Law & Policy* 8: 257–273.

Muir, W. K.
  1968   *Prayer in the Public Schools: Law and Attitude Change.* Chicago: University of Chicago Press.

Nader, L. and Todd, H. F., eds.
  1978   *The Disputing Process—Law in Ten Societies.* New York: Columbia University Press.

Rollins, J.
  1985   *Between Women: Domestics and Their Employers.* Philadelphia: Temple University Press.

Ross, H. L.
  1970   *Settled Out of Court: The Social Process of Insurance Claim Adjustment.* Chicago: Aldine.

Roth, J. A., and Witte, A. D.
  1985   Understanding Taxpayer Compliance: Major Factors and Perspectives. Unpublished paper, National Research Council, Washington, D.C.

Schmölders, G.
  1970   Survey research in public finance—a behavioral approach to fiscal theory. *Public Finance* 25:300–306.

Schur, E. M.
  1965   *Crimes Without Victims: Deviant Behavior and Public Policy.* Englewood Cliffs, N.J.: Prentice-Hall.

Schwartz, R. D. and Orleans, S.
  1967   On legal sanctions. *University of Chicago Law Review* 34: 274–300.

Strümpel, B.
  1969   The contribution of survey research to public finance. pp. 13–38 in A. T. Peacock, ed., *Quantitative Analysis in Public Finance.* New York: Praeger.

Sudnow, D.
  1965   Normal crimes: sociological features of the penal code in a public defender office. *Social Problems* 12(3): 255–276.

Tyler, T. R.
  1985   Psychological Perspectives on Normative Issues: Theoretical Implications of Citizen Concerns With Fairness. Paper presented at the annual meeting of the American Political Science Association, New Orleans.

Westat, Inc.
  1980   Self-Reported Tax Compliance: A Pilot Survey Report. Prepared for the

Internal Revenue Service, March 21, 1980, by Westat, Inc., Rockville, Md.

Witte, A. D.
1987 The nature and extent of unrecorded activity: a survey concentrating on recent U. S. research. In Sergio Alessandrini and Bruno Dallago, eds., *The Unofficial Economy: Consequences and Perspectives in Different Economic Systems*. London: Gower Publishing.

Robert A. Kagan

3. On the Visibility of Income Tax Law Violations

What determines the extent to which laws are complied with or violated? The question takes on special importance in contemporary society, where governments attempt to regulate individual behavior in countless ways and specific legal duties often seem unrelated to traditional morality. Consider these instances of legal noncompliance:

- The manager of a food processing plant, striving to meet a "rush order" production deadline, keeps the assembly line going for a full shift beyond the point at which FDA "good manufacturing practices regulations" (and company policy) call for periodic cleaning.
- On the form he files with the IRS, a housepainter does not report 20 percent of the income he has received from painting jobs during the past year.
- An individual drives home a little drunk but within the speed limit and, as he has done forty times before in the same condition, arrives safely.
- A teenager scrawls his name and street number on the wall of a New York City subway car, already defaced by twenty similar examples of graffiti.
- A woman receiving meager AFDC benefits for her family fails on her monthly form to inform the welfare office that her teenage daughter is no longer attending school and has a full-time job.

These kinds of illegal actions are not easy to prevent. They are "low-visibility" offenses; that is, the violator bears little risk that a governmental official or a third person will see him commit the offense and initiate law enforcement proceedings. For these kinds of offenses, moreover, the usual social inhibitions against breaking the law are comparatively weak, and legal penalties, when imposed, typically are not

Department of Political Science, University of California, Berkeley very severe. The primary reason, I believe, is that each particular offense inflicts no direct or immediate harm on any identifiable person. Although such "victimless" offenses, viewed cumulatively, lead to significant social harms, the individual offense, viewed in isolation, seems morally insignificant, at least in comparison to the terrible crimes, catastrophes and large-scale frauds we read about in the newspapers (see Glazer, 1979).

Nevertheless, despite the obstacles to enforcement, most people comply with the laws in question. Obviously, normative factors—such as cultural commitments to follow the law, or beliefs in the legitimacy of the overall public policy reflected in the particular regulation—play a vital role in enhancing compliance. Moreover, even the remote threat of legal penalties—with their associated social stigma—matters; small increases in the probability of detection can induce large numbers of citizens to take pains to comply, and the probability of detection can sometimes be increased substantially.

This chapter concentrates on the last-mentioned factor: Detectability, which I will refer to as the relative "visibility" of violations to law enforcement officials. My empirical focus will be failure to report taxable personal income to the Internal Revenue Service. According to IRS estimates, underreporting of personal income is the largest component of the "tax gap." For 1981, IRS researchers estimated that unreported individual income from legal sources accounted for $55.1 billion in unpaid taxes. This figure dwarfs other tax violations, such as overstated business expenses on individual returns ($6.3 billion in lost revenue), overstated personal deductions ($6.6 billion), and unreported income and overstated offsets by corporations ($6.2 billion) (IRS, 1983: Table I-1).

Drawing on the IRS's own research, the chapter demonstrates how variation in the extent to which income-generating transactions are "visible to" (or detectable by) the tax authorities has an enormously powerful effect on compliance rates. After discussing the role and limits of mandatory reporting to ensure compliance with law, the chapter will analyze (1) variations in visibility across types of income and transactions; (2) the "informal suppliers" who are associated with the "underground economy," noting the particular characteristics that reduce the visibility of their unreported income; (3) factors that tend to increase the visibility of unreported small business income; and (4) the concealment of income in ostensibly higher-visibility businesses. By speculating about the factors that increase or reduce the visibility of violations, the chapter attempts to broaden understanding of variations in compliance levels and of how noncompliance is, or might be, affected by governmental and private action.

Making Offenses Visible: Mandatory Reporting and Its Limits

To sociologist Robert Merton, the concept of "observability" of social behavior, or its "visibility" to others, is crucial in explaining the extent to which social groups cohere and display or enforce conformity to group norms. Without "direct and immediate observability," he wrote, "deviant behavior can cumulate" (Merton, 1957:320). A critical variable in social behavior, accordingly, is the existence of "structural hindrances to the flow of information" about deviant acts to those who have the inclination or duty to impose sanctions against them" (ibid.). Conversely, such social inventions as double-entry bookkeeping are mechanisms for enhancing the flow of information about role performance when direct observation is difficult (ibid.:342).

With respect to legal norms, the social institution of privacy creates a major "structural hindrance to the flow of information" about deviance to officials in charge of imposing legal sanctions, at least in wealthy, modern societies (Stinchcombe, 1963; Posner, 1981). When law violations occur in private places, as they often do, they are in an immediate sense invisible to law enforcement officials. The officials can "see" them only if (a) private victims or complainants become aware of the violations and call enforcement officials or file legal claims against the perpetrators, or (b) the government invests in costly and intrusive search or surveillance operations (see generally Black, 1973; Reiss, 1971; Kagan, 1978:26).

Offenses vary in "degree of visibility," or the *frequency and ease with which they come to the attention of and can be proved by enforcement officials.* The most visible violations are those that are easily detected by victims, provided that the victims are motivated to complain to officials (because they have a reasonable probability of obtaining some tangible benefit or remedy) and have the ability to do so at low cost (and without fear of retaliation). A repetitive or ongoing violation, evidenced by physical conditions on the violator's property (such as a dangerous unguarded machine in a factory or defective plumbing in a rental housing unit), is far more visible to enforcement officials than a violation that is fleeting, as a truck driver who drives a few hours longer than is allowed by highway safety regulations.

Of course, enforcement officials may be able to detect even "low-visibility" violations. They can interrogate a truck driver and the dispatchers at the sites where he made stops, and they can calculate, from that information and the study of maps, approximately how long he was on the road. But violations of that nature, precisely because they are more costly to detect and prove than those that leave behind more easily obtained and reliable evidence, can be thought of as "less visible." For that reason, false financial claims in a stock prospectus are more visible to the Securities and Exchange Commission than are violations of insider trading rules. Not only are false claims more likely to trigger complaints, but SEC officials can more easily establish the falsity of financial claims by publicly traded companies by comparing the prospectus to financial statements prepared by independent auditors. The SEC typically can detect insider trading, on the other hand, only by labor-intensive charting of many stock transactions over an extended period (Shapiro, 1984).[1]

For offenses such as nonpayment of taxes and some regulatory violations, law enforcement officials, unable to rely on victims to identify offenders, employ a variety of techniques designed to reduce the cost of discovering offenses and offenders. One common technique is *mandatory record keeping and reporting:* individuals or businesses are required to furnish law enforcement officials with compliance-related information. Under some pollution control laws, factories are ordered to monitor and report excessive emissions to governmental officials. Shippers of hazardous wastes must file with relevant agencies manifests documenting proper disposal. Truck drivers are required to keep logs, and in some cases to install devices that automatically record travel times and speeds for each twenty-four-hour period. Failure to report or to report honestly is a separate offense, wholly apart from the underlying illegal acts (excessive emissions, unsafe dumping or driving).

Mandatory reporting gives rise to an additional enforcement problem, however. How can enforcement officials detect failure to report fully about inherently low-visibility acts? This problem is acute in federal income tax law, where the acts to be reported—receipt of income, deductible expenditures—are not wrongful themselves. Nor is a separate report required of each transaction. Only an annual summary report is required, summarizing the cumulative results of individual income-generating transactions scattered over an entire tax year. Even if an IRS agent or an informant saw a storekeeper putting cash receipts from some sales into his pocket rather than into the cash register, the IRS could not know for certain that the storekeeper was evading his obligation to report those receipts as income until he filed his annual tax return and then an audit somehow showed that he had failed to include the pocketed cash in the "income" column. Thus, even with mandatory annual reports, nonreporting of income remains an inherently low-visibility offense, discoverable only through costly enforcement efforts. Since tax officials cannot "see" the countless "invisible" income-producing transactions, the accuracy of the report often can be determined only by comparing a full accounting of a year's worth of the taxpayer's transactions (if such an accounting can be done through auditing processes) with the sum reported in the return.

Similar problems of verification are faced by other control systems. For example, like the IRS, insurance claims offices are concerned about the accuracy of reports of expenses incurred by the insured over a period of time, such as claimed business losses due to fire, or claims for services rendered by health care providers. Purchasers of businesses and financial institutions extending credit are on guard against misrepresentation in sellers or borrowers' statements of their annual income. Welfare and disability programs worry that beneficiaries' periodic eligibility reports may understate their actual earned income.

Tax officials, however, face an even more difficult verification problem, primarily because of the sheer magnitude of the IRS's jurisdiction. Participation in its reporting system is universal and mandatory. Administrative resources for determining who has not filed, and for auditing the accuracy of the millions of reports that are filed, are limited. (In recent years, the IRS has audited less than 2 percent of the more than 100 million income tax returns filed.)[2]

In addition, in the case of private credit applications and sales of businesses, the lender or buyer can require the applicant to provide independent verification of the claims in their reports (e.g., via certified financial statements, letters from attorneys, and so forth). Insurance claims offices can withhold payment until the claimant provides required indicia of the truthfulness of his claim. In contrast, when questioning whether a return fully discloses all taxable income, the IRS shoulders the burden of providing evidence that it does not.

Welfare offices that suspect ineligible recipients of understating their income are somewhat akin to the IRS with respect to the difficulty of verification, but through monthly eligibility reports and quality control reviews, they undoubtedly maintain a higher "audit rate" than the IRS. Moreover, by computer-matching their client list against lists received from governmental and large private employers, welfare agencies have developed a tool for raising some forms of cheating to visibility (see Gardiner and Lyman, 1984:153–155). In addition, third parties, whether employers or neighbors, may be more willing to report suspected welfare cheaters than suspected tax cheaters to the government, as indicated by the success of "welfare abuse hotlines" established by some states (ibid.).

The use of third-party reports—such as certified public accountants, telephone hotlines, and computer matching—is paralleled by the IRS's most potent techniques for verifying tax returns and signaling taxpayers that unreported income will be visible to tax collectors and auditors. First in importance is the *mandatory withholding* of employee income taxes by employers and mandatory employer reports to the IRS of total income paid each employee. Second in importance are *information returns,* whereby payers of interest and dividends (primarily banks, savings and loans institutions, corporations, brokerage houses) must send to each recipient and to the IRS an annual report specifying the sum paid. More recently, information returns, identifying the recipient and amount paid, have been required of governmental payers of unemployment compensation, state and local tax refunds, and agricultural subsidies; payers of fees (greater than $600) to independent contractors; payers of royalties and alimony; distributions from cooperatives to patrons and from retirement funds to pensioners; and from stock and commodity brokers, concerning the proceeds of sales of securities, commodities and futures. These third-party reporting mechanisms, as we shall see, create large variations among kinds of unreported income with respect to their visibility to the IRS, and apparently with respect to perceived visibility in the minds of taxpayers.

Dimensions of Income Visibility

According to Feffer et al. (1983:243–313), income-producing transactions are more likely to be reported when *"they leave records in the hands of third parties or the IRS from which the fact of the transactions can be detected."* Referring to Figure 1, Feffer et al. state:

> Common sense suggests, and statistical studies confirm, that noncompliance is lowest where there is withholding (area A on the chart), and somewhat greater (but still modest) when transactions are subject to

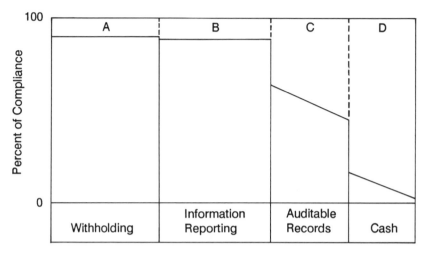

FIGURE 1. Source: Feffer et al. (1983)

information reporting (area B). When auditable records are generated by transactions but no information report is made to the IRS, noncompliance increases substantially (area C). The line slopes on the chart because the amount of noncompliance depends in large measure on such factors as the identity of the third party who has the records, the likelihood that the IRS will gain access to them, and the simplicity with which transactions can be reconstructed from them. Finally, noncompliance is obviously greatest and hardest to quantify when transactions are conducted in cash (or barter) and leave no records in the hands of third parties (area D). Again, the line slopes because noncompliance depends on such factors as the number and identities of the persons who are aware of such transactions.

The IRS's Taxpayer Compliance Measurement Program indicates that Feffer et al.'s rough diagram is basically correct, although it may overstate noncompliance for cash income. As Table 1 shows, differences in the nature of the records left behind by income-generating transactions have dramatic effects on compliance levels. For each category of income reflected in line items on individual tax returns, Table 1 displays the percentage of returns for which 1979 TCMP intensive audits discovered substantial amounts (over $500, or over $2,000) of unreported income.

The audits indicated that only 1.8 percent of taxpayers who received taxable dividends (for which payers must submit information returns to the IRS and to the taxpayer) had unreported dividend income of $2,000

TABLE 1   Unreported Income Detected by 1979 TCMP Audits

Type of income	Returns with item in exam (%)	Unreported income of $500 or more (%)	Unreported income $2001 or more (%)	Estimated number of returns
Schedule F[a]	2.8	45.7	24.0	627.620
Schedule C[b]	10.3	42.3	22.3	2,126,880
1120S Distr[c]	0.8	27.2	15.3	116,690
Rents/royalties	8.7	22.6	6.8	545,490
Form 4797[d]	1.6	20.5	11.0	166,720
Partnership distr	3.1	16.9	8.5	244,140
Schedule D[e]	9.4	12.9	5.3	455,080
Tips	2.3	11.8	4.9	102,350
Estates, trusts	0.9	5.0	2.9	22,660
Dividends	10.9	4.8	1.8	184,610
Interest	65.4	2.1	0.4	251,580
Wages and salaries	89.1	2.3	0.6	512,640

[a] Farm income
[b] Income from trade or business
[c] Income from Subchapter S partnership
[d] Capital gains on certain business property
[e] Capital gains
Source: Smith, 1985, using data from IRS, 1979 Individual Return TCMP (Phase III, Cycle 7).

or more in 1979. The comparable figure for unreported interest income was only 0.4 percent of taxpayers who had interest income in that year.

At the other end of the spectrum, over 22 percent of taxpayers who had personal income from their own (unincorporated) farm, trade or business—forms of income for which information returns usually are not filed by payers—were shown to have had more than $2,000 in unreported 1979 income.

Table 2 reflects IRS estimates of the aggregate amount of unreported income of different types: unlike Table 1, it includes nonreporting in amounts less than $500 in each category. It indicates that taxpayers report 83 to 87 percent of dividend and interest income (subject to information returns) but far less of major types of income not subject to third-party reporting—50 percent of small business income, 37 percent of rents, and 21 percent of informal supplier income.[3] Visibility, therefore, appears to be an enormously important factor—and perhaps the most important factor—in shaping compliance rates.

TABLE 2   Estimated Voluntary Reporting of Income on 1981 Individual
Income Tax Returns (in billions of dollars)

Type of income	Reported on returns	Should have been reported	Net voluntary reporting (%)
Wages and salaries	$1,455	$1,550	93.9
Interest	129	150	86.3
Dividends	45	54	83.7
Capital gains	26	44	59.4
Nonfarm proprietor income	54	107	50.3 (78.7)[a]
Small business corporation and partnership income	15	32	47.0 (78.7)[a]
Rents	3	7	37.2 (95.6)[a]
Informal supplier income	5	22	20.7

[a] Income calculated on a net basis, reflecting IRS corrections for overstated expenses. The figure in parenthesis is the estimated voluntary reporting percentage for gross income.
Source: IRS, 1983a:10, 22.

A skeptic might argue that even without information returns, recipients of dividend and interest income may be more disposed to report such income, on the average, than recipients of income from a trade, farm, or business.[4] Some IRS research, however, indicates that information returns have a strong independent effect on compliance. One IRS study was based on special audits of recipients of income from U.S. government-issued bearer bonds, which can be freely negotiated (IRS, 1982). Recipients of interest coupons on U.S. government bonds (for which the Treasury Department did not file 1099 forms) reported to the IRS 81 percent of the interest they received. Recipients of interest on U.S. Treasury bills purchased for their account by banks (also not covered by information returns) had a substantially higher voluntary compliance level, 91 percent. The VCL for holders of Treasury bills for which information returns were filed was a still higher 95.7 percent.

Note the large VCL gap between coupon bond holders (81 percent) and taxpayers whose Treasury bills were held by banks (91 percent)—neither group being subject to income reporting. The reason for the disparity, one might speculate, is that the banks probably sent regular written statements to their clients, informing the honest but perhaps disorganized taxpayer of interest credited to his account, while the coupon holders received no such reminders. Like information returns, such bank statements would enhance the salience of irregular income to the taxpayer, while signaling that a record of his income is retained by a large, bureaucratized organization that could easily be audited (even if the bank does not automatically send an information return to the tax collectors). The additional 5.7 percent VCL gap between (a) T-bill holders for which information returns were issued and (b) those whose banks generated regular records of interest paid suggests the "value added," in terms of compliance, by almost certain visibility to the IRS (produced by 1099s) as compared with potential visibility (based on the ready auditability of bank records).

The impact of visibility-enhancing information returns on compliance also is illustrated by two IRS studies of taxpayers who were treated by employers as independent contractors—and hence for whom no tax was withheld. An IRS report to Congress in 1979 followed up on payments to 7,109 "independent contractors" by employers who had been subjected to employment tax audits (IRS, 1983b). The independent contractors, viewed collectively, reported to the IRS only 76.2 percent of the compensation they received: 47 percent of the independent contractors reported *none* of that income. But markedly greater compliance was indicated by a study published in 1983, some years after employers had been required to file information returns (1099 NEC) reflecting payments larger than $600 to independent contractors. The study examined 6,418 independent contractors for whom 1099 NECs had been filed by the payers. Collectively, the independent contractors reported to the IRS 92 percent of the compensation reflected on the information returns; approximately 15 percent reported none of that income (IRS, 1983b).[5]

In sum, existing research suggests visibility matters a great deal. Different kinds of unreported income can be arrayed as in Figure 2, in a hypothetical hierarchy of visibility-to-the-IRS, based on the nature and location of the evidentiary record of the underlying transactions and the difficulty or cost to enforcement officials of reviewing that evidentiary record.

Underlying Figure 2 is the assumption that, as records of income become progressively easier for the IRS to uncover and review, it becomes riskier for the taxpayer to fail to report the income fully without triggering an audit. At lower probabilities of visibility to the IRS, nonreporting is less likely to trigger an audit, but some risk remains, for the IRS could discover records of the income should the taxpayer be subjected to a thorough audit. Finally, at the lowest levels of visibility lie forms of unreported income that are difficult for the IRS to discover without extraordinary effort, even if the taxpayer is audited. The following paragraphs note the kinds of unreported income at the level of visibility suggested by Figure 2.

PREAUDIT VISIBILITY: INFORMATION SUBMITTED DIRECTLY TO IRS

Some unreported income is visible to the IRS by virtue of documents or information submitted directly to it:

- wage, dividend, interest or other income reported on information returns submitted by payers, but not reported on taxpayer's return
- internal inconsistencies in taxpayer returns, e.g. persistent net losses in trade or business, or failure to file after some years of having reported income
- unreported income channeled into unusual "high" living, resulting in tips to the IRS by resentful neighbors, coworkers, or others
- income "skimming" reported to the IRS by disaffected employees, partners, spouses.

Degrees of visibility of unreported income		Type of unreported income
Potentially visible before audit	1.	Unreported income reflected in *documents and reports submitted directly to IRS* (1099 forms, tip-offs)
	2.	Unreported income discoverable by IRS through audit of *third party records*
Potentially visible only upon audit	3.	Unreported income discoverable only through audit of *taxpayer records* (e.g., bank statements)
	4.	Unreported income discoverable only by IRS discovery and analysis of *taxpayer assets*
Potentially invisible even upon audit	5a.	Unreported income concealed from normal audit due to *fradulent record keeping*
	5b.	Unreported income concealed from normal audit by *natural invisibility* (e.g., cash income received from households or nonroutine sources)

FIGURE 2

Preaudit Visibility: Third-Party Records

Some unreported income has a significant probability of being discovered by the IRS in the course of an audit of a third-party payer. Visibility increases with the probability of the third party's being audited, which in turn generally relates to the size of the payer.

- Substantial payments to a taxpayer treated by an employer as an "independent contractor," discovered upon audit of the employer, may be followed up by review of the taxpayer's return.
- Cash payments to a taxpayer/retailer by a wholesaler for "rebates" or "returns," observed upon audit of the wholesaler, may be followed by review of the retailer's return.

Audit-Level Visibility: Taxpayer Records

Some unreported income, though not likely to trigger an audit (as in the case of the "preaudit visibility" categories mentioned above), can be discovered relatively easily by an auditor using records in the hands of the taxpayer.

- Bank statements reflect deposits of income (including cash income) not reflected on the taxpayer's return. (Such statements are visible to the IRS either through normal audit probes or through 1099 forms filed by banks and reflecting interest paid to the taxpayer.)
- A taxpayer's books and accounts that do not balance internally or jibe with tax returns are easily spotted.

Audit-Level Visibility: Taxpayer Assets

Unreported income not revealed by third-party or taxpayer records may be inferred by an auditor from discrepancies between reported income over time and the probable costs of visible assets (such as residence, motor vehicles, business equipment) or assets discovered through verbal probes concerning taxpayer's method of conducting trade or business.

Audit-Level Invisibility

Some unreported income is not likely to be discovered through a normal audit. This category can be further divided:

FRAUDULENT INVISIBILITY.   Some income can be concealed from auditors by altering books and records (e.g., keeping two sets of books), by depositing it in secret bank accounts (e.g., accounts in the names of nominees, false names, or dummy corporations), or by elaborate conspiratorial arrangements with accomplices or associates.

NATURAL INVISIBILITY.   Some income can be concealed with little effort beyond simple failure to report. A prime example is income received in cash, or even by check, in relatively small amounts and not likely to be discovered by audit of the payer (as in the case of payments received from households for nondeductible goods and services). Another example would be occasional sale of surplus materials by a building contractor who is not generally in the business of selling materials.

Recognizing the different levels of visibility gives rise to further questions: What social and economic patterns tend to push income down to Level 5 (audit-level invisibility)? What social forces or governmental interventions might increase the proportion of income that ends up at Level 3 (audit-level visibility) or higher (preaudit visibility)? To help address these questions the next section of this chapter discusses the nature and sources of naturally invisible income—Level 5(b) in Figure 2—and then discusses trends that may affect the overall importance of this kind of income in the national economy.

Natural Invisibility: Informal Suppliers

The IRS-estimated voluntary compliance rate (VCR) for small businesses is about 79 percent (see Table 2, above), as compared with 90 percent for corporations with assets of $1 million or more (Witte, 1985a:5, citing IRS, 1983a). In terms of aggregate impact, Witte has noted,

> Unreported taxable incomes generated in small enterprises and by the self-employed are estimated to have been $90 billion in 1981 compared with only approximately $10 billion of unreported taxable income generated by large corporations.

Lower still (20.7 percent) is the estimate of voluntary reporting by taxpayers they label "informal suppliers," small businesses whose income tends to be naturally invisible, that is, received in relatively small amounts, often in cash, from households who generally do not deduct such expenditures and keep no systematic records of them. Based on surveys of consumers and their expenditure patterns, the IRS estimates that informal suppliers' unreported income exceeded $40 billion in 1981, distributed as shown in Table 3 (IRS, 1983a: Table D-2).

TABLE 3   Value of Household Purchases from Informal Vendors by Types of
Goods and Services, 1981 (millions of dollars)

Goods and services	Amount purchased
Home repair and additions	12,245
Food	9,003
Child care	4,955
Domestic service	3,882
Auto repair	2,810
Sidewalk vendor goods	1,782
Flea market goods	1,698
Lawn maintenance	1,447
Lessons	933
Fuel	749
Appliance repair	744
Adult care	442
Cosmetic service	411
Sewing and related	392
Catering	300
Total	41,793

Source: IRS 1983a: Table D-2.

Some insight into the processes by which such naturally invisible
income becomes, or might be made to become, visible to the IRS, can be
provided by an analysis of the business practices of three housepainters.

THE WAY OF INFORMAL SUPPLIERS: THREE HOUSEPAINTERS

For at least four or five years, Alan, Barney, and Carl (fictitious names),
each in his late twenties, have been self-employed housepainters in an
urban area.[6] They are all unmarried. Alan and Carl are college graduates;
Carl continued painting while pursuing further postgraduate education.
Although each has earned gross income of at least $14,000 per year, none
has paid any federal income taxes. Alan and Barney have not filed returns;
Carl usually files a return indicating he has earned about $2,000.

Alan, Barney, and Carl consciously avoid creation of records that would
provide evidence of their actual income or that make their business
potentially visible to the IRS. None of them is a licensed contractor. They
have unmarked trucks. They get jobs primarily by word of mouth,
although Carl has placed advertisements in a small newspaper circulated in
a wealthy community.

Most of their work is for homeowners, although they occasionally work for real estate investors and other businesses. Often they are paid in cash. Carl says he has no inhibitions about telling homeowners he wants to be paid in cash for tax purposes; they recognize, he believes, that it is precisely because he does not pay taxes that his bids are lower than those of licensed contractors who employ union labor. Alan has painted the buildings in which he has rented an apartment in return for forgiveness of (substantial) rent payments.

When they are paid by check, which is not uncommon, they do not deposit the check to their own bank accounts, but take the check to the payer's bank and cash it there, although that sometimes involves "hassles" with bank tellers who initially decline service.

They also try to pay for supplies in cash, or with a certified check that they purchase for cash. Carl has declined an offer of credit from a paint store, believing that purchasing on credit would entail signing receipts for supplies or leaving other records indicating the volume of his work.

They do not hire workers, recognizing that this would create additional tax obligations and fearing that it would increase the risk of detection. Instead, Carl says, he forms "loose and temporary partnerships based on profit-sharing arrangements" (what some painters call a "partnership," however, is really temporary employment of skilled coworkers).[7] Both Alan and Barney mentioned that not hiring workers reduces their profit margins and their capacity for growth and larger jobs.

Each housepainter noted that he had learned these visibility-reducing techniques from other painters and from small building contractors for whom he had worked. The subculture to which they belong conveys disapproval of painters or contractors who "go straight" and file information returns identifying subcontractors or employees to whom they make payments; filing information returns puts pressure on the recipients to file tax returns or report income more fully.[8]

ELEMENTS OF NATURAL INVISIBILITY

For an informal supplier like Alan, Barney, or Carl, even an IRS audit probably won't detect much of his unreported income. Keeping his income "invisible" does not require direct falsification of records or elaborate evasive practices. Using Alan as an example, one can see that invisibility of his income flows naturally from certain characteristics of his business and life-style.

1. Because he *minimizes bank deposits* of his receipts, Alan's bank statements (crucial to the IRS audit process) substantially understate his actual income.

For a client without a substantial bank account, moreover, no bank files a 1099 form reporting interest payments. Alan thus avoids creating a tax record of his existence and indicating the possibility of substantial business income.

2. Alan *does not keep systematic books and records* documenting his expenses. He thus eliminates another important clue to his income in case he is audited.

3. Alan *does not own substantial assets,* such as a nice home or expensive capital equipment, that would belie the appearance of low taxable income.

4. Since Alan *is an unlicensed contractor,* an IRS auditor, even one with the time, could not estimate his income by examining building permits bearing his name in county archives.

5. Alan *does not withhold income or Social Security taxes from employees.* Nor does he file 1099 forms noting payments to "independent contractors." Hence, there are no systematic IRS records of Alan's annual labor costs from which his income might be estimated. Nor does he have an employer identification number on file with the IRS.

6. Alan *purchases supplies with cash, he spreads purchases over many suppliers, and supplies are a small proportion of his total costs* (as is typical in service businesses). Thus an auditor could not easily estimate Alan's total costs of doing business, and hence his income, by examining the accounts of a small number of suppliers.

7. Alan *does many small jobs for many customers, mostly households* (rather than a few large jobs for established businesses). Hence an auditor could not easily interview customers to piece together Alan's income. Household customers, as contrasted with business customers, need not file 1099 forms informing the IRS of payments over $600 to independent contractors. Moreover, because they are households, not businesses, Alan's customers typically do not treat payments to contractors as deductible expenses; hence if one of the customers is audited, the audit is unlikely to focus attention on Alan.[9]

8. On the other hand, unlike a retail business, Alan does not have so many customers that he must hire employees to man the cash register. Hence *he does not have to keep detailed records of receipts* (analogous to cash register tapes) *to ensure that employees are not skimming.* Thus he avoids a form of income records that would be available to an auditor.

9. Because his jobs generally are of short duration, and because he often obtains partial payment in advance, at least for materials, *Alan does not need bank loans to finance material or labor costs* incurred before he is paid by his customers.

10. He has *no fixed place of business with visible assets*. (He works out of an old, unmarked truck; equipment is easily concealed).

The Dynamics of Increased Visibility: From the Informal Economy to the Record-Keeping Economy

In principle, the government might increase compliance by small entrepreneurs like Alan by threatening drastically increased penalties; by devoting vastly greater resources to detection; by requiring households or material suppliers to file information returns reporting on all substantial transactions with service providers;[10] or by some combination of penal, surveillance and visibility-enhancing methods. In practice, there would be formidable political obstacles, as well as philosophical and policy-related objections, to such an enforcement campaign.

It is important to note, therefore, the natural limitations of Alan's invisibility to the tax system. There are significant nongovernmental, market-driven factors that push informal suppliers toward the "record-keeping" or "bureaucratic" economy, making their unreported income more visible to potential auditors and hence riskier to conceal.

What increases audit-level visibility? Simply reversing Alan's practices and business characteristics suggests the following list:

1. systematic bank deposits of income;
2. systematic records of expenses;
3. ownership of substantial personal or business assets;
4. participation in a licensing or permit system that creates records of work by all licensees;
5. retention of several regular, nonfamily employees;
6. purchases of supplies from a single supplier or a small number of suppliers on open account.
7. supplies or raw material purchases making up a large proportion of total costs;
8. businesses rather than households as customers, and a few large customers accounting for a large proportion of income;
9. systematic records kept of cash receipts for internal control purposes;

10. bank loans needed to finance purchases of supplies or inventory;

11. a fixed place of business with visible assets.

The core element of most of these visibility-enhancing practices is what might be called "bureaucratization." Records of the entrepreneur's transactions are deposited in the files of larger, bureaucratized entities—banks, large suppliers or customers, licensing authorities—whose records are in principle readily available to the IRS. Or the entrepreneur, when he deals with larger numbers of employees or larger bureaucratic entities, is compelled to bureaucratize his own operation, keeping systematic written records and establishing fixed record-generating procedures; these in turn are more easily subject to effective auditing. Once these record-generating procedures and documents are in place, failure to report income entails greater risks of detection.

What spurs an informal supplier's entry into the record-keeping economy? I will discuss a number of factors: business growth, desire for economic security, private income-auditing arrangements, and third-party payment arrangements. I will then suggest some factors that may exert countervailing tendencies: generous income-replacement and insurance arrangements, and stringent regulatory programs.

BUSINESS GROWTH.   A key to the low-visibility business practices of Alan, Barney, and Carl is the small size of their operations. There is an unavoidable tension between desire for the higher income that can be produced by business growth and the desire to keep one's income invisible to tax authorities. Generally speaking, to retain invisibility an entrepreneur must sacrifice opportunities for substantial growth. The pervasive (although not universal) human desire to seize opportunities for business growth, therefore, is an important factor in encouraging more complete income reporting.[11] Consider the effects of growth, first for service businesses like Alan's, and then with respect to other kinds of business.

Service businesses. To achieve larger net income, Alan would need larger jobs and more employees. But more employees means that sooner or later some will demand workers' compensation insurance[12] and withholding of Social Security and unemployment taxes. There is also a larger risk that a disaffected employee will "snitch" to the IRS or other authorities. Larger jobs (and the capital equipment they may require) often cannot be financed without loans from banks, which probably would require the borrower to furnish systematically kept financial statements. Alan's customers for larger jobs generally would be businesses, who likely would insist (for their own legal protection) that Alan be licensed and carry workers' compensation and liability insurance. With a larger operation, even a service business probably would need more capital equipment and, for security and communications reasons, a fixed place of business.

These hypotheses are supported by an interview with a general contractor who specializes in jobs in the $1 to 6 million range and works primarily with subcontractors who employ union labor. He believes that his subcontractors don't attempt to hide much unreported income on their tax returns, at least with respect to the payments he makes to them. When asked why, he mentioned a number of factors, each of which pushes them toward systematic record keeping. Most importantly, his subcontractors' jobs were fairly large, as much as $1 million. The size-of-the-job factor had several implications:

1. Larger subcontractors often seek *bank loans* to cover labor and material expenses that run ahead of progress payments. To satisfy the banks' demands, the subcontractors must generate regular financial statements and show some profits. Some banks demand income tax returns as well.

2. The general contractor requires a *performance bond*. To get a bond from a bonding company at normal rates, the subcontractor has to be licensed and submit evidence of financial reliability.

3. The subcontractor typically has a number of workers, at least some of whom will expect tax withholding and want Social Security and unemployment and workers' compensation coverage. Although many construction workers attempt to avoid taxation by claiming unwarranted exemptions on their W-4 forms, the subcontractor must obtain an employer identification number and file regularly with the IRS and the state government.

4. The general contractor pays by *check* in order to establish proof of his expenses. The subcontractor therefore will have to maintain a bank account; on large jobs, payments are too large to risk attempting to cash such checks.

5. The general contractor files with the IRS a *1099 form* noting all payments of over $600, and sends a copy to the subcontractor.

6. On larger jobs, the subcontractor typically buys materials on credit, resulting in a book account with major suppliers (which in turn generates monthly statements easily available to tax auditors).

7. The need for internal financial control information, just to keep track of expenses in a highly competitive industry with a high rate of bankruptcy, provides large contractors an incentive for careful record keeping.

8. These pressures are stronger for subcontractors in heavy construction trades, whose contracts are larger and who must finance heavier equipment, than for, say, painters, whose capital expenses are lower, who require lower skill levels among workers, whose firms move in and out of business more rapidly, and who work on more and smaller jobs.

These observations suggest a broader generalization: a small service business's progress toward substantial growth (and hence toward substantial tax liability) moves it toward the record-keeping, "bureaucratized," auditable economy[13] and reduces the proportion of its income that is naturally invisible.

Other kinds of businesses. The shift to systematic record keeping, of course, is likely to vary by type of business. Small businesses selling goods at retail, rather than services, may make the shift at a lower level of income. Unless they restrict themselves to weekend flea markets or door-to-door sales, they have to adopt a fixed place of business, increasing the odds of state sales tax audits. To finance growing inventories, they probably turn more quickly than service companies to external finance sources.[14] Unless they can rely on family members, they must hire more sales employees, compelling them to install systems for accurate recording of cash receipts.

Manufacturers and jobbers, one would expect, tend to move quite early in their growth curve into the bureaucratized, income-recording economy. Their customers are businesses, buying in larger lots, typically by check.[15] Small manufacturers, needing equipment and inventories, often must seek credit from suppliers and bank credit (or other external financing) and hence are compelled to adopt standardized bookkeeping methods almost from the outset.

Farmers, loggers, and fishermen also generally sell in substantial lots to business customers. But in some settings, they continue to receive payments in cash, reducing the visibility of their actual income. This is most feasible, even at substantial volume, when sales are made in an open-market setting, as when fishermen sell to restaurateurs, merchants or packing house agents as their boats come into the pier (IRS, 1978a)[16] or when truck farmers sell directly at produce markets. Mississippi catfish farmers, until an IRS investigation uncovered their practices, commonly sold fish for cash to out-of-state haulers (IRS, 1978c).[17] Nevertheless, although it may occur at a later point on their growth curve than for, say, retailers, even catfish farmers, deep-sea fishermen, and loggers who seek to expand profits by developing efficiencies of scale will be pushed toward more systematic income-reporting methods as they hire more employees and seek outside financing for more modern machinery and equipment.

DESIRE FOR ECONOMIC SECURITY. For small service providers like the housepainters Alan and Barney, one of the inducements to take larger jobs, which would probably (they acknowledge) compel them to start filing tax returns, is the added security that would come from not having to look for new jobs every week or two. On the other hand, as Barney noted, with a large-scale business he would have business assets and good will to protect. As an informal supplier, without his own home and possessing few business assets other than a pickup truck and tools, he has little that the banks and the IRS could put a lien on, he points out, and he could easily move to another state "if the IRS caught on to me."

Similarly, these single housepainters indicated that they would be likely to change their taxpaying behavior once they "settled down" and had a family. To buy a house, Barney noted, he would need a bank loan. To get it, he must show the bank regularly kept records demonstrating profitability—which an IRS auditor could compare with his tax return. Moreover, with a house he would have more to lose if the IRS sought to collect unpaid taxes. And, presumably, a "family man" would be more concerned about how "trouble with the IRS" would affect his wife and children. Thus the desire for economic security (which tends to intensify as taxpayers age and take on responsibilities) pulls informal suppliers toward the higher-visibility "bureaucratic economy."[18]

PRIVATE INCOME-AUDITING SYSTEMS. In many business situations, those who extend credit to businesses insist on record keeping that facilitates accurate assessment of the debtor's compliance with his obligations. This in turn makes the debtor's income more visible to the IRS. Consider, for example, these common practices:

Partnership and formal financing arrangements. When sources of finance are not directly involved in a business's operation, they often insist on full reporting by the active partner or the operating entrepreneur and employ active auditing techniques. Banks require periodic financial statements and tax returns and, in some cases, independently audited statements. So do some suppliers who sell large amounts of raw materials or merchandise on credit. One would expect especially close monitoring of income when loans are secured by accounts receivable. Ordinarily, then, income becomes more visible as entrepreneurs obtain financing outside their families.[19]

Percentage of sales leases. Landlords are likely to require accurate record keeping and to audit income closely where retailers' rent obligations are tied to gross receipts.[20] This would also apply where operators of coin-operated vending and amusement machines lease them, paying on a percentage of income basis (IRS, 1978b) and where entertainers or producers who rent theaters pay on the basis of ticket sales.

Automatic sales-registering devices. The consecutive numbering of theater tickets is a counting device designed to prevent cheating (primarily by employees, I presume) in recording of income. Similar numbering devices to facilitate auditing of records of sales income are employed by management in parking lots, luncheonettes (numbered "checks"), and some retail stores. A related step is the use of automatic meters that count sales or total output, as in the case of taxicab meters (note, however, that drivers are often obligated to maintain handwritten logs), gasoline station pumps, turnstiles that "count" patrons, oil and gas wellhead meters, and so forth. While these systems, as well as tapes and electronic records generated by modern cash registers, may be designed primarily for internal control purposes, they also make income more visible to IRS auditors, except insofar as elaborate evasive techniques are used.[21]

Where such privately enforced income-recording systems exist, nonreporting of income, according to IRS officials, typically is limited to nonordinary sales "on the side" (e.g., merchandise acquired for cash through unusual channels or sales made at unusual outlets), repair services rather than gasoline sales in service stations, candy and popcorn sales in movie theaters, and the like. While evasion occurs, the proportion of the taxpayer's income that is naturally invisible is substantially reduced, and the pressure to report and pay taxes increases.

THIRD-PARTY PAYMENT AND RECORD KEEPING.   For many retailers, restaurateurs, motel owners, and other kinds of businesses, customer payment by means of check and credit cards has supplanted payment by cash. In one sense, the merchant initially is "paid" not by the customer but by his own bank (which credits his account after he deposits customers' checks) or by the credit card company (a bank or American Express), which pays by check. Unlike cash receipts, these payments by third parties create records both in the merchant's possession and in the hands of the third-party payers (bank, credit card companies), making the transactions at least potentially visible to IRS auditors).[22]

Use of checks and credit cards has been growing more rapidly than population and GNP, and one observer concluded they are the predominant means of payment for nonfood purchases over $10 (Ernst,

1983:308). Businesses whose transactions generally are larger than $10 are therefore more likely to generate bank records and credit card company records, both in their own hands and in third-party payers' hands, that make nondisclosure of such income riskier. Thus when entrepreneurs seek higher income through sales of "large-ticket" items or services, some portion of their income becomes more visible. Even when restaurants, motels and retailers are inclined not to report a portion of their cash sales, growth in "upscale" clientele who use checks and credit cards reduces the proportion of low-visibility income.[23]

Another third-party payment source is health insurance, both public and private, which now accounts for a very large proportion of income for many physicians, hospitals, and dentists. Third-party reimbursement means not only that the health care provider is paid by check but also that large and easily auditable insurance companies or government agencies have records from which the provider's income can be reconstructed by an auditor.

IRS investigators were able to estimate the income of Chesapeake Bay watermen, who traditionally sold their catch to packing houses for cash, by reviewing the reports that packing houses were required to send to the Maryland Department of Natural Resources (for conservation purposes) summarizing the amount, type, and origin of the seafood they purchased (IRS, 1978b).[24] This experience suggests that the visibility of a taxpayer's income is enhanced when he or she is subject to a licensing or permit regime that records licensees' total production or sales.[25]

General Trends Affecting Naturally Invisible Income

The factors that tend to increase the visibility of income—business growth, the desire for financial security, exposure to private income-auditing and third-party payment and record-keeping arrangements—all imply that "extreme" concealment of income has certain limits. It can persist as long as a taxpayer's business remains small but tends to decrease as the business, and hence the tax liability, grows. Underreporting of income thus operates like an unplanned national subsidy for very small businesses, but one that quite appropriately is "withdrawn" as businesses grow to the point of adding nonfamily employees, acquiring financing from strangers, and selling goods or services in larger units. From this perspective, the elusive nature of naturally invisible income does not pose a serious national problem and might even be regarded as economically desirable.[26]

There are significant arguments to the contrary, however. While many entrepreneurs emerge from the low-tax informal supplier "hatchery" and begin paying their taxes, many others do not.[27] Those who do move into the reporting economy may not completely renounce their former deceptive habits; the acceptability of cheating, once learned as an informal supplier, is likely to have some lingering effects. Wage-earning taxpayers, forced by withholding to pay much higher taxes than their neighbors who enjoy naturally invisible income, undoubtedly feel resentful, and they may search for their own methods of tax evasion, such as overstating personal exemptions.[28] And even if evasion by informal suppliers has some positive economic effects, there is something discomfiting, if not corrupting, about a social system that tacitly endorses widespread deception of one's government (while at the same time holding out the threat of punishment if the deceiver is betrayed by a confidant). A major argument against the underground economy, therefore, is that it encourages attitudes of guardedness and dishonesty among citizens and alienation from government.

Moreover, like unpunished graffiti painting in the subway and vandalism in the schoolyard (see Wilson and Kelling, 1982), widely observed but unpunished tax evasion has the potential to escalate. The widely observed nature of evasion is suggested by IRS estimates indicating that unrecorded income in 1981 equalled about 12 percent of recorded national income (Witte, 1985b:28).[29] The nonreporting sector of the economy seems to have grown more rapidly in the 1970s than the economy as a whole, although that is not necessarily true of nonreporting of small business income. (See Table 4.)

Is the sector of the economy that enjoys naturally invisible income likely to grow still more rapidly, spreading the culture of deception and evasion? Some structural factors may limit its rate of growth. The use of credit card, other noncash, and third-party payment arrangements and computerized recording of transactions should increase; these trends imply that the bureaucratized, record-keeping economy will gradually extend its scope and density. An IRS publication (IRS, 1983a:8) notes that pockets of notorious nonreporting of wages, such as household and agricultural workers, have become less significant in the overall economy. Significant improvements have been made recently in third-party reporting (via information returns) of interest payments, transactions that generate

TABLE 4   IRS Estimates of Unreported Income from Legal Sources (billions of dollars)

	1973	1976	1981	Increase, 1973–81 (%)
Informal suppliers	$10.3	$12.7	$17.1	66
Small nonfarm enterprises	23.9	32.6	58.4	144
Farm proprietors	5.7	4.5	9.5	67
Rents	1.3	2.4	3.0	131
Wages and salaries	33.3	46.3	94.6	184
Dividends and interest	6.4	10.4	29.2	356
Capital gains	5.0	9.9	17.7	254
Total personal income, U.S.	1065.0	1391.0	2430.0	128

Source: IRS, 1983a: Table III-1; *Economic Report of the President, 1985,* Table B-22. For all line items except "informal suppliers," the 1981 estimates of unreported income represent straight-line projections of the 1973 and 1976 figures, which were based on TCMP audits and adjustments thereto. The figures for informal suppliers in all three years are based on a 1981 survey of consumers and their reported spending habits.

capital gains, payments to independent contractors, and IRS computer-matching capacities. To the extent that increases in unrecorded income in the 1970s stemmed from high rates of inflation, rapid increases in female labor force participation (with its associated increase in part-time work and purchases of household services from informal suppliers), and sharp increases in young adults born in the baby boom that followed World War II (who are more likely to work in low-visibility firms), these trends seem at the moment to have leveled off (Witte, 1985b:37–47). Statutory increases in the personal exemption, by eliminating taxes in the lower-income brackets, presumably have eliminated some part-time workers' and informal suppliers' need to cheat. Reduction in marginal rates may induce more willingness to file tax forms and report income.

Nevertheless, certain basic structural features of the U.S. economy, it seems likely, will continue to encourage large amounts of naturally invisible income. I will discuss three such features: legal restrictions and regulatory programs; generous social insurance or income-replacement plans; and generalized affluence.

LEGAL AND REGULATORY OUTLAWS

Laws that seek to prohibit economically advantageous actions are always difficult to enforce completely. The successful evaders, compelled to maintain a low profile vis-à-vis enforcement officials, are also induced to try to shield their income-generating activities from tax collectors. The most notorious examples are manufacturers, importers, and distributors of illegal narcotics and other drugs. Two decades of intensive enforcement activities provide little reason to expect extirpation of this immense source of unreported income,[30] or of the concentric circles of intentionally low-visibility spending and investment patterns that grow up around successful drug dealers.

Similarly, the U.S., as a huge, rich, politically open nation surrounded by poorer, less free and less stable ones, inevitably will be unable to maintain full enforcement of its immigration laws. These laws thus will continue to "create" large numbers of illegal workers and informal suppliers, understandably afraid to report their income to the IRS.[31]

Governmental regulation of "ordinary" economic activities, by increasing the costs of doing business, induces some small enterprises to attempt to operate outside the law. A barber avoids the costs and burdens of licensure by cutting hair in a low-visibility setting without a license (see Wiegand, 1984). A Korean immigrant who establishes a garment business in Los Angeles survives by paying his fellow countrymen (or illegal Mexican immigrants) wages below the minimum prescribed by law in a building that does not meet the stringent (and costly) requirements of the fire and earthquake safety code. A homeowner rents out rooms in violation of municipal zoning or rent control ordinances. Such regulation-avoiding entrepreneurs, hoping to remain "invisible" to regulatory enforcement officials, also are reluctant to file a return with the IRS (even though the IRS is not likely to contact state or local regulatory authorities). As long as occupational licensure, labor law, safety and land use regulations (many of which may be entirely justifiable) continue to expand their reach and thereby "produce" violators—and in the long run they probably will expand—they provide an additional incentive for tax violations (Bardach and Kagan, 1982:14–25).

INSURANCE CHEATERS

Public and private insurance systems that pay benefits to those unable to work inevitably produce substantial numbers of cheaters.[32] Envision the injured longshoreman, receiving a generous disability pension under the federal Longshoreman and Harbor Workers' Act, whose once crippling bad back now enables him to work as a bartender; the Florida waiter who is laid off in the summer and collects unemployment insurance but nevertheless travels to Cape Cod and takes a job (see Black and Carr, 1980; Porterfield et al., 1980); the Social Security recipient, bored with retirement, who starts a small business, or the AFDC client who does the same. Here, too, once the benefit recipient commits the potentially criminal offense of not reporting his earned income to the benefit-paying organization, it would seem foolhardy to risk reporting the earned income to IRS. One can never be *sure* the benefit-paying agency will not discover the IRS data through a mysterious computer-matching program. As social and private insurance plans continue to grow, therefore, they "generate" unreported income.

SOCIETAL AFFLUENCE

Legal and regulatory outlaws and insurance cheaters tend to choose low-visibility forms of earning income—small personal service businesses, or part-time jobs with employers who themselves are informal suppliers or regulatory outlaws. As the same time, the U.S. economy has been increasingly supportive of service business and small establishments (Witte, 1985b:38–39). Moreover, growth in societal affluence seems to produce larger numbers of small-business operators like Alan the housepainter, who can afford to remain small—and hence outside the income-reporting economy. Many receive enough income from other family members, or pension plans, or student loans, or undemanding jobs, that they are satisfied with a moderate amount of supplementary income. And an affluent economy breeds demand for child care, lessons, personal services, food preparation, gardening, home remodeling, arts and crafts and other services yet to be invented that can be provided by part-time, informal suppliers. All this suggests that the low-visibility, informal sector of the economy may grow disproportionately.

Making Income Invisible in Record-Keeping Enterprises

Business growth, it was suggested earlier, induces many small enterprises to leave behind the informal supplier style of doing business, with its naturally invisible forms of income. With more employees, larger capital expenses and credit needs, and more bureaucraticized customers and suppliers, entrepreneurs are more likely to adopt systematic banking and bookkeeping practices, obtain necessary licenses and file necessary reports, maintain a fixed place of business, and regularly advertise their existence. More of their transactions leave records in the hands of third parties, where they may be encountered by IRS officials. The IRS has their employer identification numbers and employment tax returns; information returns submitted by their banks; and past years' returns to compare with the one submitted this year, making it possible to discern marked changes in reported income, profits, or relationships among line items. An auditor thus has many more tools to check the accuracy of their reported income.

But entry into the bureaucratized, recording economy, of course, does not render all unreported income visible to the auditor. The line between informal suppliers and bureaucratized establishments is not a sharp divide; some of the latter still receive a good deal of naturally invisible income. And the company with a full array of income-recording systems can learn or invent techniques for concealing unreported income. In 1981, the Voluntary Reporting Percentage for "nonfarm proprietor income and partnership and small business corporation income" was only 78.7 percent of the amount that should have been reported, according to IRS audits (IRS, 1983a:Table III-2). This was a far higher percentage than the 20.7 percent Voluntary Compliance Level for "informal suppliers," but represented, according to the audits, a far larger aggregate amount of unreported income.[33]

For businesses that maintain relatively comprehensive bookkeeping systems and file annual tax returns (whether as Schedule C on the proprietor's personal return or as separate entities), one can envision a hierarchy of types of unreported income, based on the degree of effort and boldness required to exclude the income from routine income-recording systems. The basic distinction is between malfeasance and nonfeasance. To hide unreported income from auditors, taxpayers in some settings must affirmatively falsify routine records, keep multiple sets of books, misclassify transactions, create false documents, and the like. In other situations, taxpayers may be able to simply "forget" to record "naturally" less visible income-generating transactions. The affirmative falsifications are more closely identified in popular culture with malfeasance and fraud. Moreover, if detected, they are harder to dismiss as mere forgetfulness or ignorance of proper accounting practices. Hence the affirmative acts, on the average, require more forethought, and more *chutzpah* or desperation, than simple failure to record. A smaller proportion of taxpayers, I assume, will be willing to engage in them. Let me discuss the more naturally invisible forms of nonrecording first.

NATURAL INVISIBILITY IN RECORD-KEEPING BUSINESSES: MARGINAL OR NONROUTINE CASH TRANSACTIONS

One common type of unreported income is indicated by the Special Audit Instructions in the IRS Manual used to alert IRS agents to special problems. Agents are advised that road construction and excavation companies at the end of a job often encounter the opportunity to sell fill or topsoil but then fail to record the sales price in their reported income for the job. To these contractors, the topsoil or fill is a "leftover material," its sale a "side product," tangential to their routine business. The income from selling it can be characterized as marginal to their main product line and source of income, and nonroutine in that it does not recur predictably. If omitted from the contractor's regular ledgers showing income from construction contracts, the receipts will be invisible to the auditor who seeks to verify the sums in the contractor's income ledger by comparing them with the actual contracts. If such marginal, nonroutine sales can be made for cash, as the contractor may make great efforts to do, and the cash is not deposited in his usual business bank account, the transaction has a high "invisibility quotient."

Anecdotal accounts of unreported business income often have similar marginal, nonroutine characteristics:

- A clothing manufacturer sells odd lots (imperfect garments or discounted lines) to discount retailers for cash.
- A motel operator fails to record income from the rental of rooms for midday lovers' trysts (or commercial trysts), although she keeps complete records of income and room use for routine all-night rentals.
- A construction contractor who usually does business in County A fails to record and report income from nonroutine jobs in distant towns.[34]

In the extreme case, the ancillary unreported cash sales become routine, although still secondary to the principal source of income (which is fully reported), while expenses associated with the "side business" are charged to the principal business. Ancillary income is least visible when the side business entails *services,* especially if provided to individuals (rather than to businesses). For example:

- A general contractor specializing in remodeling for real estate developers and investors, reports his income from those jobs. However, he takes on a few jobs each year for wealthy individual homeowners and does not report that income, while charging the expenses to his "main" jobs.
- A gas station owner does not report some of the cash income from nonroutine repair jobs, even though he reports all income from gasoline sales (which an auditor can check by reference to credit card records, shipping receipts, and oil company sales records).

Retail businesses, too, can conceal marginal sales amidst full reporting of income from the main business. An extreme example, recounted to me by an IRS enforcement official, was provided by a restaurant owner, who, when he began staying open for an extra night shift, did not report any of the income from the entire shift. Such efforts typically must include employees in a conspiracy not to record income; hence the taxpayer is more vulnerable to exposure by a disgruntled employee. But small retailers who rely on family members or faithful employees, and who are not quite as greedy as the above-mentioned restaurateur, can keep a significant portion of nonroutine sales invisible.

Manufacturers' reimbursements to dealers of expenses incurred in relation to sales and service, along with rebates for returns of defective products, constitute irregular forms of income to the dealer and thus provide special opportunities for nonreporting. The IRS Manual warns agents that automobile dealers may fail to report as income payments received from manufacturers, such as incentive rebates for sales of discontinued models, bonuses for meeting sales quotas, rebates for advertising expenditures, reimbursements for parts used in warranty adjustments, and reimbursement for delivery preparation costs. Retail bakeries and food stores often receive reimbursements from suppliers for returns of damaged or unsold products. These payments do not come in through the cash register and do not appear in the audit trail created by cash register tapes. Recording them requires a special effort to readjust records of purchases or inventories. Hence there is some temptation not to record them, although, as the IRS Manual suggests, some risk is entailed because the manufacturer or supplier often keeps records.

TREATING SALARY, PROFITS, OR SERVICES AS BUSINESS EXPENSES

Perhaps the most notorious form of tax evasion is the practice whereby owners of incorporated but closely held businesses charge personal expenses to their corporation. Here are examples provided by IRS officials and private accountants.

A restaurant owner takes care of his family's entire food needs by bringing home food purchased by the restaurant corporation and charged to its normal operating expenses. Under tax law, such transfers—which might be worth $5,000 or $6,000 a year—are the equivalent of payment to the owner of an additional $5,000 to $6,000 in salary or in undeclared dividends. Yet he does not declare this income on his personal tax return, and his restaurant corporation falsely deducts the $5,000 to $6,000 as business expenses, reducing its taxable income by that amount. The diversion of this money, as long as it is a small proportion of the total food budget of the restaurant, is not easily detected by an audit of the restaurant corporation.

The president of a closely held manufacturing corporation uses factory maintenance men to make repairs or installations at his own residence; the extra wages, if any, paid to them by the company are a very small proportion of the company's total monthly wage bill and are hard to detect on audit. Yet if the job is worth $5,000, in the eyes of the law that is either additional compensation to the president or an undeclared dividend. Either way, he omits this income from his return, and corporate taxable profits are illegally reduced.

The president of a small corporation pays himself extra undeclared compensation for his services by having the corporation pay for his travel and vacations as corporate sales trips, by paying for and listing his wife's car on the corporate books as a company car used for sales, by charging his child's home computer to the corporate office equipment account, and so on.

Extra, nontaxable income can be given to key employees in a similar way, i.e., by charging their personal expenses to the company's account. Here is a more elaborate mechanism, described to me by a building contractor, that also reveals how legitimate businesses can stimulate the creation of nonreporting businesses.

A sheet metal contractor provides nontaxable income to valued employees by encouraging them to take on their own small sheet metal contracting jobs in their spare time, provided they purchase their raw materials through his firm and pay him in cash. He charges these raw materials expenses to his own jobs, reducing the taxable income he derives from them, and does not report the cash income from his employees. The employees get their raw materials without leaving an audit trail, giving them somewhat more security in not reporting to the IRS the income they receive as independent contractors.

Sometimes calculated and elaborate barter techniques are used to the same end. Successful building contractors, another general contractor told me, often take advantage of their expertise in construction and repair by buying and operating rental properties as investments. This also provides a way to conceal income. An electrical contractor, for example, may do $10,000 worth of work, using his regular employees, on a building owned by his friend, the air conditioning and heating contractor, charging the materials and labor costs to Job A, on which the electrical contractor has a large contract. This reduces the taxable income he declares from Job A. In return, the air conditioning contractor at a later time does $10,000 worth of work on a building owned by the electrical contractor, charging the cost to Job B, on which he now has a substantial contract. Each has, in effect, done a $10,000 job but, having been paid in reciprocal services, does not report any taxable income, while reducing taxable income on the reported jobs by $10,000 in expenses not actually incurred on those jobs.

These barter and diversion arrangements, IRS officials acknowledge, are extremely difficult to detect without a tip from a disgruntled employee or competitor. This suggests, however, that the larger the business grows and the more extended and impersonal the web of labor and business relationships the entrepreneur is enmeshed in, the less likely such barter and diversion methods—which depend on mutual trust among bookkeepers and other employees who become aware of them—are to occur.

FALSIFYING RECORDS

Even when systematic records of income are kept, business owners can, if they are bold enough, divert some routine income away from their normal recording process, while altering the routine records to conceal their diversions. People interested in purchasing small motels, I have been told, not infrequently are shown two sets of books by the owner/seller: one showing lower income and profits, used for tax reporting and auditing purposes, and another showing the true (larger) profit picture. A recent newspaper article described an owner of a substantial lumber and building supply store who periodically intercepted occasional large checks from big customers, took them to a bank where he had a personal relationship, and cashed them for his own use; presumably he took steps back in his office to ensure that the underlying transaction was omitted from the usual records. The same article told of a storekeeper who pocketed about $50 a day

($15,000) in cash receipts; to reduce the visibility of this "skimming," he altered purchasing records, reducing them by an equivalent amount so that his record (like his tax return) would show declared sales receipts roughly in line with declared cost of goods sold.

The IRS manual, *Specialized Audit Guidelines for Auto Dealers,* alerts agents that for used-car sales, the reported sales price may be less than that actually received. A salesman may offer a buyer a discount if the buyer pays partly in cash, enabling the seller to record only the amount paid by check. The manual urges IRS agents to sample wholesale "blue book" prices. It also suggests that auto dealers, when reducing the price of a car in return for a trade-in, sometimes list the reduction on the sales record only as a "discount," with no mention of the trade-in. The dealer can then resell the traded-in vehicle without recording or reporting the income and hope to escape detection on audit. The catfish farmers of Mississippi, mentioned in the IRS investigation cited earlier, deposited payments from out-of-state haulers in special bank accounts, set up in false names or the names of nominees, in order to avoid detection.

This list of concealment devices might be multiplied endlessly without exhausting the range and inventiveness of taxpayers bent on deception. What needs to be examined is the social and economic distribution in society of these deeply fraudulent practices—the kinds of businesses and record-keeping systems in which they are and are not prevalent. IRS records on criminal prosecution by industry and occupation, which I have scrutinized, are not helpful in this regard, for they reflect special enforcement problems and priorities in referring cases to the criminal division. TCMP audits do not appear to make distinctions concerning the type of underreporting. A more complete understanding of the distribution of fraudulence, in relation to IRS audit techniques and capabilities, might be the next subject to be addressed in studying variations in visibility of unreported income.

Policy Implications

The preceding analysis suggests three broad strategies for raising the visibility of income and thereby increasing compliance with reporting laws: (1) encouraging or requiring systematic record keeping by *taxpayers;* (2) encouraging or requiring more complete record keeping and/or reporting by *payers;* (3) encouraging or requiring *third-party auditing* (which in turn would encourage systematic record keeping and better reporting by taxpayers.[35]

Some visibility-enhancing strategies, of course, create a risk of excessive paperwork, loss of privacy, and deterrence of entrepreneurial activity. These concerns deserve attention in evaluating enforcement programs. Nevertheless, there are strong "horizontal equity" arguments for considering programs that shrink the capacity of the self-employed to pay substantially lower taxes than comparable taxpayers who lack equivalent opportunities to cheat. Moreover, as noted earlier, a widespread sense that some people get away with tax evasion tends to erode their fellow citizens' commitment to "voluntary compliance." It thus encourages active deceit or at least civic disaffection, which in turn might lead to even more intrusive tax collection efforts (or to a decline in the government's ability to provide valued goods and services).

REQUIRING SYSTEMATIC RECORD KEEPING BY TAXPAYERS

One could imagine a world in which each taxpayer systematically recorded his or her income transactions and deductible expenses on pre-numbered receipts and then entered them in a computer, which in turn generated monthly income statements and balance sheets. That is to say, all taxpayers would behave as larger "bureaucratized" business entities do today. The closer we move to this full-receipt, record-keeping world—and in our highly literate society, with its ever cheaper computers, electronic communication networks, and organizational links, we may well be drifting in that direction—the higher the visibility, on audit, of unreported income.

The drift toward fully visible income could be accelerated by legal mandate. Consider a statute, for example, that required all filers of Schedule C (income from trade or business) to file annual balance sheets as well as profit and loss statements; the requirement to balance one's books would make "skimming" more complicated and difficult and would encourage systematic record keeping. More selective and indirect approaches are also possible. For example, the federal government could offer grants-in-aid to state and local licensing agencies to help defray their costs for promulgating and enforcing regulations that require occupational licensees to file annual financial statements with the state licensing agency; the obligation to produce visible financial records, even if most of those records are not sent to the IRS, would encourage more systematic recording and reporting of income.

But record-keeping and reporting requirements, it must be remembered, entail real and significant costs (Bardach, 1982). Especially in the case of small enterprises, spending time and resources recording what they have been doing takes energy and resources away from actually doing. Pushing citizens too far toward the imagined full-recording world, therefore, is politically difficult and at some point undesirable.

Nevertheless, obligations to document certain kinds of income-generating transactions might be imposed justifiably. Consider the failure to report rental income fully. Proportionately, I would speculate, the worst offenders are not full-time real estate firms or investors but middle- and upper-income taxpayers who seek some tax-sheltered "side income" from rental of units in their own houses, in second homes in vacation areas, or in small investment properties. It might seem both fair and politically acceptable to require taxpayers who claim interest deductions for loans on real estate, as a condition for claiming the deduction, to file with the IRS a schedule (a) stating the amount of the loan, the interest paid, and the name and taxpayer identification number of the lender; (b) responding to a question that asks directly if rental income was derived from the property, and if so (c) describing the number of units, the average monthly rent charged, the rent actually received, and the tenants' names. (The rent received, of course, could be checked against the schedule for reporting income from rents.) The requirement could be trimmed to exclude lower-income taxpayers or others for whom it would be burdensome or, from the IRS's standpoint, not worth administering.

To be sure, room for deception would still exist. The bold would continue to deceive. But there are many taxpayers, I assume, who are willing to commit sins of omission (not reporting side income) but who are not ready to lie in response to direct questions or to falsify records. With each additional element of visibility or potential visibility added by reporting requirements, fewer recipients of rental income would remain bold enough to cheat. And more taxpayers would feel compelled to maintain systematic records of rental receipts as a defense against the hassle of a potential audit.

Claiming the interest deduction for real estate loans could also be treated as a "privilege" that triggers an obligation to report fully sales of the underlying real estate, a type of transaction that results in considerable underreporting of capital gains (U.S. Congress, 1985:7–8).

The workability (or unworkability) of these particular ideas is less important than the general point—that reporting obligations can be designed to encourage or require documentation and systematic record keeping for commonly underreported categories of income.

MANDATORY RECORD KEEPING AND REPORTING BY PAYERS

The strong relationship between filing of information returns by payers and compliance by payees suggests expansion of this strategy. But here, too, there are practical, political, and philosophical limits. If each household and business were required to report the amounts of each purchase of goods and services, together with the name and identification number of each recipient, it would be theoretically possible for a computer in Washington to reconstruct the annual income of all sellers and providers. But in practice the IRS could not cope with the information-processing problem and, more importantly, households and most businesses would have neither the capacity nor the willingness to comply. Moreover, do we really want to create a nation of informers, dutifully recording each of their own and their fellow citizens' transactions, obediently transmitting the information to one great electronic Doomsday Book? Expansion of third-party reporting obligations, as the IRS well understands, must be highly selective.

Nevertheless, some possibilities for expanding third-party reporting are worth considering. One is suggested by the earlier discussion of nonreporting of income by informal suppliers in the residential remodeling and maintenance market. Suppose homeowners and apartment house owners were required to file a schedule listing all one-time expenditures on maintenance, repairs, or construction of $600 or more (or more ambitiously, all cumulative payments of $600 or more in any year to any supplier), along with the suppliers' names, addresses, and perhaps even their taxpayer identification numbers.[36] If this obligation were enforced, the potential visibility of suppliers' unreported income would be increased substantially.

The burden on payers, if such an obligation were imposed on an across-the-board basis, might be considered too great. Maintenance and remodeling costs would go up; reporting obligations might be evaded in return for lower prices. Perhaps a more selective version would be preferable. Perhaps third parties could be "paid" in some fashion for shouldering the burden of keeping records, reporting to the IRS, and thereby bringing recipients' income to taxable visibility.[37] The point, again, is to stimulate thought about such extensions of the third-party reporting concept.

THIRD-PARTY AUDITING

Systematic reporting of income is encouraged, I argued earlier, where third parties audit or require verification of a taxpayer's financial condition. The IRS is the indirect beneficiary of auditing conducted by landlords "enforcing" percentage-of-sales leases and by lenders that require debtors to furnish regular financial statements. Compliance presumably increases, on balance, as small proprietors and informal suppliers turn to nonfamily sources of credit or to computer firms to handle their payroll, inventory, and sales records, or even when they seek the services of accountants and income tax preparers.[38] One general compliance-enhancing strategy, therefore, would seek means of increasing the proportion of taxpayers whose accounts are examined, maintained, or verified by third parties.

One significant set of "third parties," viewing the taxpayer and the IRS as the initial dyad, are state and local sales and property tax collection agencies. The retailer who would otherwise be tempted to avoid reporting some naturally invisible income on his federal income tax return (or to avoid filing any return at all) may feel compelled to keep more honest records and report income more fully if he is regularly and effectively audited by local sales tax agencies. State and local tax auditors, in effect, are proxies for the IRS. A major weakness in this model is the notorious understaffing of state and local tax agencies. The federal government could help. Members of Congress reluctant to vote major audit staff increases directly to the IRS might be willing to vote for federal grants to local tax agencies in their own home districts. And the IRS might consider training sessions and other ways of assisting local tax agencies to coordinate their efforts with federal concerns.

ENFORCEMENT AND RESEARCH

A primary variable affecting visibility of income, and especially its perceived visibility, is the frequency and thoroughness of IRS audits. The taxpayer may regard as invisible unreported income that would be quite visible on audit, if he has learned by experience that the possibility of being audited seems remote. Most other law enforcement agencies have a similar problem; they don't have enough enforcement officials to inspect, patrol, audit, or process documents. The strategic question is how best to target their limited resources. (See Kagan, 1984; Shapiro, 1984; Bardach and Kagan, 1982:160–176.)

For the IRS, one strategy would be to emulate the Occupational Safety and Health Administration by undertaking well-publicized audit campaigns directed at particular target industries or trades; they might be motels, sheet metal contractors, loggers, used-car dealers, food purveyors, or something else. Publicized audit campaigns may stimulate self-regulatory efforts by the relevant trade associations eager to get the IRS "off their members' backs." Such campaigns may stimulate ripple effects in related trades. Both the efficiency and the political justifiability of targeted enforcement efforts, however, depend on adequate research documenting the below-average voluntary reporting rates for the trades in question. This would require a much denser trade-specific sampling strategy by the IRS's TCMP) audit program, generating comparative data on unreported income by both type and size of business. This would be expensive. But painting the contours of unreported income in more vivid detail may be an important way of bringing hidden income to light.

Conclusion

This chapter began with the query, "What determines the extent to which laws are complied with or violated?" In attempting to answer it, I have stressed the significance of "visibility" of violations—that is, the relative costs and difficulties enforcement officials face in detecting and proving offenses. Other factors matter, too, of course, such as individual attitudes toward the law in question or toward the political system as a whole, subcultural norms favoring and abetting (or deterring) compliance, the nature of the advice received from or the example set by community leaders or professionals (including professional tax return preparers), the opportunity costs to individuals in learning about and complying with legal requirements.

In the case of the federal income tax, however, visibility of violations seems to be immensely important. Taxpayers report and pay taxes on a dramatically higher percentage of their income when the income is subject to third-party reporting—that is, when the *payer* is obligated to send information returns to the IRS (as in the case of salaries, interest payments, dividends, royalties, alimony, and larger contractual payments) identifying the recipient and the amount paid. Third-party reporting—not differences in taxpayers' political attitudes, aversion to risk, or subcultural norms—accounts for the difference in compliance rates.

Moreover, regardless of social norms, individual attitudes, or other cognitive factors, the social organization of a taxpayer's income-generating activities affects the visibility of that income and hence the likelihood that the taxpayer will feel compelled to report it. For example, visibility of income increases, I have tried to demonstrate, when small business enterprises whose income previously had been naturally invisible grow to the point at which they must:

(a) hire more than a few nonfamily employees (who expect unemployment and Social Security coverage, or who cannot be trusted to maintain secrecy about nonreporting of income, or who handle cash and must be subjected to internal controls); or

(b) seek outside financing or credit from suppliers, which in turn require accurate records of the taxpayer's income and bank accounts; or

(c) engage in transactions with large, bureaucratized business clients, whose files or reports to the IRS contain easily auditable evidence of payments to the taxpayer.

Similarly, nonreporting of income by businesses that have entered the bureaucratized, record-keeping economy is more likely to occur with respect to income that is irregular or nonroutine. These "sociological" characteristics of the transactions themselves, not the attitudes of the taxpayers involved, seem to be the critical factor.

Of course, visibility of income is not the sole predictor of compliance. Not all housepainters and other informal suppliers with naturally invisible income evade their full tax obligations. Many retailers scrupulously report income from nonroutine cash sales. The concept of visibility does not explain variations in compliance among taxpayers whose income is at similar levels of visibility. To explain individual behavior, social-psychological and other models must be brought into play. The concept of visibility is meant to help explain variation in compliance across large classes of taxpayers, grouped according to source and nature of income, type and size of business, and exposure to legally required reporting rules and other enforcement programs.

The analysis of the detectability or visibility implies that changes in rates of compliance are likely to be affected by broad, unplanned changes in the social organization of the economy. Visibility of noncompliance will grow (thereby discouraging nonreporting), I have argued, with the spread of inexpensive, electronic record-keeping devices and systems, use of credit cards and other automatic payment systems, and laws extending third-party information-reporting obligations. On the other hand, and perhaps more important, some social trends suggest increases in the proportion of taxpayers with "naturally invisible income." I discuss in this regard (a) the gradual growth of social affluence (which enables taxpayers with other sources of income to settle for part-time work and small "on-the-side" businesses); (b) the growth of licensing regulations and income replacement programs, both public and private (which inevitably lead to a certain number of "regulatory outlaws," welfare or insurance cheats reluctant to disclose their sources of income).

But this analysis also suggests that compliance rates are quite sensitive to governmental interventions designed to increase the visibility of violations. In the tax area, the federal government has improved compliance greatly by requiring third-party payers to report payments to particular taxpayers with respect to a growing variety of types of income. As noted in the previous section, such obligations could in principle be extended to additional categories of payers (such as tenants, or household purchasers of services), or taxpayers themselves could be directly required to keep or report more detailed records as a condition of claiming certain deductions. The limiting factor in this regard is not the incapacity of law to affect private behavior but general public values concerning excessive paperwork, intrusions on privacy, and preservation of liberty.

Some extensions of reporting and record-keeping obligations, carefully crafted with respect for those values, probably would increase the fairness of the tax system. Taxes, unlike death, are not inevitable; cheating is inevitable. It is difficult to see, however, why the government should not try to make it equally hard for all citizens to cheat. But as always, a deeper, ethnographically grounded understanding of how citizens actually experience and adapt to new regulations and to record-keeping and reporting requirements would help ensure that the government, in its efforts to increase equity, is not squeezing liberty too tightly.

Notes

1. In recent years, apparently, enterprising private attorneys have begun to monitor stock transactions for circumstantial evidence of insider trading, and they have filed class actions for damages (and attorney fees) against the alleged securities law violators. When third-party enforcement of this nature becomes efficient and prevalent, the official costs of enforcement are small and the violations correspondingly more "visible" to the authorities.
2. As the number of federal income tax returns has increased by 17 percent in the last decade (from 87 million in 1974 to 103 million in 1984), the number of

employees in the IRS's audit (or "examination") division fell from 28,000 in 1974 to 25,500 in 1984. The audit rate declined too, from 4.2 percent in 1960 to 2.39 percent in 1974, 2.12 percent in 1980, and 1.31 percent in 1984 (U.S. Congress, Joint Committee on Taxation, 1985:33). Until recently, attempts to increase IRS audit staff resources substantially have not met with the requisite political support in Congress (Scholz, this volume, Chapter 1). The IRS has recently increased computerized checking of returns, matching them against information returns submitted by employers and payers of interest and dividends; if one were to define these checks as minimal audits, the current audit rate would be much higher.

3. In later TCMP samplings, based on 1982 returns, IRS researchers found *increases* in "voluntary reporting percentages" (VRPs) for forms of income covered by information returns (e.g., 96.9 percent for interest and dividends). But they found *declines* in VRPs for Schedule C (nonfarm proprietor income), from gross VRP of 75.8 percent in 1979 to 67.6 percent in 1982. They found a major decline in the VRP for gross income from partnerships, from 67.9 percent in 1979 to 30.3 percent in 1982, primarily due to the overstatement of net losses from partnerships set up as tax shelters (IRS, 1986:21, 23).

4. Dividend and interest recipients could well have higher incomes, on the average; some studies indicate that higher-income taxpayers have better compliance records. Dividend and interest recipients may be more averse to risk, on the average, than the small entrepreneurs who file Schedule C and F returns. Dividend and interest recipients may believe that payers (large corporations, banks, the U.S. Treasury Department) are apt to divulge the names of payees and the amounts even if no information returns are in evidence. And according to survey research responses, taxpayers "appear less willing to pay taxes on money resulting from entrepreneurial activity or extra effort than on income from other sources" (Smith and Kinsey, 1987, citing Yankelovich, Skelly, and White, 1984).

5. Of the independent contractors in the sample who filed income tax returns, only 11.6 percent reported none of the compensation reflected in information returns. My estimate in the text of 15 percent, which includes independent contractors who did not file, is based on the data in Tables 5 and 6 of the 1099 NEC Compliance Study (IRS, 1983b).

The 1099 NEC (independent contractor) studies suggest that meaningful increases in voluntary compliance would ensue from investing in auditing systems to ensure compliance by payers with information-reporting obligations (see Vitez, 1983). The 1982 Tax Equity and Fiscal Responsibility Act (TEFRA) authorized penalties of up to $50 per year for nonreporting. Since information reporting is a purely public service and is experienced by payers as an additional hidden tax on paying dividends, interest, and bills submitted by independent contractors, compliance might be increased if the IRS were to reimburse payers for at least a portion of their costs.

6. "Alan" is a personal friend of a graduate student in my department and was interviewed at length by that student. Through "Alan," contact was made with "Barney," "Carl," and "Deborah" (referred to in Note 7). They, too, were

interviewed by the graduate student, in close consultation with me. I interviewed two additional housepainters, as well as two building contractors who deal regularly with painting subcontractors. It is not suggested, of course, that these painters are statistically "representative" of any subpopulation of painters or informal suppliers. Rather, their practices are recounted as illustrative of the ways in which informal suppliers can avoid reporting income.

7. "Deborah," a housepainter I interviewed, acknowledged that while she formed "partnerships" on an *ad hoc* basis, they were not true partnerships or even subcontracts to independent contractors, for when she "gets the job," she bears full responsibility for purchasing supplies, deadlines, workmanship, collections, and the like. Her "partners" are really temporary skilled employees, as she becomes when she is a "partner" on a job they get.

8. For a published account of another subculture that maintains a high degree of invisibility from tax authorities, see Dow (1977), a description of migrants from Appalachia who work in Detroit primarily in auto repair and junk dealership, dealing entirely in cash and avoiding involvement with banks and other major institutions.

9. Because they wish to be able to document expenses, businesses typically pay by check. Alan attempts to avoid visibility by cashing such checks, rather than depositing them to his own account. It is possible, although not probable, that a diligent auditor reviewing the tax return of Alan's customer would note (in the course of "check turning" while examining the payer's bank statements) that checks to "Alan" had been cashed, not deposited, indicating the appropriateness of an audit of Alan. (Interview, R. Osterholm, San Francisco IRS District Office, July 1985).

10. Householders could even be given incentives to file information returns by making a fraction of expenditures on home improvements and maintenance deductible. Revenue losses from such a deduction, however, might almost cancel out any revenue gains from increased reporting of informal supplier income.

11. To the extent that small entrepreneurs belong to a "counterculture" that encourages a moderate-income life style, or enjoy other sources of income (which is not uncommon in an affluent society), the desire for business growth is a less potent visibility-enhancing factor.

12. "Carl" pointed out that if forced to hire more workers for larger jobs, he would increase his own risk of being sued for workers' compensation insurance in the event of an accident. To obtain workers' compensation insurance, he would have to secure the necessary contractor's license, and this, he felt, would create such a high level of visibility that he would have to withhold taxes from his workers and pay them over to the IRS, which in turn would make it too risky (he thought) not to file a personal return reporting his own income more fully.

13. It would be interesting to survey small businesses to determine at what levels of gross income (or number of employees), they tend, on average, to (a) adopt pegboard or computerized payroll and accounts receivable systems, (b) employ a bookkeeper, (c) employ an accountant, (d) obtain bank loans. Such knowledge, however, may not affect law enforcement practices; the IRS, for a variety

of reasons, is unlikely to focus audits on the small businesses whose income falls below the point at which transition to systematic record keeping tends to occur.

14. Growing retailers must purchase merchandise in larger quantities, typically from established distributors, in transactions that generate records of their purchases and from which auditors can estimate their total sales. And compared with service businesses, retailers may have to adopt more systematic record keeping earlier in their growth curve in order to plan inventory replacement and markups. Some retailers, of course, can grow while still purchasing merchandise in cash. They may purchase in odd lots from manufacturers and jobbers (see note 15, below), from illegal sources (distributors of stolen goods), individual craftsmen, or small manufacturers or distributors that operate in the underground economy to evade sales and excise taxes (e.g., cigarette distributors) or labor laws.

15. I have heard of a small "discount" clothing retailer, specializing in the sale of odd lots, factory seconds, and discontinued lines, who often offered manufacturers cash, in large amounts, for such merchandise. The manufacturers could easily have refrained reporting that irregular income.

16. Chesapeake Bay watermen investigated by the Internal Revenue Service (IRS, 1978a) evidently resisted their customers' (packing houses) desires to pay by check by boycotting firms that refused to continue to pay for the catch in cash. This kind of solidarity in resisting market pressures for more systematic recording of transactions is likely to be more common in traditional agricultural, fishing, and extractive businesses like logging, hunting, and trapping than in urban trades that bulk larger in the modern economy.

17. The ways in which the catfish farmers' income was "raised to visibility" by the IRS emphasizes the limits of invisibility when entrepreneurs sell most of their output to a small number of business customers. The IRS relied heavily on audits of the relatively small number of catfish-processing plants and their records of receipts from haulers to estimate total catfish production. Similarly, the IRS was alerted to the Chesapeake Bay watermen noncompliance by audits of packing houses that indicated substantial cash payments. (IRS, 1978c).

18. Concern for security could help explain why surveys of self-reported tax cheating or willingness to cheat show declines in cheating as age increases. These findings might be interpreted in terms of increased risk aversion as youth fades, or in terms of age-related increases in knowledge of the tax law and competence in record keeping. Barney's comments, however, suggest it might be interpreted in terms of increased de facto penalties (e.g., social stigma, as well as legally imposed monetary penalties) for those with more property and reputational interests at stake, both of which are associated with settling down and raising children. See also Klepper and Nagin (1987b), who found, based on an analysis of IRS data, that the "voluntary reporting percentage" for higher-income taxpayers tends to be higher than the VRP for lower-income taxpayers (although the absolute amount of the "tax gap" is larger for higher-income taxpayers).

19. Some revolving credit associations doing business with specific ethnic groups, however, may provide financing without requiring records of a kind easily auditable by the IRS (Light, 1985).

20. A "skimming" scheme, whereby a fashionable San Francisco clothing store allegedly failed to record over $200,000 a year in cash sales, was revealed by city auditors probing whether the store had complied with a percentage-of-sales lease in a city-owned downtown building (Farrell, 1985:1).

21. In the clothing-store skimming case mentioned in the preceding footnote, the store's former bookkeeper told law enforcement officials that the unrecorded sales, mostly to store employees and to special "preferred" customers, were written up on special receipts that were kept separate from routine sales tags, and were not entered into the cash register. The case also demonstrates the vulnerability of larger-scale skimming schemes; they require the continuing cooperation and silence of a substantial number of employees or ex-employees.

22. Martin L. Ernst has noted: "There are two broad types of financial transactions—those that involve only two parties (barter and cash) and those that involve three or more (such as checks, credit cards, and debit cards). . . . When three or more parties are involved, the presence of additional participants almost always leads to written or electronic records." (Ernst, 1983:303). The records, Ernst might have added, are typically in the hands of third parties, such as banks or credit card companies, that have little incentive to shield from IRS auditors any records of individual customers' income-generating transactions.

23. Congress and the IRS seized upon the prevalence of credit card use to make unreported income from tips more visible. TEFRA requires large food and beverage establishments to report annually their (a) gross annual income, (b) gross receipts form credit card charges on which tips were included, (c) aggregate amount of tips on charge receipts, and (d) total tip income reported by employees. If employees report tips amounting to less than 8 percent of the establishment's gross receipts, the employer "must allocate an amount equal to the difference between 8 percent . . . and the total amount reported by employees." The credit card information indicates the typical tipping rate at the establishment, which the IRS can then presumably apply to gross annual receipts to estimate gross tip income, or to support the 8 percent presumption embedded in the regulations. By the 1983 tax year, an IRS study noted, the "voluntary reporting percentage" for tip income doubled from 16 percent to at least 32 percent. (Dumais, 1986:105–110).

24. Subsequently, third-party record keeping of the volume of each waterman's activity was made less vulnerable to erosion by watermen seeking to evade taxes. State of Maryland legislation requires each waterman to obtain a prenumbered identification card and stipulates that sales to packing houses cannot take place unless the card is tendered and used to stamp daily reports of the nature and amount of the catch (IRS, 1978b).

25. As in the case of the Maryland seafood catch census, regulatory officials may be unwilling to provide data to the IRS, fearing that it will result in less accurate reporting by producers or licensees. But as the history of the Chesapeake Bay waterman project indicates, these problems often are not insoluble.

26. The argument sometimes is made that nonreporting of naturally invisible income by informal suppliers and other small businesses results in no lower taxes,

on average, than are paid by the businesses in the recording/reporting economy that hire aggressive tax lawyers. While this may be true in some cases, it probably is false in general; the tax "savings" from simply not reporting significant amounts of income are on the average proportionately larger, I suspect, than those that come from exaggerating deductions or from aggressive use of tax-sheltering methods of finance or depreciation.

27. According to "Alan", some tax-evading informal suppliers (including himself) wish to "go straight" but are afraid to begin reporting income, fearing that it will lead to punishment of their past transgressions. Many other small enterprises simply do not grow, either because of economic constraints or because they are part-time enterprises without the wish to grow.

28. According to IRS estimates, in 1981 taxpayers who filed returns claimed almost $8.1 billion in unjustified personal exemptions and $1.8 billion in overstated or unjustified statutory adjustments. (IRS, 1983a:2) This is smaller than the estimated $16 billion in overstated business expenses and much smaller than the estimated $133.8 billion in unreported income on filed returns, but it indicates that ordinary wage earners, too, can cheat in very substantial amounts.

29. About 85 percent of unrecorded income is from legal sources (as opposed to income from narcotics, gambling, prostitution, and the like), according to IRS estimates.

30. Taxable income from sales of illegal drugs in the U.S., it has been estimated, increased from $5.1 billion in 1973 to $23.4 billion in 1981, and that may underestimate the true figure. Illegal drug sales, as estimated, equal about 8 percent of the estimated total unreported income in the nation (Witte, 1985b:27, citing Carlson, 1983).

31. Some estimates hold that in the mid-1970s, there were approximately one million undocumented aliens (about half of the total in the U.S.) working exclusively in unrecorded economic activity (Simon and Witte, 1982).

32. Detailed Stanford Research Institute surveys of participants in the Seattle and Denver Income Maintenance Experiments in the 1970s found that "about one-half the households in each city had reportable income. Of these, one-quarter of the Seattle households and one-third of the Denver households reported no income to AFDC. The average amount of monthly earnings not reported to AFDC by households which reported income to SRI was $322.36 in Seattle and $354.45 in Denver." (Gardiner and Lyman, 1984:8).

33. For Schedule F (farm income) and Schedule C (income from trade or business) returns in the TCMP Phase III, Cycle 7 audit, the IRS cross-tabulated VCL by three-digit industry classification codes. Among those categories with the lowest VCLs (less than 60 percent) were hunting and trapping, commodity contract brokers, liquor stores, builders, drinking places, roofing contractors, and bowling alleys; among the highest (over 94 percent) were veterinary services, hardware and plumbing wholesalers, new-car dealers, hotels, medical laboratories, merchandising machine operators, and travel agents. But the sample sizes for each type of business were too small to allow us to place any confidence in the figures or even in the gross relationship among them, as emphasized by numerous inexplicable disparities in VCL among similar kinds of businesses.

34. See IRS manual, *Audit Techniques Handbook for Specialized Industries,* Sec. 4232.7—Construction (IRS, 1985), advising auditors to be on guard against such practices.

35. A broader implication of the above analysis, one reviewer of this chapter suggested, would be to shift a much larger proportion of national tax obligation from individuals to large corporations—bureaucratized entities whose income is more visible and easily audited than that of the nonbureaucratized household and small business sector. However, in view of the uncertainty about who ultimately bears the corporate income tax burden (consumers in the form of higher prices, workers in the form of lower benefits, shareholders, or someone else), and in view of the issues of international competitiveness raised by pushing corporate income tax rates, already high in comparison to most industrialized nations, to even higher levels, there may be overriding policy arguments against such a shift.

36. This reporting obligation could either be imposed on all homeowners and apartment owners or, more modestly (and as a sort of *quid pro quo*), only on those who claim a deduction for property maintenance or casualty losses, for interest on real estate loans, or for depreciation on the property.

It is noteworthy in this regard that IRS regulations promulgated in 1984 require taxpayers who wish to deduct alimony payments to report to the IRS the Social Security number of the alimony recipient, thereby facilitating an IRS computerized alimony deduction/alimony income matching program. (Before this requirement, the estimated voluntary reporting percentage for alimony recipients who filed returns was 56 percent.) (IRS, 1986:184).

37. Information reporting by payers, along with the additional record keeping and other efforts it entails, might be considered an uncompensated public service. It surely is experienced as such by many payers. Those who are asked to assume this burden, therefore, might be granted a tax credit for at least a portion of their costs. Whether this would be cost effective for the revenue system depends on the level of compliance to be expected for payers (especially individual taxpayers and small businesses, as contrasted with bureaucratized businesses) obligated to file information returns.

38. Some accountants and preparers, of course, may suggest new ways of reducing tax payments, both legitimate and illegitimate. But in general, this chapter's perspective suggests, the larger the number of persons aware of the taxpayer's true income (including accountants and tax advisors), the riskier it will seem to the taxpayer to fail to report income, at least for the majority of taxpayers (see Klepper and Nagin, 1987a; Kinsey, 1987.)

References

Bardach, E.
    1982   Self-regulation and regulatory paperwork. Pp. 315–340 in E. Bardach and R. Kagan, eds., *Social Regulation: Strategies and Reform.* San Francisco:Institute for Contemporary Studies.

Bardach, E., and Kagan, R.A.
   1982   *Going by the Book: The Problem of Regulatory Unreasonableness.* Philadelphia: Temple University Press. A Twentieth Century Fund Report.
Black, D.J.
   1973   The mobilization of law. *Journal of Legal Studies* 2:125–149.
Black, D.J., and Carr
   1980   An analysis of income misreporting. In National Commission on Unemployment Compensation, *Unemployment Compensation: Studies and Research.* Vol. 2.

Carlson, K.
   1983   *Unreported Taxable Income from Selected Illegal Activities.* Vol. I. Cambridge, Mass.: Abt Associates.

Dow. L.M.Jr.
   1977   High weeds in Detroit: the irregular economy among a network of Appalachian migrants. *Urban Anthropology* 6:111–128.
Dumais, J.
   1986   The impact of TEFRA on tip income reporting. Pp. 105–110 in Internal Revenue Service, *Trend analysis and Related Statistics.* 1986 Update. (See entry, IRS, 1986.)

Ernst, M.L.
   1983   Transaction records and their role in compliance. In P. Sawicki, ed., *Income Tax Compliance: A Report of the ABA Section on Taxation, Invitational Conference on Income Tax Compliance.* Washington, D.C.: American Bar Association.

Farrell, D.
   1985   Bashford 'skimming' charged. *San Francisco Chronicle* December 17, 1985: 1.
Feffer, G.A., Timbie, R.E., Weiner, A.J., and Ernst, M.L.
   1983   Proposals to deter and detect the underground cash economy. Pp. 293–316 in P. Sawicki, ed., *Income Tax Compliance: A Report of the ABA Section on Taxation, Invitational Conference on Income Tax Compliance.* Washington, D.C.: American Bar Association.

Gardiner, J.A., and Lyman, T.R.
   1984   *The Fraud Control Game.* Bloomington: Indiana University Press.
Glazer, N.
   1979   On subway graffiti in New York. *The Public Interest,* Winter:3–11.

Internal Revenue Service
   1978a   Watermen project. IRS Criminal Investigation Division. Attachment 8 in *Planning Model Study.* Washington, D.C.: U.S. Department of the Treasury.
   1978b   Coin operated gaming devices study. IRS Criminal Investigation Division. Attachment 8 in *Planning Model Study.* Washington, D.C.: U.S. Department of the Treasury.
   1978c   Catfish project. IRS Criminal Investigation Division. Attachment 8 in

Planning Model Study. Washington, D.C.: U.S. Department of the Treasury.

1982   *Report on Bearer Obligation Interest Compliance*. Research Division, Office of Planning, Finance and Research, Internal Revenue Service. Washington, D.C.: U.S. Department of the Treasury.

1983a   *Income Tax Compliance Research: Estimates for 1973–1981*. Office of Assistant Commissioner (Planning, Finance and Research), Internal Revenue Service, Washington D.C.: U.S. Department of the Treasury.

1983b   *Form 1099 NEC Compliance Study*. IRS Research Division. Office of Assistant Commissioner (Planning, Finance and Research), Internal Revenue Service, Washington D.C.: U.S. Department of the Treasury.

1985   *Internal Revenue Manual, Audit Techniques Handbook for Specialized Industries*. Washington, D.C.: U.S. Department of the Treasury.

1986   Trend Analyses and Related Statistics, United States, Districts, Regions, and Service Centers, 1986 Update. Office of Assistant Commissioner (Planning, Finance and Research), Internal Revenue Service, U.S. Department of the Treasury.

Kagan, R.A.
1984   On regulatory inspectorates and police. In K. Hawkins and J.M. Thomas, eds., *Enforcing Regulation*. Boston: Kluwer-Nijhoff Publishing.

1978   *Regulatory Justice: Implementing a Wage-Price Freeze*. New York: Russell Sage Foundation.

Kinsey, K.A.
1987   Advocacy and Perception: The Structure of Tax Practice. American Bar Foundation Working Paper. American Bar Association, Washington, D.C.

Klepper, S., and Nagin, D.
1987a   The Role of Tax Practitioners in Tax Compliance. Unpublished paper, Department of Statistics and School of Urban and Public Affairs, Carnegie-Mellon University.

1987b   The Anatomy of Tax Evasion. Unpublished paper, Department of Statistics and School of Urban and Public Affairs, Carnegie-Mellon University.

Light, I.
1985   Immigrant entrepreneurs in America: Koreans in Los Angeles. In N. Glazer, ed., *Clamor at the Gates: The New American Immigration*. San Francisco: Institute for Contemporary Policy.

Merton, R.K.
1957   *Social Theory and Social Structure*. Glencoe, Ill.: Free Press.

Porterfield, et al.
1980   Selecting Claimants for Audit of Unreported Earnings. In National Commission in Unemployment Compensation, *Unemployment Compensation: Studies and Research*.

Posner, R.A.
   1981   *The Economics of Justice*. Cambridge, Mass.: Harvard University Press.
Reiss, A.J., Jr.
   1971   *The Police and the Public*. New Haven, Conn.: Yale University Press.
Scholz, J.T.
   1989   Compliance Research and the political context of tax administration. Chapter 1 in this volume.
Shapiro, S.
   1984   *Wayward Capitalists: Targets of the Securities and Exchange Commission*. New Haven, Conn.: Yale University Press.
Simon, C.P., and Witte, A.D.
   1982   *Beating the System: The Underground Economy*. Boston: Auburn House.
Smith, K.W.
   1985   Line by Line TCMP Distributions. Unpublished paper, American Bar Association, Washington, D.C.
Smith, K.W. and Kinsey, K.A.
   1987   Understanding taxpaying behavior: a conceptual framework with implications for research. *Law and Society* 21:639.
Stinchcombe, A.L.
   1963   Institutions of privacy in the determination of police administration practice. *American Journal of Sociology* 69:150.
U.S. Congress
   1985   *Tax Reform Proposals: Compliance and Tax Administration*. Joint Committee on Taxation, U.S. Congress, July 30, 1985. Washington D.C.: U.S. Government Printing Office.
Vitez, T.G.
   1983   Information reporting and withholding as stimulants of voluntary compliance. Pp. 191–216 in P. Sawicki, ed., *Income Tax Compliance: A Report of the ABA Section on Taxation, Invitational Conference on Income Tax Compliance*. Washington, D.C.: American Bar Association.
Wiegand, R.B.
   1984   Dimensions of the Shadow Economy. Unpublished Ph.D. dissertation, Department of Sociology, Vanderbilt University.
Wilson, J.Q. and Kelling, G.
   1982   Broken windows. *Atlantic Monthly*. March: 29–38.
Witte, A.D.
   1985a The nature and extent of unrecorded activity: a survey concentrating on recent U.S. research. In Sergio Alessandrini and Bruno Dallago, eds., *The Unofficial Economy: Consequences and Perspectives in Different Economic Systems*. London: Gower Publishing.
   1985b The Underground Economy in the U.S. and Western Europe: Estimates of Size and Trends and Suggestions for Research. Department of Economics, Wellesley College.

Yankelovich, Skelly, and White, Inc.
1984   Taxpayer Attitudes Study: Final Report. Public opinion survey prepared
        for the Public Affairs Division, Internal Revenue Service, December 1984,
        by Yankelovich, Skelly, and White, Inc., New York.

Steven Klepper and Daniel Nagin

4. The Criminal Deterrence Literature: Implications for Research on Taxpayer Compliance

In the past two decades there has been a literal flood of studies on the deterrent effect of criminal and civil sanctions. These studies have focused on a broad spectrum of illegal behaviors ranging from speeding to homicide and on a comparably broad spectrum of sanctions ranging from fines to execution. The disciplinary perspectives and methodologies of economists, psychologists, and sociologists, among others, have contributed to this literature. Analytic approaches ranging from simple correlations to complex econometric analyses have been employed. Our challenge is to distill from this far-flung literature a manageable number of insights concerning both substance and methodology which are relevant to the emerging literature on taxpayer compliance.

A useful point of departure is a comparison, in general terms, between tax compliance and conformance with the behavioral prohibitions catalogued in society's lengthy criminal and civil code. Reflections reveal some similarities but many more differences. Like many instances of property crime, the motivation for tax evasion is pecuniary. Like a handful of nontax infractions, such as speeding, drunk driving, and drug use, tax evasion is common behavior throughout society. This scant list of similarities only serves to emphasize the differences. Some of these are obvious. The motivation for most assaultive violence is not pecuniary, and even for many property crimes, material gain may be only a partial or secondary motivating factor. Many property crimes committed by juveniles lack a substantial acquisitive motive. Juvenile crime also points to another obvious difference between tax noncompliance and property and violent crime—tax evasion is

Steven Klepper, Department of Economics and Social Science, Carnegie-Mellon University; Daniel Nagin, School of Urban and Public Affairs, Carnegie-Mellon University.

common behavior throughout society, whereas the perpetrators of property and violent crimes are overwhelmingly young, male, and poor.

Beyond these obvious differences are several less obvious ones that contribute to some of the major themes of this chapter. First, tax compliance requires affirmative and repeated action on the part of over 100 million Americans. At a minimum, a tax return must be filed by all individuals with taxable income above very low thresholds if only to declare that liability equals tax withheld. For many others compliance requires an honest accounting of all relevant income and expenses and payment of any outstanding liability. For most Americans, this responsibility must be met every year of their adult lives. In contrast, conformance with the litany of requirements catalogued in our nontax criminal and civil codes simply involves restraint from certain behaviors.

A second important difference is that matters of tax noncompliance remain confidential until they have moved to some fairly advanced state of enforcement (e.g., lien filed, bank account seized). Such confidentiality is unique to tax compliance and contrasts sharply with the public character of criminal and civil enforcement against other legal infractions.

A third distinguishing characteristic is that the primary enforcement arrows in the tax administrator's quiver are administrative and civil, not criminal. For nearly all instances of tax noncompliance, the chance that criminal remedies will be sought is negligible. Since the empirical literature on deterrence focuses primarily on the deterrent effects of arrest, conviction, imprisonment or length of imprisonment, it has little direct relevance to most types of tax noncompliance.

In light of the very substantial differences in the ecologies of tax evasion and the illegal behaviors that have been the topic of most deterrence research,[1] are any findings from the latter literature transferable to the former? From a narrow empirical perspective the answer is obviously no. None of the estimates that purport to measure the elasticity of some crime with respect to some sanction are even remotely transferable to the tax compliance problem. However, we believe that some of the theoretical insights from the criminal deterrence literature and the methodological issues confronting deterrence research are relevant to research on tax compliance; tax compliance, after all, is a case, albeit a very special case, of conformance with legal obligations.

The main purpose of our chapter is to extract a series of lessons from the general deterrence literature that can be usefully applied to the study of tax compliance. The chapter is organized as follows. The second section describes the enforcement tools available to tax administrators and the alternative conceptions of tax compliance that shape their use. This serves to establish the nature of the questions that need to be addressed in order to formulate tax compliance policy. The third section briefly reviews the deterrence literature and draws some substantive and methodological lessons that are relevant to the study of tax compliance. The fourth section summarizes major findings of the tax compliance literature and critiques these findings in the context of the lessons drawn from the deterrence literature. The fifth section lays out a research agenda for exploring some issues of promising relevance for tax administration policy which emerge from the prior sections. Concluding remarks are offered in the sixth section.

The Tax Administrator's Perspective on Compliance

In this section we describe the array of compliance tools available to tax administrators and the different conceptions of tax compliance that underlie them. If research on compliance behavior is to inform policy, it must sort out the relative importance of these different conceptions of compliance.

COMPLIANCE FUNCTIONS

Compliance activities can be characterized in any number of ways. One that is useful for our purposes distinguishes the following functions:

- Taxpayer information programs—The objective of information programs is to provide taxpayers with the means to comply (e.g., tax returns), the information necessary to comply (e.g., instructions, regulations, and notification of statutory changes), and knowledge of the consequences of not complying (e.g., publicity concerning sanctions against noncompliance).
- Detection of noncompliance—A large and growing arsenal of methods are available for detecting noncompliance, including checks on the arithmetic accuracy of returns, computer cross-matches with other data sources, a wide variety of audit tactics, and techniques such as undercover investigations.
- Punishment of noncompliance—Punishment options range from nominal fines to serious civil action or criminal prosecution.
- Proposition of statutory changes in the law—Examples of possible changes in the law include increasing penalty charges and expanding information-reporting and withholding requirements.

The emphasis placed on each of these functions and the tactics used to execute them often reflect competing models of noncompliance. We next illustrate some of these tactics and the alternative conceptions of compliance behavior which motivate them.

INFORMATION PROGRAMS. Noncompliance may stem alternatively from ignorance, confusion, or conscious attempts to exploit attractive opportunities. The ever-increasing complexity of federal, state, and local tax codes increases both the likelihood of nonwillful noncompliance and the opportunity for aggressive and calculated forms of noncompliance. The dilemma confronting tax administrators is to design a communication program to impede these two very different forms of noncompliance. A program designed to combat nonwillful noncompliance would explain the requirements of the tax law in as clear, simple, and nonthreatening a manner as possible. Such a program would be characterized by a commitment to simplifying instructions and regulations, intensive use of the media to educate the public on the requirements of the law, and an extensive network of service centers for answering taxpayer questions and assisting taxpayers in preparing tax returns.

Alternatively, an information program building from a perspective that noncompliance most commonly reflects a conscious exploitation of attractive evasion opportunities would carefully delimit the boundaries of compliance and the penalties for crossing these boundaries. Such a program would attempt to create an image of a threatening and vigilant revenue agency.

DETECTION OF NONCOMPLIANCE. An impressive array of tools are available for detecting noncompliance. Besides the standard arsenal of auditing techniques, advances in computer technology provide growing opportunities to inspect returns for anomalous patterns and to detect persons or businesses who fail to file. While tax administrators have a broad arsenal of detection tools, tight resource constraints demand strategic choices of which enforcement tools to emphasize, in what circumstances, and by what methods. We illustrate such strategic choices with two examples: audit selection and depth versus breadth audit techniques.

Audit opportunities far outstrip any agency's auditing capacity. By and large, audit selections are driven by the direct recovery motive, namely picking targets likely to yield the largest dollar deficiency. However, selection decisions are also influenced by behavioral considerations. An audit may have a specific deterrent effect on the future noncompliance of the auditee, or it may affect the behavior of other taxpayers, or both. An audit strategy designed to exploit specific deterrent effects would select for audit individuals or businesses who persistently engage in noncompliance, even if the noncompliance is not egregious. For example, it might focus on individuals with modest as well as substantial amounts of income not subject to withholding or information reporting. Such an audit selection strategy sacrifices some short-term direct recovery on the assumption that an audit will have a chastening effect on chronic noncompliance behavior, whether moderate or severe. Alternatively, an audit strategy designed to exploit general deterrent effects would select for audit "well-connected" targets, who might report their experience to others. For example, if tax preparers were perceived as important conduits of information, this strategy might concentrate on auditing selected tax preparers.

The abundance of audit targets also creates an ongoing tension between depth versus breadth audit strategies. The depth strategy argues for thorough and exacting audits. In contrast, the breadth strategy argues for maximizing the number of audit contacts by restricting audits to a few simple tests unless a more thorough examination appears warranted.

The depth strategy emphasizes the importance of "educating" taxpayers. A thorough audit is a taxing agency's best tool for demonstrating the agency's ability to detect noncompliance and enforce all relevant aspects of the tax code. The argument for depth audits can be illustrated by an IRS study concluding that audits from the Taxpayer Compliance Measurement Program (TCMP), renowned for their thoroughness, failed to identify about 75 percent of unreported 1099 income (IRS, 1983:52). This poor success rate stemmed from auditors having little independent information (e.g., preaudit compilations of 1099s) about an auditee's unreported income. An advocate of the depth strategy would argue that the lopsided quality of TCMP audits has the perverse effect of encouraging noncompliers to adjust their noncompliance strategies by emphasizing income nonreporting tactics and deemphasizing deduction overstatement tactics. He might suggest conducting fewer, more thorough audits using techniques such as cash flow and net worth analysis[2] and undercover investigations.

The breadth audit strategy builds from a very different perspective on taxpayer psychology. First, in-depth audits, which of necessity are time consuming, disruptive, and inherently menacing because of their thoroughness, are perceived to jeopardize the goodwill of complying taxpayers and perhaps even taxpayers committing only minor, nonsystematic infractions. Second, only a small fraction of taxpayers are thought to be as calculating as depth advocates suggest. It is anticipated that most auditees respond to audits that fail to detect some element of noncompliance not so much by exploiting the apparent weakness in detection procedures, but rather by concluding that they may not be so lucky the next time. The very act of auditing a taxpayer, even if it is relatively narrow or superficial, sends a tangible signal that the taxing agency reviews returns and takes compliance seriously enough to initiate person-to-person audits. A breadth audit strategy maximizes the number of such signals.

PUNISHMENT OF NONCOMPLIERS.   A large arsenal of punishments of different severity is available for penalizing noncompliers, ranging from nominal fines to civil and criminal prosecution. Choices about punishment are affected by legal considerations, direct recovery, and behavioral assumptions. One punishment with potentially far-reaching consequences is civil or criminal prosecution. While use of this option typically is sparing, it is widely believed that exemplary penalties have an important behavioral impact. The high cost of being the target of such remedies is the tax administrator's main counterweight to certain difficult-to-identify forms of noncompliance. These costs include not only the statutorily prescribed penalties for serious breaches of tax law, but also the stigma attached to their imposition—loss of prestige and the attendant losses in economic and social opportunities. The importance of exemplary punishment may also be magnified by confidentiality requirements. Matters of tax noncompliance remain confidential until they have moved to a fairly advanced state of enforcement. Imposition of exemplary penalties provides tax administrators with their only opportunity to pierce the veil of confidentiality and make a public statement about the potentially serious costs of noncompliance.

The effectiveness of exemplary punishment as a deterrent to noncompliance depends upon how it is deployed. Currently, IRS's use of criminal prosecution is narrowly targeted to drug traffickers and tax protesters. Implicit in this choice is the assumption that the message transmitted by exemplary punishment is lost if the targets of the punishment are too diffuse. State tax administration also tends to target criminal prosecution, but less narrowly than the IRS. A favored target of states with aggressive enforcement programs is individuals who collect and fail to remit trust fund taxes, a much larger class of taxpayers than drug traffickers and tax protesters.

STATUTORY CHANGES.   The final vehicle for advancing compliance is statutory changes. Such changes can raise the cost of noncompliance by increasing civil and criminal penalties or by reducing opportunities and incentives for noncompliance. (Incentive can be reduced by, for example, lowering the tax rate). Examples of statutory changes to reduce opportunity are two provisions of the Tax Equity and Fiscal Responsibility Act of 1982. One extended 1099 information reporting to most securities transactions. The other was an ill-fated provision requiring withholding on dividend and interest income.

In defining a legislative agenda, the tax administrator's dilemma is deciding which of a limitless number of initiatives to push in the legislative process. Legislatures typically have short attention spans and a tax administrator's political capital is limited, necessitating strategic choices.

Alternative Conceptions of Noncompliance

Our brief review of the enforcement tools available to tax administrators indicates some of the issues that need to be resolved in order to formulate tax compliance policy. Many of these issues center around two questions: (1) Exactly how cunning are taxpayers?; and (2) How does experience with tax enforcement affect compliance?

The design of taxpayer information programs illustrates the significance of the first question. If taxpayers are thought to be predisposed to comply with the tax laws based on a sense of moral obligation to comply with legal requirements, information programs need only provide clear direction about what is required. Alternatively, if taxpayers are thought to have little moral commitment to tax compliance, information programs should carefully delimit the boundaries of noncompliance and the consequences of crossing the boundaries.

The discussion of audit selection illustrates the importance of the second question. Since most routine enforcement activities, including audits, are exercised in confidence, audit selection strategies that focus on persistent noncompliers exploit the assumed specific deterrent effect of an audit. Such strategies assume that auditees engage in a limited amount of communication of their experiences to others, a necessary antecedent to gaining a general deterrent effect. Alternatively, selection strategies designed to select "well-connected" targets are more optimistic than an audit experience will be communicated either directly by auditees or by passive observation (e.g., merchants in a mall observing that auditors have visited a fellow merchant).

Another aspect of experience is illustrated in the depth advocate's conception of noncompliance. Depth audit strategies assume taxpayers cunningly exploit all available opportunities. Such taxpayers are expected to respond to less than thorough audits either by continuing their aggressive exploitation of undetected facets of their noncompliance or by adjusting their strategies to take full advantage of weaknesses they perceive in the course of audits. Such taxpayers may also tell others of the weakness in detection procedures, thereby exacerbating noncompliance.

An even more pessimistic conception of the cunning taxpayer is that routinely employed penalties for noncompliance, which by and large are quite nominal, are insufficient to deter noncompliance in areas inherently difficult to detect (e.g., underreporting of proprietorship income, especially from cash sources). This conception of noncompliance argues for increased emphasis on criminal prosecution or serious civil remedies. Such a strategy would not only increase the direct monetary costs of noncompliance but would also emphasize the few tax enforcement tools that are both highly visible and stigmatizing.

The most extreme conception of noncompliance behavior is nihilistic. Taxpayers are perceived as aggressively exploiting opportunities for noncompliance that have very little chance of detection. This view argues for a legislative fix to the noncompliance problem by expanding withholding and information-reporting requirements to the maximum possible extent.

These alternative views of taxpayer behavior are reminiscent of themes in the general deterrence literature. They raise issues of:

- General versus specific deterrence;
- The importance of opportunities and incentives;
- The role of morality;
- The importance of informal sanctions;
- The importance of experience.

We turn now to the deterrence literature to examine what can be learned about these issues, both from a substantive as well as a methodological perspective.

A Review of the Major Findings of the Deterrence Literature and Their Applicability to the Study of Tax Compliance

This section is divided into two parts. The first discusses the principal findings of the criminal deterrence literature. The second discusses general lessons that emerge from this literature and their implications for the study of tax compliance. The first part is further subdivided to reflect the distinction between specific and general deterrence.

REVIEW OF THE DETERRENCE LITERATURE

GENERAL DETERRENCE.   The early studies on general deterrence appear in the sociology literature. They focus on the effect of certainty and severity of punishment on criminal behavior (Gibbs, 1968; Tittle, 1969). Using a variety of statistical methods, they explore the association between official police data on the incidence of crime and various measures of sanction risk and sanction severity. The predominant, but by no means universal, finding of these studies is that crime rates are inversely associated with the certainty of punishment but not generally related to the severity of punishment. Some have interpreted these results as suggesting that certainty of punishment deters crime but severity of punishment does not.

The next wave of general deterrence studies in the sociology literature probed this conclusion further using self-reported data on crime, perceived certainty and severity of punishment, moral beliefs about crime, and experience with offenders (Waldo and Chiricos, 1972; Gibbs, 1975; Silberman, 1976; Erickson, Gibbs, and Jensen, 1977; Meier and Johnson, 1977; Minor, 1977; Akers et al., 1979; Grasmick and Bryjak, 1980; Grasmick and Green, 1980; Tittle, 1980). The predominant findings of these studies are: (1) Crime is inversely related to the perceived severity of informal sanctions, such as loss of respect of family, friends, and peers, but is not strongly related to perceptions about the severity of formal sanctions. (2) Crime is inversely related to perceived certainty of detection. (3) Experience with other criminal offenders is associated with greater criminal involvement. (4) Beliefs about the legitimacy of laws and moral attitudes concerning criminal behavior are important determinants of criminal behavior; those experiencing less guilt from breaking a law, either because of a lesser sense of moral obligation to uphold the law or because of a greater ability to rationalize breaking the law, are more likely to violate the law.

The most recent wave of general deterrence studies in the sociology literature uses panel data, either from official sources or from repeated surveys of individuals over time, to explore principally the effect on crime of perceptions of certainty and severity of punishment, experience with offenders, and moral beliefs (Greenberg, Kessler, and Logan, 1979; Greenberg and Kessler, 1982; Minor and Harry, 1982; Paternoster et al., 1983; Saltzman et al., 1982; Liska and Reed, 1985). The findings of these studies suggest that much of the association between crime, beliefs, and perceptions of sanction certainty and severity may result from the effect of criminal involvement on perceptions and beliefs rather than the reverse. When past involvement in crime is controlled for, perceptions of certainty no longer seem to be related to criminal involvement; and the importance of moral beliefs, perceptions about informal sanctions, and a number of other determinants of criminal behavior is reduced.

A separate set of general deterrence studies have also emerged in the economics literature. In addition to stressing the role of sanction risk and severity on criminal behavior, these studies also emphasize the importance of incentives and opportunities to commit crime (Ehrlich, 1973; Sjoquist, 1973; Heineke, 1978). Besides marshalling support for the importance of formal sanctions, these studies present evidence suggesting that the incidence of crime is inversely related to the returns from legal activity, represented by the legal wage rate and the prospects for employment.

SPECIFIC DETERRENCE.   Most of the literature examining the behavior of punished offenders focuses on the efficacy of rehabilitation. The predominant findings of this literature are that rehabilitative efforts have virtually no effect on recidivism (Sechrest, White, and Brown, 1979). There are very few studies of the effect of punishment on recidivism, although there is some evidence suggesting that punishment may affect the subsequent involvement of offenders for specific crimes (Lempert, 1981). The dearth of studies on specific deterrence suggests that punishment is not viewed as an effective means of deterring offenders from committing subsequent crimes. One possible explanation of this is that once an individual experiences the social stigma associated with criminal enforcement, punishment may cease to have a significant deterrent effect. This would be consistent with labeling theories that suggest that individuals commit more crimes once they have been "labeled" as criminals.

GENERAL LESSONS AND THEIR TRANSFERABILITY TO THE STUDY OF TAX COMPLIANCE

SUBSTANTIVE FINDINGS.   One important conclusion of the earlier deterrence literature is that certainty of punishment appeared to be a much more important deterrent to criminal behavior than severity of formal sanctions. This conclusion has been challenged for a variety of reasons (Cook, 1977; Nagin, 1978; Blumstein, Cohen, and Nagin, 1978) which we allude to below. However, even if it is deemed correct, we suspect it has only limited applicability to tax compliance policy. A widely held explanation for the deterrent effect of certainty is that targets of criminal justice enforcement are stigmatized by the public character of the enforcement. However, since most tax enforcement is conducted privately, it is unlikely that detection of tax offenses will stigmatize offenders and thus deter noncompliance. Furthermore, unlike most crimes, sanctions for tax offenses are measured in the same units as the principal benefits of tax noncompliance, namely monetary ones. We suspect this greatly heightens the importance of sanctions for tax offenses relative to most other crimes.

A second finding of the general deterrence literature is that offenders appear to be responsive to the severity of informal sanctions, such as loss of the respect of family and friends, but not particularly responsive to formal sanctions. This is also consistent with the explanation for the deterrent effect of certainty—it isn't formal sanctions but rather the stigma associated with being identified publicly as a criminal that deters crime. Applying this reasoning to tax compliance suggests that fear of stigma may be an important factor in deterring more serious tax offenses that sometimes result in criminal enforcement, such as failure to file a return, failure to report large sums of money, and fraudulent declaration of deductions. This suggests it might be productive to study the deterrent effect of exemplary punishment on tax compliance.

A third finding of the deterrence literature, or at least the economic studies of crime, is the importance of incentives and opportunities to commit crime. While the relevance of economic incentives and opportunity for explaining many forms of criminal behavior may be limited, we believe these two themes are extremely relevant for the study of tax evasion. The tax saving from noncompliance is a direct function of the marginal tax rate, which suggests that incentives for noncompliance should be related to the marginal tax rate. Since the tax rate has varied over time and clearly varies considerably across individuals, this may be an important factor explaining both cross-sectional and temporal variation in tax compliance.[3] Opportunities for tax noncompliance are also likely to vary considerably across individuals and over time. For example, individuals with income not subject to withholding or information reporting are in a much better position to avoid detection of unreported income than individuals receiving primarily wage and salary income. Differences in audit probabilities across income levels and types of returns also give rise to variation in the likelihood of detection of noncompliance across individuals. Since reasonably reliable measures of both incentives and opportunities for tax noncompliance at the individual level can be constructed from audited tax returns, studies of the effect of incentives and opportunities on tax compliance are feasible and may prove to be very fruitful.

A fourth finding of the deterrence literature is that experience with offenders appears to be associated with greater criminal involvement. There are multiple explanations for this association. Experience with offenders may provide information about the nature of criminal enforcement. If uncertainty about the likelihood and consequences of such enforcement is a major deterrent to crime, resolving this uncertainty may lead to greater criminal involvement. Alternatively, experience with offenders may condition an individual's moral attitudes about the law or change his perceptions about the nature of informal sanctions that would result if he were detected violating the law. A third explanation for the association is that it may be a manifestation rather than a cause of criminal involvement. Either of the first two explanations suggest that it would be worthwhile to study networks of taxpayers. It would be interesting to analyze how punishing one offender affects the subsequent behavior of others in the same network.

A fifth finding of the deterrence literature is the limited efficacy of specific deterrence. We suspect this finding is of limited relevance to the study of tax compliance. One reason why punishment of offenders in most crimes may have little effect on their subsequent behavior is because the social stigma associated with being the target of public enforcement is a lesser concern to those who have already been labeled as criminals. However, for most tax offenses enforcement is private and thus no labeling occurs. Consequently, prior enforcement is not likely to undo the deterrent effects of punishment. Moreover, tax offenders may fear that repeated offenses, even of a relatively small amount, may constitute grounds for civil or criminal prosecution. Westat, Inc.'s (1980b:18–24) survey of taxpayers suggests that individuals have a very high esteem for IRS's ability to monitor the behavior of taxpayers over time and to detect repeated noncompliance. If in fact individuals fear public enforcement for repeated offenses, nonpublic enforcement may serve as a forceful deterrent to subsequent noncompliance.

Specific deterrence can have a substantial effect on tax compliance only if a large number of taxpayers are subjected to tax enforcement. The fact that IRS audits only about 2 percent of returns each year suggests a limited role for specific deterrence. However, if there is not too much overlap in audit targets from year to year, many taxpayers may be audited at least once in an extended interval. Indeed, Song and Yarbrough (1978:448) report that a little less than 30 percent of the respondents to their survey on taxpayer ethics and attitudes reported that their tax return had been audited in the past. Moreover, IRS sends out millions of notices of tax deficiency after a preliminary computer review of returns. Individuals also have contact with IRS through corporate audits and with state tax administration through audits of state tax returns. These observations suggest a potentially important role for specific deterrence.

The last major finding of the deterrence literature we consider concerns moral beliefs. While moral beliefs appear to play an important role in inhibiting involvement in many crimes, we do not think they play a comparably pronounced role in deterring tax noncompliance. Most of the survey evidence on tax noncompliance suggests that even fairly large amounts of noncompliance are not generally perceived as highly immoral acts. For example, Westat, Inc. (1980a:74) found that a majority of respondents viewed evading $500 in taxes as less serious than taking $500 that did not belong to them. Song and Yarborough (1978:445) found that tax evasion was viewed as only slightly more serious than stealing a bicycle. Many individuals perceive tax compliance to be a game, a battle of wits between the taxpayer and IRS (Westat, Inc., 1980a:54–57). All of this suggests that moral beliefs about breaking the law are likely to play a less important role in deterring tax noncompliance than most other crimes.

METHODOLOGICAL LESSONS.   A number of important methodological lessons emerge from the deterrence literature that are likely to be relevant to the study of tax noncompliance. The first concerns the simultaneous determination of the crime rate and sanction risks and levels. Using cross-sectional data, the early studies of crime examined the relationship across jurisdictions between crime and certainty and severity of punishment assuming that causality flowed exclusively from certainty and severity to crime. However, plausible theories were advanced that crime rates might also affect the certainty and severity of punishment.[4] Sorting out the contribution of the deterrent effect of sanctions from the observed negative association between the crime rate and sanction risk requires the imposition of so-called identification restrictions. Deterrence studies using aggregate data on crime rates and sanctions have been hobbled by the inability of researchers to set forth widely accepted identification restrictions (Blumstein et al., 1978; Fisher and Nagin, 1978).

We raise the issue of simultaneity because revenue agencies and IRS in particular allocate their enforcement resources according to estimates of noncompliance. This suggests that aggregate measures of tax noncompliance and revenue agency enforcement levels may be simultaneously determined. Consequently, studies of tax compliance based on aggregate data must confront the identification problem that has so troubled deterrence research.

A major motivation for individual survey studies in the deterrence literature is to circumvent this simultaneity problem. However, they too are plagued by a simultaneity problem. Early researchers using survey data noted that perceptions and beliefs might be as much caused by crime as causes of crime, although they did little to deal with the problem. Recent studies using panel data suggest that neglecting the influence of crime on perceptions and beliefs can lead to seriously distorted results (Minor and Harry, 1982; Paternoster et al., 1983; Saltzman et al., 1982; Liska and Reed, 1985). While panel data can be used to cope with this problem, they too require restrictive assumptions to identify the nature of the causal process (Greenberg and Kessler, 1982:25–46). These issues are directly relevant to tax compliance studies using survey data.

The second methodological lesson concerns interactive effects. A number of deterrence studies using a utilitarian perspective (e.g., Grasmick and Bryjak, 1980) argue that the influence on crime of factors affecting the costs of crime should depend upon the benefits from crime, and vice versa. This is likely to be an important point for the study of tax noncompliance. For example, the tax rate might be expected to have a more pronounced influence on underreported income for individuals earning income not subject to withholding or information reporting; in the extreme case where all of an individual's income is in the form of wages and salaries, he is likely to report all his income regardless of the tax rate he faces. This suggests that tax rates and opportunities, among other variables, should be examined in an interactive setting.

The third methodological lesson concerns biases in measures of crime. It is well known that official crime rates understate the true incidence of crime because victims do not detect all crimes and fail to report all crimes to the police and because police departments fail to record all reported crime. Similarly, revenue agencies fail to detect all forms of tax noncompliance, even when in-depth audits are employed. The understatement of crime rates in the general deterrence literature is thought to exaggerate the inverse association between crime and certainty of punishment (Nagin, 1978:97). While in tax compliance studies the nature of the bias due to underestimates of noncompliance will not necessarily take this same form, these studies should be sensitive to the kinds of biases underestimates might induce.

A more directly relevant lesson concerning biases in crime measures involves the use of survey data. Because of recall, veracity, and nonresponse problems, survey data tend to underestimate the crime rate. Nonresponse may be particularly serious if individuals who commit the most crime or who have distinctive motives for committing crimes disproportionately fail to respond to surveys. If in fact respondents to tax surveys are not represen-tative, the results of studies using survey data will be distorted (Roth and Witte, 1985:21).

The last methodological problem pertains to the study of specific deterrence, where the major problem is the development of a suitable control group. Ideally, it would be desirable to compare the behavior of identical groups of offenders receiving different punishments. However, offenders receiving different punishment generally differ on characteristics that may independently influence their subsequent criminal involvement. Efforts to assess the effects of punishment on tax offenders who are nonran-domly subjected to some kind of enforcement will likely be affected by this problem.

Review of Tax Compliance Studies

In this section we apply the lessons of the general deterrence literature to studies of tax compliance. The lessons are especially relevant to the two principal types of studies of determinants of tax compliance— nonexperimental studies using IRS data and analyses of self-reported tax compliance. We also review the few experimental studies that have been done on tax compliance. We conclude the section with an assessment of the state of research on tax compliance and productive directions in which it might be extended.

NONEXPERIMENTAL STUDIES USING IRS DATA

There are three nonexperimental studies using IRS data (Clotfelter, 1983; Witte and Woodbury, 1984; Slemrod, 1985). The basic approach of each study is to model tax evasion as a problem of maximizing expected utility. Individuals are assumed to choose a level of noncompliance for which the benefits from the last dollar of noncompliance are equal to the costs. The optimal level of noncompliance is shown to depend upon factors that affect the (marginal) benefits and costs of noncompliance. These factors include: the probability of an audit, which depends upon income, type of return (e.g., whether substantial Schedule C or F income is re-ported), the historical audit rate, and presumably the level of noncom-pliance; the probability of detection if an audit is made, which is deter-mined by such things as the type of income of the taxpayer (e.g., whether it is subject to withholding or information reporting) and possibly the level of noncompliance; the monetary savings from noncompliance, which depend on the marginal tax rate; the nature of sanctions if noncompliance is detected, which is related to the historical use of different sanctions; and demographic factors such as age, sex, marital status, and geographic region of the country.

Each of the studies uses data compiled by the IRS. Clotfelter looks at the determinants of unreported income on individual income tax returns audited randomly in the 1969 Taxpayer Compliance Measurement Program (TCMP). Witte and Woodbury use the same underlying data as Clotfelter aggregated to the three-digit zip code level. They also focus on the compliance level, defined as the ratio of total taxes paid to total taxes owed, rather than just unreported income. Slemrod analyzes data from the 1977 stratified sample of tax returns. He exploits the fact that when the tax table is used, tax liability is the same for all returns with adjusted income in the same $50 bracket. He argues theoretically that noncompliers have an incentive to report adjusted income in the upper part of a $50 bracket whereas compliers do not. His analysis focuses on the determinants of the position of taxable income within a $50 income bracket across a large sample of individual returns.

Perhaps the principal finding of all three studies is the importance of opportunity. Clotfelter finds greater compliance for returns with both greater wage and salary income and greater dividend and interest income. Witte and Woodbury find greater compliance in jurisdictions with a greater fraction of employment accounted for by manufacturing, presumably because manufacturing income is more likely to be subject to withholding than other types of income. Slemrod finds greater compliance for taxpayers who have no adjustments to income, do not itemize deductions, and do not report any self-employment, small business, or estate and trust income. All of these results are consistent with simple summaries of the TCMP indicating that reporting rates are highest for income subject to withholding or 1099 reporting and lowest for other types of income such as proprietorship, farm, and capital gains income.

The three studies also examine the relationship between income and compliance. However, because income and the marginal federal tax rate are so highly correlated, it is difficult to interpret estimates of the partial effect of income on compliance when the tax rate is not controlled for or when it is represented by the marginal federal tax rate. Only Clotfelter is able to cope with this problem. Representing the tax rate as the sum of the marginal federal and state tax rates and, where relevant, the self-employment tax rate, he finds a direct relationship between total unreported income and both the tax rate and true income. However, he finds that the tax rate does not have a comparable effect on overstated business expenses or on overstatement of the charitable deduction.

Witte and Woodbury examine the relationship between compliance and sanction certainty and severity. They find that compliance is directly related to past audit rates and the number of notices sent by IRS as a result of data-processing efforts. In contrast, compliance is not related to their measure of the probability of criminal sanctions or to the severity of criminal fraud penalties for all but one of the classes of taxpayers they examine. Moreover, compliance is significantly (statistically) related to the probability of a civil fraud penalty in a way contrary to expectations.

Thus, the principal finding of the three studies is the importance of opportunity as embodied in the type of income received by the taxpayer. The results concerning other variables are mixed, especially regarding the importance of certainty and severity of sanctions.

In light of the methodological problems plaguing general deterrence studies, it might be the case that the findings concerning opportunity and incentives are spurious. In particular, three of the methodological lessons extracted from the general deterrence literature seem relevant: the bias in official estimates of crime, interactive effects between the costs and benefits of crime, and the simultaneous determination of aggregate measures of crime and sanction risk and severity. Somewhat surprisingly, however, our analysis suggests that, if anything, these methodological problems cause the importance of opportunity and incentives to be *underestimated* in the three studies.

Consider first the problem of measuring the extent of noncompliance. The IRS postaudit of the fraction of unreported 1099 income detected in the 1976 TCMP and independent estimates of unreported capital gains income (Hinrichs, 1964) and farm and rental income (Groves, 1958) suggest that noncompliance is underestimated in the TCMP. This implies that the measures of noncompliance used by both Clotfelter and Witte and Woodbury are downwardly biased, especially for returns with substantial income not from wages or salary. Both studies thus are likely to underestimate the strength of the relationship between compliance and measures of opportunity (e.g., the proportion of income subject to withholding).

A second limitation of all three studies is the lack of interaction between the tax rate and income variables on the one hand and variables representing opportunity on the other hand. As we noted when reviewing the general deterrence literature, if tax rates influence compliance decisions, they are likely to have a greater effect on compliance the greater the probability of escaping detection. Similarly, variables representing the probability of escaping detection are likely to have a greater effect on compliance when the tax rate is greater. This suggests that the tax rate and variables representing opportunity should be interacted, which none of the studies do. Consequently, the influence of taxes and opportunities reported in the studies is likely to be underestimated for individuals with both a high tax rate and low detection risk opportunities. Since these individuals are likely to account for a disproportionate share of noncompliance, estimates of average effects of taxes and opportunities across all taxpayers are likely to understate the policy relevance of both factors.

A third methodological implication of the general deterrence studies is that at the jurisdictional level noncompliance rates, sanction certainty, and sanction severity are likely to be simultaneously determined. Even if sanction certainty and severity have no effect on compliance, the fact that IRS allocates its resources where it anticipates the greatest noncompliance suggests that sanction certainty and severity will be highest in jurisdictions where noncompliance is greatest. Failure to take this into account is likely to lead to a downwardly biased estimate of the (absolute) effect of sanction certainty and severity on compliance, causing the deterrent effect of sanctions to be underestimated. This suggests that Witte and Woodbury underestimate the deterrent effect on compliance of the audit probability and the incidence and severity of different types of sanctions.

In conclusion, the studies using IRS data on individual returns suggest that opportunity and incentive are important determinants of compliance. If their studies err, it is likely that they underestimate the importance of these factors.

SURVEY STUDIES OF COMPLIANCE

We reviewed the survey studies of Vogel (1974), Spicer and Lundstedt (1976), Minor (1977), Mason and Calvin (1978, 1984), Tittle (1980), Westat, Inc. (1980a, b), Scott and Grasmick (1981), Grasmick and Scott (1982), Thurman, St. John, and Riggs (1984), and Yankelovich, Skelly, and White, Inc. (1984). The findings of these studies vary somewhat, but in general they are similar to the findings of the survey studies in the general deterrence literature. The following factors were found to be significant determinants of compliance. (1) Perceptions of the probability of detection of compliance. Mason and Calvin (1978) found this to dominate all other factors in importance. (2) Severity of informal sanctions. Presumably this was relevant only for individuals expecting public revelation of detected noncompliance. (3) Moral beliefs about violating the tax laws: Although moral beliefs acted to constrain noncompliance, evidence was found suggesting that guilt feelings associated with noncompliance (as a result of committing an immoral act) could be neutralized by certain types of excuses for noncompliance, such as paying an unfair amount of taxes. (4) Experience with other noncompliers and past experience with IRS enforcement. Greater experience both with other noncompliers and with past IRS enforcement was associated with greater noncompliance. (5) Demographics. Older individuals were found to engage in less noncompliance.

Like the survey studies in the general deterrence literature, these studies are subject to a number of methodological problems that call into question the reliability of their findings. First, the quality of the data employed in the studies is suspect. The self-reported incidence of noncompliance in a number of studies seems low relative to TCMP and other estimates of noncompliance. This may be because of veracity and recall problems. Alternatively, it may be because nonrespondents to the surveys on average engage in a greater amount of compliance than respondents. If in addition nonrespondents are less likely to have a moral justification (in their eyes) for noncompliance and are more likely not to comply because of good opportunities and incentives for noncompliance, then surveys are likely to overestimate the role of moral beliefs and underestimate the importance of opportunities and incentives.

Another problem with the survey studies is the frequent failure to control for all relevant determinants of compliance. Many studies use bivariate correlations to analyze the role of individual factors, despite the fact that across individuals factors like age, sex, and many perceptual variables are likely to be correlated with each other as well as with incentives and opportunities. Even studies using more sophisticated methods often do not adequately control for opportunities.

Perhaps the most serious limitation of the survey studies is the failure to probe the direction of causality between compliance and its correlates. The general deterrence studies suggest that crime may be a more important determinant of perceptions and beliefs than perceptions and beliefs are determinants of crime. Yet this possibility seems to have been neglected in the survey studies on tax compliance. Consequently, it is unclear to what extent perceptions and beliefs actually contribute to tax noncompliance rather than are the result of tax noncompliance.

EXPERIMENTAL STUDIES

We reviewed three experimental studies of tax compliance. Two of the studies, Friedland, Maital, and Rutenberg (1978) and Spicer and Becker (1980), use a laboratory setting to study income reporting. Experimental subjects are given a certain amount of money per period and must decide how much of it to report. Dollars reported are subject to a fractional tax rate of t. Unreported dollars are not subject to any tax if undetected but are subject to a tax and a penalty equal to pt if detected, where $1/p$ is the probability of detection. This setup insures that no matter what the values of p and t, nonreporting is always an even gamble.

Spicer and Becker find that subjects misled to think they face a higher tax rate than other subjects report less income while those misled to think they face a lower tax rate than other subjects report more income. They interpret this as suggesting that perceived fairness of the tax system affects compliance. Friedland et al. find that on average the greater the tax rate the smaller the reported income. They also find that raising the penalty, p, for nonreporting, which involves lowering the probability of detection (without affecting the evenness of the nonreporting gamble), leads to greater reported income.

The third experimental study, by Schwartz and Orleans (1967), administers three different types of surveys to random samples of high-income taxpayers prior to the filing of their tax returns. One group is subjected to a survey emphasizing the moral duty to pay taxes, the second to a survey emphasizing the sanctions against noncompliance, and the third group to a neutral survey. Schwartz and Orleans find that taxpayers subjected to the "morality" survey increased reported income relative to the prior year's tax return by a greater amount than either of the other two groups and by a greater amount than a fourth, unsurveyed group.

We suggest caution about drawing strong conclusions from these studies. None of the findings concerning equity and morality is significant statistically at conventional levels. Furthermore, there is a certain artificiality about each of the studies that may limit the generality of the results. The environment in the Spicer and Becker and the Friedland et al. studies, where nonreporting is an even gamble and there is no uncertainty regarding the enforcement process, is very different from the normal circumstances facing taxpayers. In the Schwartz and Orleans study, a close reading of the morality and sanction surveys raises questions about whether these labels clearly reflect the messages conveyed by the surveys. Despite our concerns, however, we are impressed with the potential experiments have for illuminating the motives for tax compliance. In particular, we think the methodology employed by Schwartz and Orleans can be productively applied not only to experimental, but also to actual, interventions such as audits. We pursue this theme further in the next section.

WHERE DO WE GO FROM HERE?

One implication of the tax compliance studies using IRS data is that the role of opportunities and incentives seem worth studying in much more detail. To date, tax compliance has been studied at an extremely high level of aggregation. There may be different types of opportunities and incentives that pertain to different items on the tax return. A promising direction for future research would be to use IRS data from the TCMP to investigate the importance of opportunity and incentives for each line item on the tax return.

We are less sanguine about the value of studying further the role of moral beliefs, at least using survey approaches. Our bias is that morality is not an especially important factor affecting compliance. Notwithstanding our bias, we feel that survey approaches, at least the way they have been practiced to date, are not a very reliable method for learning about the role of morality. One solution to the methodological problems plaguing survey studies is to survey individuals repeatedly over time in order to create a panel. However, we suspect few individuals would be willing to discuss honestly their tax behavior on a repeated basis, and those that would be willing are likely to be unrepresentative.

We think that some of the themes raised in the review of the general deterrence literature suggest promising avenues for future research. We suggested that specific deterrence might be an important source of deterrence in the tax compliance area. The abundance of IRS data on audited individuals has received little attention to date. We also suggested that experience with the tax system and with other noncompliers might be an important factor affecting tax compliance. It might be worthwhile to study the behavior of networks of taxpayers after one member of the network has been subjected to some kind of enforcement. We also noted the potential importance of exemplary punishment, which to date has also received little attention.

In the next section we describe a series of research projects that begin to address a number of these themes. We suggest these projects not so much to propose a specific research agenda for the study of tax compliance but rather to illustrate the sorts of projects we think might be illuminating.

Research Agenda

Our proposed research projects involve using data on individual compliance to address two central questions on tax compliance: (1) To what extent can existing patterns of noncompliance be explained in terms of calculated responses to opportunity and incentive? and (2) To what extent can compliance behavior be modified by the activities of revenue agencies? The proposed projects are representative of the ways we think these questions can be fruitfully explored.

ECOLOGY OF NONCOMPLIANCE

Currently, little is known about the nature, or as we call it, the ecology, of tax noncompliance. For example, little is known about the following issues. To what extent do individuals fully exploit specific low-detection risk opportunities (such as the nonreporting of capital gains)? Are low-detection risk opportunities exploited before high-detection risk opportunities? Are there systematic patterns of noncompliance across income, marginal tax rate, and demographic groups conditioned on the availability of different types of opportunities? What strategies do taxpayers use in exploiting opportunities for noncompliance?

Answers to these questions would be helpful in designing a model of tax compliance. Indeed, currently one of the biggest obstacles to building such a model is the lack of stylized facts concerning tax compliance. Since the TCMP involves random audits of taxpayers, it provides a rich set of data for the development of such stylized facts. The following types of analyses could be done with the TCMP data:

- Relative frequency functions could be computed for the ratio of unreported tax liability to true tax liability across all TCMP audits in a given year. This same density function conditioned alternatively on such factors as total income, the marginal tax rate (perhaps computed as in Clotfelter, 1983), type of income, occupation, and demographic characteristics, could be computed.

- A similar analysis could be conducted for each line item of the tax return. For example, relative frequency functions of the ratio of unreported to true tax liability could be analyzed individually for different types of income (such as wages and salaries, income subject to 1099 reporting, and cash income), different types of adjustments to income, different types of business expenses, different itemized deductions, and so forth. Again, various conditional relative frequency functions could also be reported. In addition to the factors cited above, it might also be valuable to condition on the ratio of unreported to true tax liability for other categories of income, deductions, expenses, etc. For example, the frequency function of the ratio of unreported to total 1099 income, conditional on the ratio of reported business expenses to true expenses, could be computed.

• Deficient filers (above a certain amount) could be compared with nonfilers in terms of such things as income, sources of income, marginal or average tax rate, prior filing history, and demographic characteristics.

Analyses like these could greatly inform models of tax compliance. For example, suppose it were learned that a large majority of taxpayers were fully compliant even for categories of liability such as cash income, where noncompliance is difficult to detect. This would suggest to us that much compliance is induced by moral beliefs about the importance of paying taxes. Alternatively, suppose it were learned that most taxpayers were not fully compliant but few engaged in egregious noncompliance. If in addition it were found that the fraction of income not reported was inversely related to the ratio of overstated to true deductions, we would conclude that taxpayers cunningly restrict noncompliance below some threshhold level. Such behavior might reflect a fear of exemplary punishment for egregious noncompliance. Alternatively, it might reflect the belief that excessive noncompliance greatly raises the probability of detection.

We suspect analyses like these could be extremely revealing about the motives for noncompliance and the factors that constrain it. The proposed analyses are merely representative of the types of analyses we think could serve this function.

STUDIES OF THE SPECIFIC DETERRENT EFFECT OF AGENCY
ENFORCEMENT ACTIONS

We noted earlier that IRS enforcement may have a substantial chastening effect on offending taxpayers and this might be an important factor restraining noncompliance. The fact that tax returns must be processed through a lengthy pipeline provides an excellent opportunity to study the effect of different types of enforcements. For example, consider the CP-2000 programs for the tax year 1983. This program notifies taxpayers of taxes owed on 1983 income reported by payers on 1099 forms but not reported by the taxpayer on his 1983 tax return. Because of the length of time it takes to process returns, as of this writing IRS has not yet completed

CP-2000 processing of 1983 tax returns. This provides an opportunity for a simple experiment to assess the behavioral effects of the CP-2000 program. Changes in reported income, deductions, and other factors from the 1983 to the 1984 tax return could be compared for taxpayers receiving deficiency notices concerning their 1983 reported income before versus those receiving notices after April 15, 1985, the filing deadline for (unextended) 1984 personal tax returns. Any effects of the program should be reflected in differences in the reporting behavior of the two groups.

A similar strategy could be used to probe the effects of other types of IRS enforcement such as requests for further documentation, deficiency notices resulting from arithmetic errors, automated collections, liens and seizures, and audits. The results of studies like these could help tax administrators gauge the specific deterrent effects of alternative enforcement tools.

THE ROLE OF DIRECT EXPERIENCE: A CLOSE LOOK AT THE
SPECIFIC DETERRENT EFFECT OF A TCMP AUDIT
Because of their breadth and detail, TCMP audits provide an excellent opportunity for studying behavioral responses to a full range of audit findings. Moreover, the internal IRS postaudit of the adequacy of the 1976 TCMP procedures for detecting unreported income provides a unique opportunity for studying the response of taxpayers to inadequacies in audit procedures. As previously discussed, that postaudit revealed that 75 percent of income covered by 1099 reporting was not detected by the TCMP audit.

The experimental group for the study would be a sample of 1976 TCMP auditees. The necessary data would be the auditees' reported income, deductions, and relevant demographic data from their 1976 and 1977 tax returns, TCMP adjustments to the 1976 returns, and the post-TCMP findings on unreported income not detected in the TCMP. The control group would be a sample of non-TCMP auditees selected by the same sampling procedures used to pick TCMP auditees. Necessary data for the control group would include income and deduction items and relevant demographics from their 1976 and 1977 tax returns. A record of any routine enforcement actions taken against this group would also be necessary.[5]

Some interesting issues which could be explored include:

1. Did the percentage of change in reported tax liability for TCMP auditees exceed that for the control group? Is there any evidence that

responses vary depending on income, marginal tax rate, and demographic characteristics of the auditee?

2. For TCMP auditees who were identified as having underreported some specific category of income in 1976, does 1977 reporting behavior suggest a more accurate accounting on that specific item? Is there evidence of a behavioral impact where no deficiency was identified?

3. Did the percentage of change in reported income for TCMP auditees with undetected unreported 1099 income exceed that for TCMP auditees with no undetected unreported 1099 income?

The results of this study might be extremely valuable in clarifying some of the tension underlying the depth versus breadth audit debate discussed under "The Tax Administrator's Perspective on Compliance" above.

General Deterrent Effect of Tax Enforcement Activities: the Role of Indirect Experience and Stigma

As we noted earlier, one way to assess the general deterrent effects of tax enforcements is to examine networks of taxpayers and see how behavior in a network is affected by an enforcement against one of its members. Networks of friends, peers, associates, and so on could be identified. For example, partners in a law or accounting firm, neighbors, corporate colleagues, and members of a social club or business association might be considered networks. Another especially interesting network is the clients of a specific tax preparer. An array of different types of enforcement could be considered.

Selecting an appropriate control group represents perhaps the greatest methodological challenge to the study of networks. Ideally, the control group should be randomly drawn from the same population as the experimental group; the only difference should be their ignorance of the enforcement against the target. In practice it is likely to be difficult to identify such a group and the control group will most likely have to be constructed from individuals in other, similar networks. The problem this raises is that individuals in either the experimental or control groups, being members of a common network, may all have experienced a common event, such as a tip on a good investment, that will not be shared by members of the other group. Differences in behavior of the two groups will then reflect not only the effect of the enforcement studied but also these commonly shared experiences. Researchers will have to be alert to such possibilities.

Note that our proposed approach to studying the general deterrent effect of enforcement interventions relies on individual tax return data and thus circumvents the simultaneity problem plaguing the general deterrence studies of other crimes. As we noted in Section 3, studies using both aggregate and self-reported data are plagued by this simultaneity problem. Tax return data, in contrast, can be used to measure individual behavior, as well as a number of the determinants of tax compliance, without having to rely on self-reports. Consequently, inferring the direction of causality in our proposed study, as well as in others using a similar methodology, is likely to be a much less formidable task than in the typical general deterrence study.

Conclusion

Our review of the general deterrence literature suggested a number of substantive and methodological lessons that are relevant for research on tax compliance. These lessons were used to critique the different types of research on tax compliance and to suggest productive directions for future study. We suggested a series of specific studies that are representative of a much broader class of studies that can be performed using data on both individual and business returns available at the federal, state, and local level. We are confident that studies like these can help clarify the motives for tax noncompliance and provide considerable insight into the efficacy of different tax enforcement strategies.

Notes

1. These are primarily the FBI index crimes of murder, rape, robbery, aggravated assault, burglary, larceny, and auto theft.

2. A cash flow analysis compares reported income with banking records of deposits and withdrawals. A net worth analysis compares reported income with the sum of consumption and the change in net worth.

3. However, we note that in the U.S. monetary penalties are also proportional to the tax rate. As a result, extant theory does not conclude that higher tax rates are an incentive for greater noncompliance (Roth and Witte, 1985).

4. These theories built on the observation that because of resource constraints (e.g., limited personnel and prison capacity), high crime rates might overwhelm the criminal justice system's capacity to take action against criminals. As a result, high crime rates could lead to a smaller fraction of offenders being prosecuted and possibly even less severe punishment of convicted offenders.

5. The fact that controls may also have been the target of routine enforcement activities complicates the analysis. If this factor is neglected then the measured difference between the experimental and control groups will underestimate the impact of the TCMP intervention. One strategy for avoiding this downward bias is to distinguish individuals in the control group who were the subject of routine enforcement (C1) from those who were not (C2) and use measures such as DIF scores to segregate TCMP auditees who would have been targets for routine enforcement (T1) from those who would not have been (T2). Comparison of the reporting behavior of groups C2 and T2 would measure the effects of TCMP audits on individuals who are already relatively compliant, at least as measured by DIF scores. Without further information on the type of enforcement intervention exercised against the C1 group, it is difficult to speculate on the interpretation of a C1/T1 comparison. However, to the extent that the most common intervention was a regular audit, the C1/T1 comparison might provide some perspective on the impact of depth versus breadth audits.

References

Akers, R. L., Krohn, M. D., Lonn, L.-K., and Radocevich, M.
    1979   Social learning and deviant behavior: a specific test of a general theory. *American Sociological Review* 44: 636–655.
Blumstein, A., Cohen, J., and Nagin, D., eds.
    1978   *Deterrence and Incapacitation: Estimating the Effects of Criminal Sanctions on Crime Rates.* Panel on Research on Deterrent and Incapacitative Effects, National Research Council. Washington, D. C.: National Academy of Sciences.
Clotfelter, T.
    1983   Tax evasion and tax rates: an analysis of individual returns. *Review of Economics and Statistics* 65(3): 363–373.
Cook, P. J.
    1977   Punishment and crime: a critique of current findings concerning the preventive effects of punishment. *Law and Contemporary Problems* 41(1): 164–204.
Ehrlich, I.
    1973   Participation in illegitimate activities: a theoretical and empirical investigation. *Journal of Political Economy* 81(3): 521–565.
Erickson, M. L., Gibbs, J. P., and Jensen, G. F.
    1977   The deterrence doctrine and the perceived certainty of legal punishments. *American Sociological Review* 42: 305–317.
Fisher, F. M., and Nagin, D.
    1978   On the feasibility of identifying the crime function in a simultaneous model of crime rates and sanction levels. In A. Blumstein, J. Cohen, and D. Nagin, eds., *Deterrence and Incapacitation: Estimating the Effects of*

Criminal Sanctions on Crime Rates. National Research Council. Washington, D.C.: National Academy of Sciences.

Friedland, N., Maital, S., and Rutenberg, A.
1978   A simulation study of income tax evasion. *Journal of Public Economics* 10: 107–116.

Gibbs, J. P.
1968   On crime, punishment and deterrence. *Southwestern Social Science Quarterly* 49 (March): 157–162.
1975   *Crime, Punishment, and Deterrence.* New York: Elsevier.

Grasmick, H. G., and Bryjak, G. J.
1980   The Deterrent Effect of perceived severity of punishment. *Social Forces* 62(2): 471–491.

Grasmick, H. G., and Green, D. E.
1980   Legal punishment, social disapproval and internalization of inhibitors of illegal behavior. *Journal of Criminal Law and Criminology* 71(3): 325–335.

Grasmick, H. G., and Scott, W. J.
1982   Tax evasion and mechanisms of social control: a comparison with grand and petty theft. *Journal of Economic Psychology* 2: 213–230.

Greenberg, D. F., and Kessler, R. C.
1982   The effect of arrests on crime: a multivariate panel analysis. *Social Forces* 60: 771–790.

Greenberg, D. F., Kessler, R. C., and Logan, C. H.
1979   A panel model of crime rates and arrest rates. *American Sociological Review* 44: 843–850.

Groves, H. M.
1958   Empirical studies of income tax compliance. *National Tax Journal* 11(December): 291–301.

Heineke, J. M.
1978   Substitution among crimes and the question of deterrence: an indirect utility function approach to the supply of legal and illegal activity. Pp. 153–209 in J. M. Heineke, ed., *Economic Models of Criminal Behavior* Amsterdam: North-Holland.

Hinrichs, H. H.
1964   Unreporting of capital gains on tax returns or how to succeed in gainsmainship without actually paying taxes. *National Tax Journal* 17: 158–163.

Internal Revenue Service.
1983   *Income Tax Compliance Research, Estimates for 1973–1981.* Office of Assistant Commissioner (Planning, Finance and Research), Internal Revenue Service. Washington, D.C.: U.S. Department of the Treasury.

Lempert, R.
1981   Organizing for deterrence: lessons from a study of child support. *Law and Society Review* 16: 513–568.

Liska, A. E., and Reed, M. D.
1985   Ties to conventional institutions and delinquency: estimating reciprocal effects. *American Sociological Review* 50: 547–560.

Mason, R., and Calvin, L. D.
  1978   A study of admitted income tax evasion. *Law and Society Review* 13(Fall): 73–89.
  1984   Public confidence and admitted tax evasion. *National Tax Journal* 37: 489–496.
Meier, R. F., and Johnson, W. T.
  1977   Deterrence as social control: the legal and extralegal production of conformity. *American Sociological Review* 42: 292–304.
Minor, W. W.
  1977   A deterrence-control theory of crime. Pp 117–137 in R. F. Meier, ed., *Theory in Criminology: Contemporary Views.* Beverly Hills, Calif.: Sage Publications.
Minor, W. W., and Harry, J.
  1982   Deterrent and experiential effects in research: a replication and extension. *Journal of Research on Crime and Delinquency* 19: 190–203.
Nagin, D.
  1978   General deterrence: a review of the empirical evidence. In A. Blumstein, J. Cohen, and D. Nagin, eds.), *Deterrence and Incapacitation: Estimating the Effects of Criminal Sanctions on Crime Rates.* Panel on Research on Deterrent and Incapacitative Effects, National Research Council. Washington, D.C.: National Academy of Sciences.
Paternoster, R., Saltzman, L. E., Waldo, G. P., and Chiricos, T. G.
  1983   Perceived risk and social control: do sanctions really deter? *Law and Society Review* 17: 457–479.
Roth, J. A., and Witte, A. D.
  1985   Understanding Taxpayer Compliance: Major Factors and Perspectives. Unpublished paper, National Research Council, Washington, D.C.
Saltzman, L. E., Paternoster, R., Waldo, G. P., and Chiricos, T. G.
  1982   Deterrent and experiential effects: the problem of causal order in perceptual deterrence research. *Journal of Research on Crime and Delinquency* 19: 172–189.
Schwartz, R. D., and Orleans, S.
  1967   On legal sanctions. *University of Chicago Law Review* 34: 274–300.
Scott, W. J., and Grasmick, H. G.
  1981   Deterrence and income tax cheating: testing interaction hypotheses in utilitarian theories. *Journal of Applied Behavioral Science* 17: 395–408.
Sechrest, L., White, S. O., and Brown, E. D., eds.
  1979   *The Rehabilitation of Criminal Offenders: Problems and Prospects.* Washington, D.C.: National Academy of Sciences.
Sherman, L. W., and Berk, R. A.
  1984   The specific deterrent effects of arrest for domestic assault. *American Sociological Review* 49: 261–272.
Silberman, M.
  1976   Toward a theory of criminal deterrence. *American Sociological Review* 41: 442–461.

Sjoquist, D. L.
   1973   Property crime and economic behavior: some empirical results. *American Economic Review* 63: 439–446.
Slemrod, J.
   1985   An empirical test for tax evasion. *Review of Economics and Statistics* 67(2): 232–238.
Song, Y.-D., and Yarborough, T. E.
   1978   Tax ethics and taxpayer attitudes: a survey. *Public Administration Review* 38(Sept./Oct.): 442–452.
Spicer, M. W., and Becker, L. A.
   1980   Fiscal inequity and tax evasion: an experimental approach. *National Tax Journal* 33(2): 171–175.
Spicer, M. W., and Lundstedt, S. B.
   1976   Understanding tax evasion. *Public Finance* 31(2): 295–305.
Thurman, Q. C., St. John, C., and Riggs, L.
   1984   Neutralization and tax evasion: how effective would a moral appeal be in improving compliance to tax laws? *Law and Policy* 6: 309–327.
Tittle, C. R.
   1969   Crime rates and legal sanctions. *Social Problems* 16(Spring): 409–423.
   1980   *Sanctions and Social Deviance: The Question of Deterrence.* New York: Praeger.
Vogel, J.
   1974   Taxation and public opinion in Sweden: an interpretation of recent survey data. *National Tax Journal* 27(December): 499–513.
Waldo, G. P., and Chiricos, T. G.
   1972   Perceived penal sanction and self-reported criminality: a neglected approach to deterrence research. *Social Problems* 19: 522–540.
Westat, Inc.
   1980a Self-Reported Tax Compliance: A Pilot Survey Report. Prepared for the Internal Revenue Service, March 21, 1980, by Westat, Inc., Rockville, Md.
   1980b Individual Income Tax Compliance Factors Study: Qualitative Research Results. Prepared for the Internal Revenue Service, March 21, 1980, by Westat, Inc., Rockville, Md.
Witte, A. D., and Woodbury, D. F.
   1985   The effect of tax laws and tax administration on tax compliance: the case of the U.S. individual income tax. *National Tax Journal* 38(1): 1–14.
Yankelovich, Skelly, and White, Inc.
   1984   Taxpayer Attitudes Study: Final Report. Public opinion survey prepared for the Public Affairs Division, Internal Revenue Service, December 1984, by Yankelovich, Skelly, and White, Inc., New York.

Joel Slemrod

5. Complexity, Compliance Costs, and Tax Evasion

Let me begin by posing and then answering the broad policy question that the research this paper discusses is designed to address the question: Can simplifying the tax system reduce the extent of noncompliance? The answer to this question is clearly yes. Several alternative tax systems would constitute simplification by any reasonable definition and would also almost certainly reduce noncompliance below its current level. The obvious candidates are radical reforms such as a comprehensive value-added tax or a Hall-Rabushka type flat-rate tax.

One lesson of the recent debate about tax reform that culminated in the Tax Reform Act of 1986 is, though, that change in the tax system will be closer to piecemeal than radical. In this event it is important to recognize that simplification is not necessarily consistent with improved compliance and to identify what aspects of simplification and what specific kinds of simplification would serve to reduce tax evasion.

The plan of this chapter is as follows. The first section discusses various aspects of the concept of complexity and the relationship of complexity to compliance costs; it also reviews evidence of the magnitude and nature of compliance costs in the current U.S. individual income tax system. The second section reviews and places within a common framework the existing theoretical models of evasion and compliance costs. This serves as a basis for the subsequent discussion, in the third section, of the various links between noncompliance and complexity. As each link is discussed, the relevance of past research is assessed and promising directions for future research are investigated. The final section summarizes and organizes suggestions concerning the direction of future research.

Department of Economics, University of Michigan. Helpful comments on an earlier draft of this paper were received from Harvey Galper.

Complexity and Compliance Costs

Different aspects of complexity are important to different participants in the tax system and have different relationships to the issue of noncompliance. An important issue to the tax lawyer is the certainty, or *predictability,* of the tax law. To the tax collection agency, complexity in large part relates to the administrative cost of raising revenue, or the *enforceability* of the tax law, and in particular relates to the encouragement that some tax provisions provide for the use of complicated schemes to avoid tax payments. For the taxpayer himself, the critical aspect of complexity is the time and expense involved in completing the tax return, or compliance cost, including not only complying with the filing requirement, but also identifying and documenting the deductions, credits, and reductions in taxable income to which he is entitled. This aspect can be further divided into the cost required to comply with the law, due to its *difficulty,* and the cost incurred by taxpayers in an effort to reduce taxable income, due to the tax system's *manipulability.* The administrative cost, compliance cost, and costs borne by third parties in the tax collection process (e.g., employers operating the withholding system) make up the total resource costs of collecting taxes.

Complexity of a tax system cannot usefully be defined independently of the characteristics of the potential taxpaying population. The difficulty of a step in the tax-filing process depends on the cognitive skills of those who must complete the step. Similarly, the total cost of tax collection is an outcome of the interaction between the complexity of the tax system, the preferences of the potential taxpayers, and other characteristics of the tax system. How much time and money is spent on tax matters depends on how individuals value time spent on their tax affairs, how risk-averse they are, and their marginal tax rate.

In an earlier paper (Slemrod, 1983), I proposed that the total cost of collection is a useful index of the complexity of a tax system. Evaluating the strengths and weaknesses of this index is helpful to understanding the relationship between complexity and collection costs. First of all, note that this index does not distinguish on the taxpayer side between collection costs due to difficulty, which must be expended in order to comply with the law, and collection costs due to manipulability, which are incurred in an effort to reduce one's tax liability, whether through legal or illegal means. Nor, on the tax collection agency's side, does it distinguish between the cost of administering the tax system and the cost of enforcing it—that is, dealing with potential evaders of the tax law. As I will argue below, these distinctions are important to make in any analytical treatment of simplification. However, all are costs of operating the tax system and should be considered in an assessment of how simply it operates.

In some cases this index of complexity may conflict with intuition. As an example, consider that the record-keeping and calculation requirements of a particular credit are loosened so that only half as much resources as before are required to calculate and qualify for the credit. Suppose that as a result there is a quadrupling of the number of households who apply for and receive the credit and that any changes needed to make up the lost revenue have no collection cost implications. According to the cost-based index, the tax system has become more complicated. The credit procedure itself has become simpler to understand, but the system as a whole is, by the index of costliness, more complex, since the total number of hours spent on that line item has increased.

A more extreme example of the same problem is a case where the cost-based measure of complexity may seem clearly misleading. The U.S. General Accounting Office (1979) estimated that in 1976 over six million taxpayers who should have filed income tax returns did not do so. Its finding that the average educational level of the nonfilers was below the national norm suggested to them that the reason for nonfiling was often that the process was too complicated to be understood. Assuming that the IRS makes no effort to uncover the nonfilers, the collection cost associated with this group is approximately zero. Furthermore, a change in the tax system which, by making the process easier to comprehend, induces those currently not filing to file would almost certainly add to total privately borne compliance costs. This increase may be somewhat offset by a decline in the amount of IRS resources devoted to pursuing nonfilers. If the increase in compliance cost dominates, then although the tax system may have become simpler to understand, revenue collection has become more complicated (that is, more costly). The cost-based measure of complexity embraces the latter judgment.

This measure of complexity was designed to be calculable and therefore useful in assessing tax policy's inevitable trade-offs among its several goals, including efficiency, equity, and simplicity. It is valuable for that purpose but inadequate for the analysis at hand. Because the relationship between complexity and compliance depends on the source of the compliance cost, it will be important to maintain the distinctions among predictability, enforceability, difficulty, and manipulability. These aspects are discussed in more detail under "The Relationship of Tax Evasion to Complexity and Compliance Costs" below.

Although it is important for conceptual purposes to distinguish the four aspects of complexity, what empirical evidence exists generally does not correspond to these categories. Instead, it refers to total resource costs of compliance, regardless of source. One goal of future data collection should be to try to distinguish collection costs according to the conceptual categories discussed above. What follows is a review of the existing evidence on total compliance and collection costs.

The most careful and exhaustive English language study of compliance costs to date is that of Sandford (1973). Unfortunately for present purposes, the object of Sandford's investigation was the income tax system of the United Kingdom, which differs in some critical aspects from that of the United States. For example, the majority of taxpayers in the U.K. are required to fill out an income tax form only one year in five. Sandford studied compliance costs by conducting surveys of professional tax advisors and individual taxpayers and an analysis of tax-related inquiries to press bureaus and public tax advice clinics. Based on the survey of individual taxpayers, Sandford estimated that compliance costs amounted to between 1.9 and 3.4 percent of individual income tax revenue collected. He also concluded that low-income people had, on average, higher compliance costs as a fraction of income than higher-income people. Because the U.K.'s tax system places less responsibility for calculation on the taxpayer than does the U.S. system, the compliance cost in the United States is likely to be higher than that in the United Kingdom. Thus Sandford's estimates are at best a lower-bound figure for the United States.

A study in progress promises to provide extensive data on compliance costs in the United States. The IRS has commissioned Arthur D. Little, Inc., to conduct a study of the paperwork burden imposed on the public by the federal tax system. The study's goals include providing an estimate of the aggregate burden and also an understanding of the relationship between the burden and the detailed characteristics of the tax-filing process, so as to be able to estimate the impact of change in the filing process. The final report of this project is not yet public information.

The data for this analysis is to be obtained from two national taxpayer surveys. The first is a diary study of nearly 750 taxpayers who were asked to keep track daily of the time spent in completing federal tax returns. The second survey is a retrospective mail questionnaire sent out to a large sample of taxpayers.

In advance of collecting the survey evidence, the research team conducted some group interviews ("focus groups") in order to determine the feasibility of the subsequent diary and survey analysis. The report on these focus groups reveals several interesting patterns. First, the individuals appeared to be able to estimate the amount of time they spend preparing their tax returns and did not consider a fairly accurate answer difficult to reach. Second, when asked to think about the time spent on tax matters on a piecemeal basis (record keeping, research, return preparation, and so on), people reported more total time by a factor of two than they initially estimated before the component activities were separately considered. Finally, the individuals were unable to accurately estimate the time spent on individual forms and schedules, or the time spent specifically on the state tax form.

A recent comprehensive study of the compliance cost of the U.S. income tax system is that of Slemrod and Sorum (1984). The data for this study were drawn from a mail survey of Minnesota households' tax-filing behavior. Immediately after the deadline for filing 1982 tax returns (April 15, 1983), a four-page questionnaire was mailed to a random sample of 2,000 Minnesota residents. The 653 questionnaires returned represented a 32.65 percent response rate. Of these, 41 were from people not required to file 1982 state or federal tax returns, and 38 questionnaires were eliminated from the sample because of incompleteness, leaving a total of 574 usable responses.

The questionnaire's first section asked for some demographic information, in particular the respondent's sex, age, level of education completed, income, employment status, occupation, and wage rate or reservation wage. Because the cover letter pointedly asked that the addressee refer the questionnaire to the "person in (the) household most familiar with filing (the) income tax returns," the distribution of demographic characteristics would not be expected to precisely replicate the population distribution of characteristics. In particular answers to questions about sex and education would be expected to be biased if, as the data indicate, males tend to be more familiar with the returns or, as is likely, the most educated household member is most familiar with the filing process.

The next section of the questionnaire solicited information about the household's income tax return itself. The taxpayer was asked which, if any, of the three federal tax returns and which, if either, of the two Minnesota state tax forms were filed. In addition, responses were sought concerning whether the return featured itemized deductions, whether it was a joint return, and which of several sources of income were received.

The remainder of the questionnaire was devoted to collecting information about the household's cost of filing tax returns. This section asked how many hours were spent during the year and requested a breakdown of the hours into various categories. In addition, any money spent on tax assistance or otherwise spent on filing returns was solicited. A question on the individual's attitude toward filing returns was included, as was a question designed to elicit a dollar figure for the value of all time, effort, and money spent on tax affairs. Finally, the taxpayer was asked whether he or she had ever chosen not to undertake some business activity because of the hassle or expense of complying with tax laws.

Note that the findings of the group interviews conducted by Arthur D. Little, Inc., support some of the methodological choices made by Slemrod and Sorum: i.e., a survey study that differentiated components of the tax-filing process such as record keeping, research, and return completion but did not attempt to differentiate resources spent on federal versus state returns.

The survey results indicated that the average taxpayer spent 21.7 hours of their own time on tax filing, valued (using after-tax wage rates) at $231, and $44 in additional expenses, for a total of $275 per household. Applying these averages to an estimated 97 million taxpaying units in 1982 yielded aggregate estimates of 2.13 billion hours and a total resource cost of $26.7 billion. This cost is approximately 1.4 percent of aggregate adjusted gross income, and more than 7 percent of total federal and state income tax revenue.

Nearly two-thirds of the time spent on filing was devoted to record keeping, with actual preparation of the return accounting for about one-fifth, and research about one-tenth, of total time. Slightly less than half of all households (45.9 percent) hired professional tax assistance. This figure is consistent with the fact that 44.1 percent of federal returns in 1982 were co-signed by a professional tax advisor (IRS, 1985:85). For those who used assistance, the average payment for it was $76. About three-quarters of the households spent less than twenty hours on tax matters, and a similar fraction spent less than $50 for tax assistance. However, over 13 percent of households spent at least fifty hours on tax compliance, and 13 percent spent more than $100.

The distribution with respect to income of the taxpayer's time spent on tax matters was found to be U-shaped. However, the relatively high figures for the low-income group are somewhat suspect, due to the low number of respondents in the group (15) and the likelihood that many of these households are in occupations which have high income variability (e.g., farming or other self-employment) and large record-keeping requirements; many people in their occupations also experienced temporarily low income in 1982, although their usual income is not low. The allocation of time spent among the various categories was relatively constant among income groups, although research and record keeping were relatively more important for the highest (and lowest) income groups, and actual preparation time was relatively more important for the $5,000–$20,000 income households. The proportion of households who paid for professional assistance generally increased with income, rising from about 35 percent for the lowest two classes to about 50 percent for the middle-income groups and climbing to 78 percent for households earning more than $50,000 of income. Except for the lowest two classes, the average amount spent by those who use assistance rose as well, peaking at nearly $200 for the highest income class.

The total resource cost of compliance has a U-shaped relationship with income. For households with over $50,000 income, the average resource cost exceeded $1,400. As a percentage of tax liability, though, there was no obvious pattern except a high percentage for the lowest two income groups. Measured as a percentage of income, the cost for the highest group (1.7 percent) was significantly higher than for any of the other groups except the lowest two.

More educated taxpayers tended to spend more time on their tax affairs and were less likely to purchase professional tax advice. In the lowest educational attainment group, over 55 percent of households paid for assistance, compared to less than 50 percent for college graduates and less than 40 percent for those with a graduate level education. However, the average amount spent by those who paid for assistance rose monotonically from about $50 for the lowest group to over $120 for the highest group. The total resource cost of compliance generally increased with educational attainment; this was due both to a greater number of hours spent and a higher average valuation of an hour by more educated households.

Finally, the self-employed exhibited much higher compliance costs than employees. They spent more than three times as much of their on time, were about twice as likely to use professional assistance, and had an average resource cost of compliance of more than $800.

One shortcoming of drawing conclusions about the nature of compliance costs on the basis of the patterns discussed above is that they do not account for potential interrelationships among the variables and thus may misrepresent the causal associations. For example, the apparent positive relationship between education and time spent on compliance may be due to an actual causal association between income and compliance time plus a correlation between income and educational attainment. In other words, households of the same income with different levels of education may have no tendency to behave differently. In order to investigate the relationhip between compliance behavior and any demographic variable, holding all other variables constant, an ordinary least-squares regression analysis with dummy independent variables for household characteristics was employed.

The simple relationships observed above with respect to income generally remained when other demographic variables were held constant. Being in the lowest income class was associated with relatively high compliance cost, as was being in the highest income class. The predominantly positive simple relationship between compliance costs and educational attainment did not strongly appear in the regression analysis. The magnitude of the extra costs incurred by the most educated was smaller than those observed above, and the estimates were for the most part not statistically significant. It thus appears that most of the observed difference in costs can be better explained by differences in income, wage rate, or employment status. Education level is supposed to be a proxy for skill in dealing with tax matters, but these other variables, especially the wage rate, may be superior indicators of that skill.

The strong relationship between self-employment and compliance costs clearly showed up in the regression analysis. Holding other demographic factors equal, the self-employed spent thirty-five more hours, spent $69 more, and had over $400 more in total resource cost than the reference group of employees.

Slemrod (1985) used the same set of data to further investigate the relationship between compliance costs and particular sources of income. The ordinary least-squares estimates presented there confirm the strong positive relationship between self-employment and compliance cost. In addition, receiving capital gains income was significantly positively correlated with both own time spent and the amount of professional assistance purchased. Having rental income was significantly positively associated with the amount spent on professional assistance, but not with own time spent.

Little definitive information exists on the compliance costs borne by employers in administering the withholding system for wages and the costs borne by other third parties (e.g., brokers) in complying with the information return requirements. The most helpful study in this area refers to the

British tax system. Godwin, Hardwick, and Sandford (1983) surveyed over nine hundred employers about the cost to them of operating the income tax withholding system and the national insurance tax system; they had determined in prior interviews that most employers were unable to separate out the costs of complying with each system.

Godwin et al. concluded that aggregate compliance costs in the financial year 1981–1982 amounted to £450 million, or just over one percent of the sum of income tax and national insurance payments. About 80 percent of the cost represented staff time. The costs are borne proportionately more heavily by small compared to large businesses.

An extrapolation of these results to the U.S. tax system is not straightforward. On one hand, the British system of cumulative account withholding, in which more than half of taxpayers need not file a return more than once every five years, is more complicated for firms than the U.S. system and therefore is likely to have higher compliance costs. Furthermore, Godwin et al. found that there are substantial fixed costs per establishment, so that the larger average size of establishment in the United States suggests smaller average compliance costs. On the other hand, wage rates are higher in the United States, so that the resource cost per hour of employee time spent on compliance is likely to be higher. To what extent these considerations offset each other is not known.

Existing Theoretical Models of Noncompliance and Compliance Costs

This section reviews some of the theoretical models that have been developed to analyze tax evasion and compliance cost issues, and attempts to integrate the approaches. The integrated model will then serve as the formal underpinning for the discussion in the next section of the relationship of tax evasion to complexity and compliance costs.

The seminal paper of Allingham and Sandmo (1972) posed the question of the taxpayer's decision concerning evasion within the standard economic model of choice under uncertainty, first applied to criminal behavior by Becker (1967). In this model, the taxpayer chooses the amount of income to report to the tax authority with the objective of maximizing expected utility. There is a discrete probability that an act of evasion will be detected and subject to a known penalty. A simple version of the individual's problem can be written as:

(1) Maximize $(1 - p)U[\Upsilon - T(\Upsilon - E)]$
      E
           $+ pU[\Upsilon - T(\Upsilon - E) - F(T(\Upsilon) - T(\Upsilon - E))]$,

where p is the probability than an act of evasion will be detected and punished, U is the cardinal utility function that embodies the taxpayer's attitudes toward risk, Υ is true taxable income, E is the taxable income understatement, T is the tax function, and F is the penalty function. Both the T and F functions are general so that they can represent proportional tax or penalty functions or more complicated formulae.

The optimal amount of evasion (assuming it is nonzero) is characterized by the marginal expected utility of the income increase due to successful evasion being equal to the marginal expected disutility of the penalty incurred in the event the evasion is detected. The optimal decision depends on the individual's attitude toward risk as well as the tax and penalty structure and the probability of detection.

Cross and Shaw (1981, 1982) proposed that the taxpayer choice of whether and how much to evade should be treated jointly with the decision about how much to invest in legal tax avoidance measures. The taxpayer's maximization problem they suggest can be written in consistent notation as follows:

(2) Maximize $(1 - p)U[\Upsilon - T(\Upsilon - E - A) - C(E, A)]$
    E, A
          $+ pU[\Upsilon - T(\Upsilon - E - A) - F(T(\Upsilon - A) - T(\Upsilon - E - A))$
                  $- C(E, A)]$,

where A is the amount of taxable income reduction due to legal avoidance; E is the amount of illegally understated income; C is the expenditure on avoidance and evasion, which is a positive function of both E and A; and Υ is taxable income in the absence of any expenditure on either evasion or avoidance.

The innovation here is that in order to discover and (in the case of avoidance) to document both avoidance and evasion activities, expenditures are required. Two avenues of interaction between avoidance and evasion become relevant. First, in a progressive tax system, expenditures on avoidance (evasion) reduce the marginal tax rate, thus reducing the return to engaging in evasion (avoidance). Second, depending on the characteristics of the cost function C, investment in avoidance may reduce the marginal cost of evasion, or vice versa. For example, while investigating a legal real estate tax shelter, a sure-fire abusive tax shelter arrangement may be uncovered without much additional investment of time.

The cost of achieving given levels of E and A may include income foregone in the effort to reduce tax liability. For example, purchasing tax-exempt bonds reduces taxable income, but also reduces pre-tax income as long as the rate of interest on tax-exempt bonds is less than the rate of return on taxable bonds.

A critical but implicit assumption of the Cross and Shaw model is that, *ceteris paribus,* more evasion requires more expenditure by the taxpayer, presumably to investigate promising evasion opportunities and to camouflage evasion. Alternatively, more evasion could be associated with *less* cost. For example, not bothering to trace a miscellaneous source of income is less costly than tracking down whatever receipt or Form 1099 would document the income. The extreme example of this possibility, discussed more fully in the next section under "Complexity as a Barrier to Compliance," is not filing a return at all. This is the ultimate act of evasion, and it also happens to minimize compliance cost. When the relationship between cost and evasion is not straightforward, applying the calculus to the individual's decision process is problematic. Corner solutions become possible, as do discrete changes in behavior resulting from small changes in the environment.

A useful extension of both the Allingham and Sandmo as well as the Cross and Shaw models is to allow the probability of detection and penalty to depend on the actions of the taxpayer. It is reasonable to suppose that the probability of detection depends, *ceteris paribus,* positively on the amount of evasion and may also depend positively on avoidance. In a more detailed model, the cost accompanying an act of evasion or avoidance may be varied so that more expenditures for given E and A reduce the probability of detection—they are "cover-up" costs. When p is endogenous, the characterization of the consumer optimum must also consider the induced change in p resulting from varying E or A.

Slemrod (1985), in a study of the effect of tax reform on compliance costs, presents a model of a household's choices concerning its tax filing behavior. The household must choose how much of its own time to spend on tax matters and how much, if any, professional tax advice to purchase. It is assumed that both of these activities uncover legitimate ways to reduce taxable income and thereby reduce tax liability. The model thus abstracts from the possibility of evasion. This assumption allows the consumer problem to be posed as one of complete certainty. Utility is a function of two arguments: consumption and labor supply adjusted for the hours spent on tax matters. Consumption equals gross income, which consists of exogenously given nonlabor income and labor income, minus tax paid, payments for professional tax assistance, and income foregone due to avoidance and evasion.

Adapting the notation used earlier and integrating Slemrod's model into the tax evasion model of Allingham and Sandmo, as extended by Cross and Shaw, yields the following problem:

(3) Maximize $(1 - p)U[Y - T(Y - E - A) - B, L + zH]$
    $\underset{E,A,H,B,L,G.}{}$
$$+ pU[\Upsilon - T(\Upsilon - E - A) - B - F(T(\Upsilon - A) - T(\Upsilon - E - A)),$$
$$L + zH],$$
where $\Upsilon = D + wL - G$ and $f(E,A,H,B,G,R,N,X) = 0$.

Here B is expenditure on professional tax assistance, L is hours of labor supply, z is the labor equivalent of one hour of one's own time spent on tax matters, H is hours of own time spent on tax matters, D is nonlabor income, w is the wage rate, and G is income foregone in the process of avoidance and evasion.

The f function represents the tax reduction technology and replaces the cost function of expression (2). It embodies the relationship between the desired output—taxable income reduction via evasion or avoidance—that is detectable with probability p and the inputs to this process—own time, professional assistance, and foregone income. It states that legal reductions in taxable income claimed and evasion depend on the amount of own time spent on uncovering, documenting, and camouflaging them (H), the amount of professional assistance purchased (B), foregone income (G), the sources of income of the household (indexed by R), some personal characteristics (indexed by N) such as age, level of education completed, and attitude toward tax matters, and the tax law itself (X). In my 1985 paper, time and money spent on uncovering and documenting deductions were treated distinctly from resources spent on finding reductions in taxable income because the former activities are worthwhile only if the household chooses to itemize deductions, while the latter may be worthwhile to any household which has a nonzero marginal tax rate; this aspect of the model is not treated explicitly here. In the maximization problem of (3), the R variable captures the influence of itemization on the return to investment of time and money.

In this integrated model compliance cost is determined endogenously as a result of the decisions of the taxpayer choosing H, B, and G. Evasion is also a choice variable of the individual. The interactions between evasion and avoidance are also present. The spirit of Cross and Shaw is maintained as compliance cost is modeled to be discretionary and undertaken in order to reduce tax liability. The cost function approach of Cross and Shaw is replaced by an explicit representation of the compliance technology which highlights the alternatives of own time and professional assistance and the role of individual characteristics as well as the structure of the tax code.

Using the terminology of model (3), this chapter is concerned with the effect of the tax law, represented by X, on evasion, denoted E. How can policy, by altering the complexity of the tax law, induce taxpayers to increase their compliance rate? In this context, X is properly thought of as a vector of characteristics of the tax law. The logical next step in the development of this model is to expand the variable so that it separately identifies the four aspects of complexity (enforceability, unpredictability, difficulty, and manipulability) and to be able to trace the impact upon tax evasion of changes in these different aspects of tax complexity. This is the task of the next section.

The Relationship of Tax Evasion to Complexity and Compliance Costs

COMPLEXITY AS A BARRIER TO COMPLIANCE

This section investigates the hypothesis that because complexity increases the cost of complying with the tax law, it discourages compliance. An important special case of this hypothesis is the phenomenon of nonfilers who, according to this argument, prefer not filing to undertaking the complicated task of filing.

I consider first the case of nonfilers. In terms of model (3), the nonfiling phenomenon would be represented by a discontinuous f function, where zero input of H, B, and G can produce a value of E equal to Y, regardless of the value of N. In general the probability of conviction would also be a discontinuous function of its arguments at this point. Due to the discontinuity of these functions, the nonfiling decision cannot be analyzed using the calculus but rather entails a comparison between the expected utility under the nonfiling option and the expected utility under the filing option, given optimal conditional choices of the decision variables.

No explicit model is required to establish the proposition that, in a decision about whether to file, anything that increases the cost of filing will induce some households otherwise at the margin not to file a return. What remains are empirical questions about the magnitude of the relationship between the cost of filing and the extent of nonfiling and also what particular aspects of complexity are critical for the cost of filing. Several comments are in order.

The cost of filing to an individual due to the difficulty of the tax system depends both on the filing process and on characteristics of the individual. Less educated individuals may find the same process to be more demanding in terms of time spent compared with more educated individuals. Individuals also certainly differ in how they value the time spent on tax matters.

Note, though, that all individuals have the option of seeking IRS assistance for their returns or hiring professional assistance. The typical professional fee to file a 1040EZ or 1040A return is on the order of $10. Thus, even if the difficulty in comprehending and executing the filing requirements implies a large cost for the act of filing one's own return, the option of assistance provides an upper bound on the cost of filing. In fact, professional assistance is utilized for even the simplest of returns. According to preliminary IRS data for 1983 (IRS, 1985), overall 45 percent of all returns had a paid preparer signature, including 25 percent of 1040A returns and even 5 percent of 1040EZ returns.

Evidence about the characteristics of nonfilers from the U.S. General Accounting Office's (1979) study can shed light on the hypothesis that difficulty of the tax system is a significant cause of nonfiling. One of its findings was that nonfilers tend to have lower educational attainment than filers, which is consistent with the nonfilers' perception that the tax-filing process is more imposing a requirement. This finding is not explainable according to an alternative hypothesis that nonfilers are predominantly those who, due to the characteristics of their income sources, are less likely to be detected not filing. However, this empirical finding could also be due to the fact that less educated individuals tend to have lower income, and are therefore more likely to be near the filing threshold income and uncertain of their need to file a return. A more sophisticated multivariate analysis of the characteristics of nonfilers would shed more light on this hypothesis.

The findings of Slemrod and Sorum are relevant here. They found that more educated taxpayers spend more time on their tax affairs and are slightly less likely to purchase professional assistance than the average. The lowest educational group were by far the most likely to purchase professional assistance. However, holding other demographic variables such as household income constant, no strong relationship between educational attainment and compliance cost emerged. Thus, though there is an *a priori* reason to believe education and therefore difficulty in filing will be correlated with nonfiling, no convincing empirical evidence of the magnitude of this link as yet exists.

Empirical research into the influence on nonfiling behavior is hindered by the current absence of and the difficulty of ever obtaining reliable data on the nonfiling population. A possible alternative research strategy is to assemble time-series evidence on the number and characteristics of low-income filers and to concentrate analysis on the years following the introduction of the simplified tax forms 1040A and 1040EZ. The hypothesis to be investigated is that the introduction of these forms induced households to file who otherwise would not have; it should be detectable in the time trends of the characteristics of the filing population. After all, given the population of those who should file, the filing population is a perfect complement to the nonfiling population.

Other than the filing decision, how does difficulty relate to tax evasion? In the terms of model (3), difficulty is represented by the productivity of H and B in "producing" A. In other words, how much time and effort does it take to document and establish legitimate deductions? Higher values of these productivity measures (so that a given amount of taxable income reduction requires less time and money) correspond to less difficult tax systems.

This is tricky ground, though, because what may appear to be a reduction in difficulty can lead to either an increase or decline in the amount of resources expended. If the marginal productivity of H and B in terms of A increases for all values of H and B, then certainly both the resources expended and the magnitude of A will increase. By making it more productive to spend time on tax matters, more time is spent. In this case, difficulty is just the obverse of productivity. Another possibility is that an apparent reduction in difficulty may increase the marginal productivity of H and B for low values of H and B, but reduce the marginal productivity for higher values as the opportunities for avoidance are depleted. As an example, consider the effect of relaxing the requirements for documentation of itemized expenses. This would increase the number of items per hour that can be documented for low values of time spent. Once all deductible items are dealt with, though, additional time (at lower values of time than previously chosen) is no longer helpful. In this case, simplification would increase A but probably decrease H and B.

Thus, the effect of changes in difficulty on avoidance depends on the precise way that difficulty is reduced. However, any reduction in difficulty would, by increasing A and therefore reducing the marginal tax rate, tend to reduce the incentive to evade taxes. If, though, increased avoidance provides information that facilitates evasion, as suggested by Cross and Shaw, a reduction in difficulty that causes an increase in H and B might increase evasion. What happens in this case is that, by making the rules for legally reducing taxable income more accessible, taxpayers are induced to invest more time in learning about them. One side effect is that they become more sophisticated about tax evasion opportunities, and take more advantage of them, even though their marginal tax rate has been reduced by the increased avoidance. Note, though, that if difficulty declines in such a way that the resources spent on avoidance decline (as in the itemization example), both the marginal tax rate effect and the complementarity of avoidance and evasion activities will cause less evasion.

When there is no unique true tax liability, it becomes somewhat problematic to differentiate precisely between difficulty and manipulability. The distinction is similar to the distinction between nondiscretionary and discretionary costs. The problem in definition is that the absolute minimal compliance cost is certainly quite low, if one is willing to forego the benefits attendant to itemized deductions, adjustments to income, credits, and expenses incurred for self-employment income. In other words, it is generally quite easy to comply with the legal filing requirement. If the costs of legally filing a return are the only nondiscretionary costs of compliance, then the vast majority of costs are discretionary. I have in mind a more useful distinction between the costs of establishing what would generally be considered the appropriate tax liability and the costs of aggressively pursuing tax minimization activities. Because "appropriate" cannot be defined precisely, neither can these costs be distinguished precisely. Nevertheless, I believe it is an instructive distinction. Aaron and Galper (1985:28) apparently have a similar distinction in mind when they identify two forms of tax simplification:

> "legal simplification," which would ease taxpayer comprehension, compliance, and administration; and "transactional simplification," which is the reduction of the number and complexity of transactions undertaken to avoid taxes. (p. 28)

This notion of transactional simplicity is similar to my concept of (lack of) manipulability.

To help fix the two concepts, suppose that there is some tax liability that is generally considered to be the unmanipulated liability. Then "difficulty" refers to the cost of establishing that liability, and "manipulability" refers to the cost of establishing a lower liability.

It is certainly possible that tax systems, or aspects of tax systems, can be difficult but not manipulable, or manipulable but not difficult. What are the operational differences between difficulty and manipulability?

One is that investment in moving tax liability *below* the "unmanipulated" level is likely to have a greater cross effect on the return to effort aimed at evasion than would investment in reducing tax liability *toward* the unmanipulated level. In other words, manipulating your tax affairs (by, for example, arranging a legal tax shelter) is closer to evasion than doing the standard procedures such as itemizing deductions. This implies that reducing manipulability would be a more effective policy than reducing difficulty, because it would reduce the incentive to acquire information that might prove useful for evasion.

As an offsetting factor, it may be that individuals resent the resources they must expend to reach their unmanipulated tax liability more than the resources they are induced to expend in order to reduce their tax liability even further. Thus, to the extent that negative attitudes toward the tax-filing process induce evasion, reducing difficulty would be more effective in reducing evasion than reducing manipulability.

The effect of difficulty and manipulability on noncompliance is ultimately an empirical question. As measures of the difficulty and manipulability of particular provisions are refined, it may be instructive to correlate them with known measures of compliance (i.e., what fraction of particular income sources are reported). One such measure, albeit crude, is the total compliance cost. Slemrod (1985) identified the following high compliance cost sources of income: income from self-employment, capital gains, and rental income (for professional assistance purchased only). According to the IRS (1983:22), the voluntary reporting percentage of net income in 1981 for filers and nonfilers combined was 50.3 percent for nonfarm proprietor income, 47.0 percent for partnerships and small business corporations (two categories akin to self-employment), 59.4 percent for capital gains, and 37.2 percent for rental income. These figures compare to 87.2 percent overall, so that all three sources have significantly lower reporting fractions than average. Note, though, that the voluntary reporting percentages for gross income were much higher in some cases. For example, gross rental income had the highest voluntary reporting percentage (95.6 percent) of any category (IRS, 1983:10), suggesting that the deductions were so generous that reporting the gross income did not imply large additional tax burden. Because one of the objectives of the Arthur D. Little, Inc., study discussed above is to obtain compliance cost estimates for detailed parts of the tax-filing process, more extensive correlations like this will be possible.

Of course, the observed simple correlation between compliance cost and noncompliance does not necessarily indicate the presence of a causal relationship. The correlation may be due to a third factor that influences both compliance cost and the extent of reporting. This suggests using a multivariate statistical technique and accounting for other characteristics of particular aspects of the tax code, such as the likelihood that an act of evasion will be detected by the IRS.

Another potential source of information is the TCMP data set. This data set contains information on a stratified sample of taxpayers' returns and the results of an intensive IRS audit. It has been used by Clotfelter (1983), Witte and Woodbury (1985), and Slemrod (1988) to investigate the relationship between noncompliance and aspects of the taxpayer's decision problem such as the marginal tax rate, the probability of detection, and so forth. Hypotheses suggested in this chapter could be studied by examining the relationship between evasion and avoidance behavior, the latter appropriately defined. For example, an observation that, *ceteris paribus,* individuals who avoid taxes also evade taxes is consistent with the hypothesis that there is significant complementarity between resources invested in avoidance and resources invested in evasion. In this case, reducing manipulability is an appropriate goal for tax reform.

Difficulty can induce overpayment of taxes as well as underpayment. A substantial number of taxpayers would pay lower taxes if they itemized deductions but do not because of the documentation requirements. Pitt and Slemrod (1988) used evidence from tax returns to estimate that in 1982, 679,000 taxpayers were in this situation, foregoing a total of $196 million in tax reduction due to the cost of compliance. Another good example of individuals passing up tax savings is the now-repealed income-averaging provision, which could in the past save taxpayers with highly fluctuating income substantial sums but which required relatively complicated record keeping and calculations. Steuerle, McHugh, and Sunley (1978) found that of those eligible for income averaging in 1971, only 31.1 percent elected to take advantage of it. The average foregone tax saving of those eligible but not income-averaging was $114, compared to the average realized tax saving of $499 for those who did income-average.

Difficulty may affect not only filing behavior, but also investment and other economic decisions. For example, the prospect of keeping extended records may dissuade some people from purchasing real estate and obtaining preferential tax treatment.

Reducing complexity can reduce noncompliance if it takes the form of declaring certain kinds of income nontaxable or eliminating restrictions on allowable deductions. Examples of the former are the nontaxation under current law of fringe benefits and the nontaxation a few years back of employment compensation and Social Security Benefits. This reduces noncompliance in the same way legalizing marijuana would reduce the extent of illegal drug activity.

Complexity and Uncertainty of True Liability

One dimension of complexity is the predictability of tax liability, i.e., whether the "correct" tax liability is clearly defined. Long (1981) argues that the IRS exploits the unpredictability of tax liability to enhance its powers by using it as a license to decide cases in whatever way serves the government's interests at the time. She also notes that unpredictability makes the IRS's burden in proving criminal intent (rather than inadvertent errors) more difficult.

Uncertainty of true tax liability can be modeled by extending the Allingham and Sandmo framework. For simplicity, assume that the assessed tax liability is symmetrically centered around Y and will be $Y + k$ or $Y - k$ with an equal probability of one-half. The concept of income understatement, formerly denoted E, now becomes problematic because the taxpayer is uncertain whether any given income declaration is correct or not. Instead I will use Y^* to denote declared taxable income. Then the taxpayer's problem becomes:

(4) Maximize $(1 - p)U[Y - T(Y^*)] + \frac{1}{2} pU[Y - T(Y^*) - F(T(Y-k) - T(Y^*))]$
Y^*

$$+ \frac{1}{2} pU[Y - T(Y^*) - F(T(Y+k) - T(Y^*))],$$

where $F(Z) = 0$ if $Z \leq 0$.

There are now three possible outcomes that the taxpayer must consider. If the return is not audited (with probability $1 - p$), true taxable income is irrelevant—the taxpayer merely pays the tax due on his declared taxable income. If the return is audited, there are two possible outcomes, depending on what the assessed tax liability turns out to be.

Scotchmer and Slemrod (1988) show that, unless the taxpayer is reporting exactly $Y - k$, increasing the dispersion of possible assessed taxable incomes induces increased compliance, given weak conditions about the taxpayer's attitudes toward risk. The intuition is that, for a given reported income (Y^*), a high value of k lowers income in the least desirable state of the world, when the taxpayer is audited and his taxable income is determined to be $Y + k$. This increases the marginal utility of income in that state of the world, which is accomplished by increasing Y^* and thus subjecting oneself to a lower penalty in the event this state of the world occurs. As long as the taxpayer exhibits declining absolute risk aversion (a reasonable condition that implies that as wealth increases, desired risk does not decline), increasing the report is the optimal response.

Beck and Jung (1987a) show that this conclusion may not hold when there is a continuous range of possible taxable income assessments. In this case one marginal benefit of increasing the income report is that it reduces the probability that a fine will be assessed. (In Scotchmer and Slemrod, this probability may be reduced only when Y^* is raised from below to above $Y - k$.) For a taxpayer reporting income below the mean of possible assessment, an increased dispersion of possible assessed incomes decreases the likelihood that the income report will be declared insufficient and a fine assessed, so that this component of marginal benefit is reduced. Thus it is theoretically possible that increased dispersion will cause lower reports. Beck and Jung (1987b) conclude, though, that for reasonable parameters the effect of increasing taxpayer uncertainty about assessed taxable income is to induce greater compliance.

Another dimension of uncertainty is uncertainty about the penalty structure itself, including both the likelihood of a given evasion being detected, and the penalty for any given detected evasion. Constructing a rigorous economic model to analyze this issue is not a trivial matter. There is some empirical evidence that individuals' perceptions are biased toward overestimating the probability of detection (Aitken and Bonneville, 1980:47). However, because the probability of detection varies greatly depending on the type of evasion, this apparent finding may be due to an imprecise phrasing of the question and subsequent misinterpretation of the results.

Note that uncertainty does not reduce tax evasion by as much as it reduces aggregate noncompliance in the sense of *true* aggregate tax liability minus tax paid. This is because one effect of uncertainty is to induce some taxpayers to pay *more* tax than they are legally obligated to pay, which reduces aggregate noncompliance but not the amount of individual tax evasion.

A desirable extension of this model is to allow for the possibility that, by expending resources, the uncertainty can be reduced. The resources can be in the form of research by the taxpayer himself or in the form of professional assistance hired. The model structure is then modified by allowing k and possibly also p to depend on expenditure, which is a cost to the taxpayer regardless of what state of the world occurs. In this case the cost of unpredictability includes not only the disutility caused by uncertain tax liability but also the resources expended to reduce the uncertainty. The chapter by Suzanne Scotchmer in this volume analyzes a model of this type.

The introduction of unpredictability into model (3) presented above is not straightforward because its effect is to blur the distinction between evasion and avoidance. In general the probability of incurring a penalty depends in a complicated way on what particular income sources are reported, which deductions are claimed, and how well they are documented, how much effort has gone into camouflaging possibly illegal activities, and so on.

COMPLEXITY AND LIMITED IRS RESOURCES—THE ISSUE OF ENFORCEABILITY

A more complex tax system spreads more thinly the resources of the IRS. The more items per tax return that must be verified, the lower the probability that any one item will be subject to examination. Former IRS Commissioner Roscoe L. Egger, Jr., acknowledged this linkage when he stated that "one reason we are auditing fewer returns is that they have become more complex and take longer to examine" (*U.S. News and World Report,* April 19, 1982, p. 46).

Thus, there is a potentially important link between complexity in the sense of enforceability and the probability of detection of a given act of evasion. A recent example of this phenomenon is the crackdown on abusive tax shelters, which has apparently been successful in limiting evasion in this area, but at the cost of reducing the resources devoted to other areas of noncompliance. If the law were changed to eliminate the possibility of tax-sheltering arrangements, then the probability of detection of other kinds of evasion could be increased, with the presumed result of less evasion in those areas.

It is difficult to argue with the broad proposition that if the IRS had less to do, it could accomplish its remaining tasks better. The tasks for research are to identify those aspects of the tax system for which improvements in enforceability would be most valuable—and to pursue how best to effect improvements in enforceability. Presumably the latter is one of the principal ongoing efforts of the IRS. The former task probably is not given as much attention by the IRS, and some insight may be gained from analytical modeling.

The model I envision would attempt to draw inferences about the appropriate targets for improving enforceability from data on current IRS resource allocation decisions. In the model, the IRS is assumed to be maximizing a certain objective function, which would certainly include revenue recovered and evasion deterred, subject to certain constraints, including a binding one on total resources. Optimal resource allocation would then be characterized by certain conditions such as, in a simple version of this model, equal marginal revenue per dollar expended in every use.

The next step is to assume that the IRS actually operates optimally. With certain further assumptions about the form of certain functions (e.g., the marginal revenue pickup with respect to increases in the probability of detection), it may be possible to assign priorities to areas of the tax code where increased enforceability would be most valuable.

Obviously I have presented a sketch of a model rather than a model itself, but this is an area where analytical work could prove to be valuable. Most academic research up to now has focused on the taxpayer. More emphasis on the tax collection agency is probably in order.

COMPLEXITY AND ATTITUDES TOWARD THE TAX SYSTEM

Many researchers have investigated the hypothesis than an individual's attitude about the tax system and the operation of government in general influences his willingness to evade taxes; this hypothesis links negative feelings to greater willingness to evade. Evidence supporting this hypothesis has been offered by, for example, Spicer and Lundstedt (1976), although Mason and Calvin (1984) and others have found no effect of dissatisfaction with the tax system on the prevalence of noncompliance.

Complexity in the tax system may be a source of frustration and resentment about the tax code and may thereby increase noncompliance. This hypothesis can be studied in future surveys and interviews by specifically asking how complex or time-consuming the tax-filing process is, and whether these factors contribute materially to any sense of dissatisfaction with the tax system. To be most helpful, the various aspects of complexity that directly affect the individual taxpayer should be distinguished—its predictability, difficulty, and manipulability.

Summary

This chapter is misleading if it suggests to the reader that much is known about the relationship between complexity and noncompliance. Objective measures of certain aspects of the complexity of the tax code exist (e.g., number of lines in the 1040 form, number of tax forms, percentage of taxpayers that use professional assistance). Measures of the total resource cost of collecting taxes have recently been developed, and research is in progress to estimate the cost of individual provisions. Much research on the extent of noncompliance now exists. But only recently has research been focused on the relationship between complexity, compliance costs, and tax evasion.

One reason for this lack of progress is that the formidable constraints on noncompliance research discussed by Roth (1984) apply with equal force to research into the links between complexity and noncompliance. Good data are hard to come by, as is information about the procedures of the IRS.

It is hoped that this chapter's attempt to clarify issues, review some of the literature, and raise some pertinent points has suggested promising directions for future research. In what follows these suggestions are summarized and organized with the goal of identifying where the payoff to future research is likely to be the largest.

Better data would be helpful to understand all the links between complexity and noncompliance discussed here. Interview studies should incorporate questions about complexity and the relationship between complexity and attitudes toward the tax system; ideally they should distinguish among the aspects of complexity discussed in this chapter. Subjects should be asked about the total time and expenses involved in filing, and how much of these costs were incurred to establish a reasonable (unmanipulated) tax liability and how much to push the tax liability below the unmanipulated level.

A time series of the characteristics of low-income filers could prove helpful in understanding the role of complexity in nonfiling phenomena. Because this filing population is the complement to the nonfiling population, a careful tracking of the characteristics of the former might provide insight into the characteristics of the latter.

Most currently available data on the complexity of the tax system focus on the cost of compliance. As noted earlier in this paper, this measure of complexity is an incomplete basis for analysis of the issue at hand. A promising future direction for data gathering is to focus on separate measurements of the predictability, difficulty, and manipulability of components of the tax law because their effects on noncompliance are likely to be different. A notable recent approach to this problem is Klepper and Nagin (1987), which develops proxies for the "traceability, deniability, and ambiguity" of individual line items on the tax return and relates these to the level of noncompliance on the line item. Valuable information could also be collected in a taxpayer survey such as the one undertaken in Slemrod and Sorum. However, it may be difficult to obtain quantitative responses of the kind that would be useful for econometric analysis.

In two particular areas there may be a payoff to analytical work. One is extending the model of taxpayer choice to incorporate uncertainty about true tax liability, the probability of audit, and the penalty structure for detected evasion. The second is developing a model of optimal IRS resource allocation behavior. The latter could be especially helpful in identifying the areas on which to focus measures to improve enforceability.

My guess is that the largest payoff is likely to come through sophisticated statistical analysis of existing and newly developed data sources. I have suggested three studies of possible interest. The first is a time-series analysis of how the aggregate characteristics of low-income filers (and, by complementarity, nonfilers) have responded to changes in the tax-filing process aimed at encouraging compliance, such as the introduction of the 1040A and 1040EZ forms. The second is a study of the relationship between individuals' choices concerning evasion and their choices concerning avoidance, using micro-unit data of the TCMP variety. Such a study could shed light on the quantitatively important interactions between the process of complying with the tax law and the decision not to comply. Finally, the detailed data on the compliance cost of specific provisions that will soon be publicly available could be matched with the data on the extent of noncompliance by source of income. Casual inspection reveals a strong positive relationship between the cost of compliance and the extent of noncompliance, but a careful multivariate econometric analysis is required to distinguish precisely among hypotheses about the relationship between complexity and noncompliance.

References

Aaron, H., and Galper, H.
    1985 *Assessing Tax Reform*. Washington, D.C.: Brookings Institution.

Aitken, S. S., and Bonneville, L.
  1980   A General Taxpayer Opinion Survey. Prepared for Office of Planning and
         Research, Internal Revenue Service, March 1980, by CSR Incorporated,
         Washington, D.C. (Contract No. TIR-79-21)
Allingham, M. G., and Sandmo, A.
  1972   Income tax evasion: a theoretical analysis. *Journal of Public Economics*
         1:323–338.
Arthur D. Little, Inc.
  1984   Development of Methodology for Estimating the Taxpayer Paperwork
         Burden. Phase I Report to the Internal Revenue Service, IRS Contract
         No. TIR 83-234, by Arthur D. Little, Inc.

Beck, P., and Jung, W.-O.
  1987a Taxpayer Compliance Under Complexity and Uncertainty. Revised.
         Unpublished paper, College of Commerce, University of Illinois.
  1987b Taxpayer Compliance Under Uncertainty. Revised. Unpublished paper,
         College of Commerce, University of Illinois.
Becker, G. S.
  1967   Crime and punishment: an economic approach. *Journal of Political Econ-
         omy* 78(2):526–536.

Clotfelter, C. T.
  1983   Tax evasion and tax rates: an analysis of individual returns. *Review of
         Economics and Statistics* 65(3):363–373.
Cross, R., and Shaw, G. K.
  1981   The evasion-avoidance choice: a suggested approach. *National Tax Jour-
         nal* 34:489–491.
  1982   On the economics of tax aversion. *Public Finance* 37:36–47

Godwin, M., Hardwick, P., and Sandford, C.
  1983   PAYE: costs v. benefits. *Accountancy* (November):107–112.

Internal Revenue Service
  1983   *Income Tax Compliance Research: Estimates for 1973–1981.* Office of Assis-
         tant Commissioner (Planning, Finance and Research), Internal Revenue
         Service. Washington, D.C.: U.S. Department of the Treasury.
  1985   *Statistics of Income Bulletin* 4. Washington, D.C.: U.S. Department of the
         Treasury.

Klepper, S., and Nagin, D.
  1987   The Anatomy of Tax Evasion. Unpublished paper, Department of Statis-
         tics and School of Urban and Public Affairs, Carnegie-Mellon University.

Long, S. B.
  1981   Social control in the civil law: the case of income tax enforcement. Pp.
         185–214 in H. L. Ross, ed., *Law and Deviance.* Beverly Hills, Calif.: Sage
         Publications.

Mason, R., and Calvin, L. D.
  1984   Public confidence and admitted tax evasion. *National Tax Journal* 37:489–
         496.

Pitt, M., and Slemrod, J.
1988   The Compliance Cost of Itemizing Deductions: Evidence from Individual Tax Returns. Unpublished paper, University of Michigan.
Roberts, S. I.
1979   Overview: the viewpoint of the tax lawyer. Pp. 137–159 in C. H. Gustafson, ed., *Federal Income Tax Simplification*. Philadelphia: American Law Institute.
Roth, J. A.
1984   Understanding Taxpayer Compliance: Can the Social Scientist Help the Tax Collector? Unpublished paper, National Research Council, Washington, D.C.
Sandford, C.
1973   *The Hidden Costs of Taxation*. London: Institute for Fiscal Studies.
Scotchmer, S., and Slemrod, J.
1988   Randomness in Tax Enforcement. Unpublished paper, University of Michigan.
Slemrod, J.
1983   Optimal tax simplification: toward a framework for analysis. *Proceedings of the 76th Annual Conference of the National Tax Association* :158–162.
1985   The Return to Tax Simplification: An Econometric Analysis. National Bureau of Economic Research Working Paper No. 1756, Cambridge, Mass.
1988   Are Estimated Tax Elasticities Really Just Tax Evasion Elasticities? The Case of Charitable Contributions. Unpublished paper, University of Michigan.
Slemrod, J., and Sorum, N.
1984   The compliance cost of the U.S. individual income tax system. *National Tax Journal* 37:461–474.
Spicer, M. W., and Lundstedt, S. B.
1976   Understanding tax evasion. *Public Finance* 31(2):295–305.
Steuerle, C. E., McHugh, R., and Sunley, E.
1978   Who benefits from income averaging? *National Tax Journal* 31:19–32.
U.S. General Accounting Office
1979   *Who's Not Filing Income Tax Returns? IRS Needs Better Ways to Find Them and Collect Their Taxes*. Report to Congress, July 11, 1979. GGD-79-69. Washington, D.C.: U.S. General Accounting Office.
Witte, A. D., and Woodbury, D. F.
1985   The effect of tax laws and tax administration on tax compliance: the case of the U.S. individual income tax. *National Tax Journal* 38(1):1–14.

Suzanne Scotchmer

6. The Effect of Tax Advisors on Tax Compliance

Tax preparation and related financial advice has become a large industry in the United States. A much-quoted round number is that nearly half of all federal tax returns are prepared with the help of third parties.[1] IRS data reveal that the dollar amounts of adjustment to returns prepared by third parties are much larger than those to individually prepared returns.[2] This degree of involvement suggests it might be fruitful to enlist third-party preparers and advisors in the war on noncompliance.

Policy changes might have an impact on third parties by encouraging or discouraging taxpayers from seeking tax advice, by eliciting more truthful reporting from those taxpayers who do seek tax advice, or by facilitating the tax preparer's ability to elicit the relevant information from the client. In this chapter I assess the desirability of these goals from the point of view of three possibly conflicting criteria: enhancing revenue or reducing the enforcement budget, social efficiency, and equity. "Social efficiency" means minimizing the total cost (resource cost and risk-bearing cost) of enforcing the tax code or collecting the required amount of revenue. One component of this total social cost, the resources spent auditing taxpayers, is readily apparent. This chapter draws attention to a less apparent social cost that should also be considered; namely the amount of risk that taxpayers bear. Equity means that the true tax distribution, net of enforcement, is as intended by the Congress.

In order to study these issues, it is necessary to understand the incentives and optimal responses of taxpayers and tax preparers, and also to sort out what feasible policy instruments might achieve the three goals.

Services provided by third parties include (i) filling out forms, (ii)

Graduate School of Public Policy, University of California, Berkeley. I am very grateful to Eugene Bardach, Jerry Green, Daniel Nagin, and Joel Slemrod for their useful and detailed comments. This research was supported by the IRS and by the NSF, Grant SES 86 10021.

resolving the taxpayer's uncertainty about tax treatment of ambiguous or confusing tax issues, (iii) planning tax payments or investments to minimize tax liability, and (iv) representing taxpayers before the IRS in case of audit.[3] Some of these have social value in the sense of reducing the resource cost of administering and enforcing the tax code, or in the sense of reducing taxpayers' risk, while others may be a social waste.

Services (i) and (ii) clearly have social value in the sense of being economically efficient. It is cheaper to have tax preparers learn the tax code and apply their knowledge to many tax returns than to have each taxpayer learn it. The public interest and the private interest of taxpayers coincide in that taxpayers seek professional help precisely when it is socially efficient to do so.[4] In addition, as discussed below, there is an intangible benefit to resolving a risk-averse taxpayer's uncertainty about ambiguous tax items and thereby reducing his or her risk.

Neither benefit—reduced risk-bearing nor reduction in preparation cost—is observable, and the efficiency benefits of (i) and (ii) might be overlooked by the enforcement agency, since they cannot be quantified. Furthermore, I discuss below that (ii), resolving uncertainty, will often be revenue reducing for the Treasury (unless other enforcement effort, such as the probability of audit, changes), and the goal of revenue enhancement may therefore conflict with the goal of economic efficiency.[5]

Services of type (iii) save money for individual taxpayers, but do not save social resources in aggregate. A taxpayer's saving due to sheltering income, or buying and selling assets at strategic times to take advantage of capital gains treatment, transfers funds from the public coffers to the taxpayer's bank account but does not save real resources in the economy. But we would not say that these costs are a total social waste, since the provisions of the tax code that permit these savings achieve equity or incentive goals, such as encouraging investment. The proper use of these provisions is consonant with the intentions of Congress, even if it reduces revenue or costs real resources to implement. I will not focus on tax services designed legally to shelter income.

The function (iv) of representing taxpayers in proceedings with the IRS is a legal function closely related to the rest of the legal industry. While it is legitimate and important to ask whether it is necessary for Americans to devote vast sums to litigation, as they do, that question is not substantially different for representation in tax court or audits than for other legal matters. While reducing complexity of the tax code might reduce expenditures on legal matters, since there would be less to argue about, this is a problem of tax design and not of tax compliance; I discuss it only briefly in the conclusion.

The first and second sections of this chapter discuss the incentives, respectively, of taxpayers and tax advisors. I show that if penalties and probabilities of audit do not depend on whether tax advice is sought, then in plausible cases the Treasury's revenue will decrease when taxpayers seek advice to resolve their uncertainty about taxable income, but social welfare increases, since taxpayers bear less involuntary risk. The third section discusses three roles of preparer penalties. In addition to causing taxpayers who seek advice to cheat less, preparer penalties may also dissuade taxpayers from seeking advice. The third role has to do with quality assurance, given that taxpayers cannot perfectly distinguish tax advisors who give accurate advice from those who do not. The fourth section discusses policy implications.

Incentives of Taxpayers

Most of the tax compliance literature written by economists presumes that taxpayers have no commitment to honesty and report income only to the extent that reporting is in their utility-maximizing interest. The primary means of persuasion is threat of penalty.[6] The extension of this idea to an environment with tax advisors must presume that in the decision whether to seek tax advice, the taxpayer considers the tax preparer's own incentives and possible penalties and whether, as a result, the taxpayer might be better off filing individually.

Although the taxpayer saves personal costs by having the advisor fill out forms efficiently, probably the most important service of tax advisors for taxpayers with complicated affairs is telling them how the tax code applies to their income and deductions. The tax advisor resolves the taxpayer's uncertainty about tax issues and informs the taxpayer of his or her true taxable income. Rather than paying an advisor to resolve his or her uncertainty before filing the return, the taxpayer could alternatively make a best guess (which might mean best cheat) and then be surprised (pleasantly or unpleasantly) at the assessed tax liability when and if an audit occurs.[7]

If the taxpayer is uncertain of true tax liability, as when he or she is uncertain what deductions are legitimate, the idea of "honest reporting" has no meaning.[8] For any amount of reported income, an auditor will either disallow some deductions or declare that additional legitimate deductions are available. The taxpayer's obligation to resolve uncertainties by seeking tax advice is unclear. On the one hand, a general legal principle is that ignorance of the law is no defense (else it would become an absolute defense!). On the other hand, the IRS looks leniently on errors relating to ambiguous tax items, and applies low civil penalties[9] rather than prosecuting for fraud when irregularities turn up in an audit.

Complexity in the tax code which causes the taxpayer to be confused about true taxable income therefore imposes a choice between two costs, in addition to the tax liability: he or she can pay a tax advisor to resolve uncertainty or make a "best guess" and bear risk. Even though these two private costs are also social costs, we cannot conclude that the taxpayer's cost-minimizing choice is necessarily in the public interest. There is also an effect on revenue. If the taxpayer's cost-minimizing choice causes revenue to fall, then costly enforcement effort must be raised.

With a view toward assessing whether taxpayers should be encouraged to seek third-party advice, the remainder of this section asks whether, when they do so, the Treasury's revenue is likely to go up or down. I show conditions in which revenue will go down.

As a benchmark to sort out incentives, I shall assume first that preparer penalties are seldom imposed,[10] so that fines for underreporting income do not depend on whether tax advice was sought. In the following section I discuss preparers' incentives, including penalties. For analytical simplicity I assume a constant tax rate t on assessed or reported income. I let p represent the probability that a return is audited. I also take the maximum fine rate f on undeclared tax liability to be fixed by statute and assume this maximum is always imposed. The enforcement agency's ability to set fines is restricted both by the Congress[11] and by administrative law. Large fines would be subject to appeal through the court system and would be reduced because of the legal doctrine that penalties should fit the crime. Thus, even though the enforcement agency could always increase reported income by increasing fine rates, exorbitant penalties are not observed.

In deciding whether to seek advice, the taxpayer compares the *ex ante* expected utility achieved by resolving and not resolving uncertainty, assuming that he or she reports the optimal amount of income in each case. When uncertainty is not resolved, the taxpayer chooses a report R that maximizes expression (1) below, which is expected utility. The first term represents the taxpayer's utility when no audit occurs, and the last two terms represent the taxpayer's expected utility if audited. M is the taxpayer's gross income. $F(i)$ describes the distribution of taxable incomes i that the

IRS might assess. If the assessed income i turns out to be higher than R (the second term), then the taxpayer will owe unpaid tax plus a fine: namely $t(1 + f)$ $(i - R)$. If the assessed income i turns out to be lower than reported income R (the third term), then the taxpayer will be rebated overpaid tax, but will not be "rewarded" at the fine rate.

(1) $(1 - p)U[M - tR]$

$$+ p\int_R^\infty U[M - ti - tf(i - R)]dF(i) + p\int_0^R U[M - ti]dF(i) .$$

The first-order condition describing the uncertain taxpayer's optimal report, R^*, is[12]

(2) $- (1 - p)U'[M - tR^*] + pf\int_{R^*}^\infty U'[M - ti - tf(i - R^*)]dF(i) = 0 .$

If the taxpayer resolves uncertainty before filing the tax return, he or she will choose an optimal report that depends on the true taxable income, i, that the tax advisor discovers. The taxpayer chooses $r \leq i$ to maximize:

(3) $(1 - p) U[M - tr] + p U[M - ti - tf(i - r)].$

In order to isolate the effect of uncertainty itself, I shall assume for the moment that there are no preparer penalties. The tax advisor informs the taxpayer of true taxable income and allows the taxpayer to underreport income optimally. Then the f in expressions (1) and (3) are the same. The taxpayer chooses a report, $r(i)$ (that is, the optimal reported income depends on the true taxable income i), that satisfies:[13]

(4) $- (1 - p)U'[M - tr(i)] + pfU'[M - ti - tf(i - r(i))] = 0.$

If tax advice were costless and did not alter the penalty for underreporting, the taxpayer would always choose to resolve uncertainty. This is because, for most taxable incomes i, the optimal report $r(i)$ provides more expected utility than R^*, which the informed taxpayer could alternatively report. Thus, the value of (1) is smaller for each R than the *ex ante* expected utility,

$$\int \{(1 - p)U[M - tr(i)] + pU[M - ti - tf(i - r(i))]\} dF(i).$$

The more confused or risk averse the taxpayer is (e.g., the higher the variance of i), the more valuable advice is. We would thus expect to observe that taxpayers with complicated returns seek tax advice. This phenomenon shows up in several empirical investigations. In a study using Minnesota survey data, Slemrod (1985) showed that itemizers are more likely to seek advice than nonitemizers, and this likelihood is increased if the taxpayer had capital gains or losses. Self-employment income also increases the amount of money spent on tax advice. Long and Caudill (1987) show that the probability of using a preparer increased by about 10 percent (in some range) with each additional supporting schedule. Mazur and Nagin (1987) show that taxpayers with more "ambiguous"[14] income are more likely to seek tax advice, and among those who seek tax advice, lawyers and CPAs are used by those with the most ambiguous income.

Resolving uncertainty affects revenue (expected payments) in two ways. First, imperfectly informed taxpayers will occasionally "overreport" income. The optimal report R^* of imperfectly informed taxpayers will typically be somewhere interior to the support of i, and some taxpayers will find out at audit that $R^* > i$. Since fines are asymmetric, one dollar of overreported income is more valuable to the Treasury Department than one dollar of underreported income is costly. Therefore, if the imperfectly informed taxpayer reported more than the average of what he would report after resolving uncertainty, the Treasury Department would achieve more expected revenue. Secondly, the imperfectly informed risk-averse taxpayer bears involuntary risk, unlike the perfectly informed taxpayer, who has the option of avoiding all risk. The risk-averse taxpayer may cope with involuntary risk by reporting conservatively. Whether this occurs depends on details of the taxpayer's risk aversion which I have not specified.

We want to know when the following inequality holds:

$$(5) \quad tR^* + pt(1+f)\int_0^\infty (i-R^*)dF(i) - ptf\int_0^{R^*}(i-R^*)dF(i)$$

$$\geq t\,E[r(i)] + pt(1+f)\int_0^\infty (i-r(i))dF(i).$$

The left-hand side is the expected revenue collected by the Treasury when taxpayers remain imperfectly informed and report R^*, while the right-hand side is expected revenue when taxpayers resolve uncertainty and report the amounts $\{r(i)\}$. The left-hand side is larger than the right-hand side when

$$(6) \quad -ptf\int_0^{R^*}(i-R^*)dF(i) \geq t[1-p(1+f)]\,[E[r(i)]-R^*].$$

Since the left-hand side of (6) is positive, if $R^* > E[r(i)]$, then imperfectly informed taxpayers reporting R^* pay more on average than perfectly informed taxpayers reporting $\{r(i)\}$. The interpretation that resolving uncertainty reduces revenue assumes that taxpayers' subjective distribution $F(i)$ is unbiased in the sense that, if the pool of taxpayers with the same initial uncertainty all resolved their uncertainty, the distribution of true income would also be $F(i)$.

When $R^* < E[r(i)]$, both sides of the inequality (6) are positive, provided $(1 - p)/p \geq f$ or $p \leq 1/(1 + f)$. The latter means that underreporting income is better than a "fair bet," and taxpayers will then hold some of the risky asset, underreported income, if perfectly informed.[15]

It follows from equations (2) and (4) that, as pf increases relative to $(1 - p)$, R^* and each $r(i)$ increase and the left-hand side of (6) increases. The first term of the right-hand side decreases, and the difference $E[r(i)] - R^*$ may increase or decrease. But since $E[r(i)]$ is bounded by mean assessable income $E[i]$, while R^* becomes close to the maximum income in the support of F when pf becomes close to $(1 - p)$, it follows that:

Proposition. For large enough f (at fixed p) or for large enough p (at fixed f) (but still maintaining $p \leq 1/(1 + f)$), the amount of revenue collected from taxpayers who are uncertain of their true taxable incomes exceeds the amount collected from perfectly informed taxpayers.

When taxpayers are risk neutral, maximizing expected utility is equivalent to minimizing expected payments to the government. Since taxpayers' interests (to minimize expected payments) and the Treasury Department's interests (to maximize expected payments) are directly opposed, anything that improves the ability of taxpayers to minimize payments also reduces revenue. In another paper (1987), I have shown that, when taxpayers are risk neutral and the probability of audit can depend on reported income (unlike the case here),[16] maximum revenue, net of enforcement costs, requires the government to audit third-party returns and individual returns with different probabilities. The audit functions that elicit maximum revenue have the property that some taxpayers do not resolve their uncertainty.

The loss of revenue when risk-neutral taxpayers resolve uncertainty is entirely due to the asymmetry of fines: when uncertain taxpayers are discovered to have overreported income, they are not rebated a "reward" at the fine rate. Since this asymmetry of fines is also present for risk-averse taxpayers, R^* would have to be considerably less than $E[r(i)]$ in order for the Treasury Department to collect more revenue with perfectly informed taxpayers reporting $\{r(i)\}$ than with imperfectly informed taxpayers reporting $R*$. Further research is required to understand how and whether this may occur, but it does not seem plausible.

The Legal Environment and Incentives for Third Parties[17]

Legal duties determine whether it is in the interest of tax advisors to assist taxpayers in strategically underreporting income. Although lawyers and CPAs belong to professional associations with strict codes of ethics, and are bound as well by rules of the IRS and the common law not to act fraudulently, it is not required that a tax preparer belong to any professional association. Since professional codes of conduct are enforceable by the professional associations (e.g., attorneys can be disbarred), different types of preparers may therefore be bound by different legal duties.

Legal duties to the IRS of all tax preparers are codified in Treasury Circular 230. All tax preparers are subject to the same penalties for misrepresenting a client's financial position before the IRS, and these vary according to whether the oversight is deemed negligent, willful, or "aiding and abetting." While the legal duty to the IRS is the same for all preparers, there are differences in the ethics preparers are required to endorse. Accountants and attorneys are bound by codes of ethics, but there is no code of ethics for the many independent tax preparers who are allowed to practice before the IRS simply by passing a test.

Attorneys have legal duties codified in American Bar Association Opinion 314, as modified in Opinion 352, July 1985, which states

> A lawyer may advise reporting a position on a tax return so long as the lawyer believes in good faith that the position is warranted in existing law or can be supported by a good faith argument for an extension, modification or reversal of existing law and there is some realistic possibility of success if the matter is litigated.

That is, the tax position must have "reasonable basis in law." The professional standards of the American Institute of Certified Public Accountants impose a similar test: "a member may resolve doubt in favor of his client as long as there is reasonable support for his position."

The IRS Code and the professional codes for lawyers and CPAs all prohibit the tax advisor or preparer from advising the client illegally to evade taxes or underreport income. In fact, they all impose a duty to advise a client *against* illegal or fraudulent actions. And of course these codes all prohibit preparers from willfully deceiving the IRS about the true financial position of the client. In addition to the IRS's ability to penalize preparers or disbar them from tax court, the ABA and AICPA can also take disciplinary action for violation of ethics, although this seems to occur rarely.

Differences between the professional codes of conduct and the IRS code seem to be ones of nuance. A "reasonable basis in law" is explicitly not probabilistic; that is, the attorney does not need to think he or she has a high probability of winning the point with the IRS or in Tax Court in order to have a reasonable basis. And while the attorney or CPA has a duty to advise the client against fraud or underreporting, there is no duty to report the client's fraud to the IRS if the client ignores the advice. While these seem to be loopholes in the tax advisor's responsibilities, it should also be pointed out that attorneys are explicitly barred by both Treasury Circular 230 and their own professional code from "playing the tax lottery." The only consideration in whether a tax position may be taken is "reasonable basis." Tax advisors are not supposed to consider whether the tax position may trigger an audit or whether underreported income is likely to be discovered.

Tax advisors have what may appear to be conflicting legal responsibilities to clients and the IRS, the violation of which may result in penalties, malpractice suits, or disbarment. With respect to the client, the attorney faces malpractice awards if he or she fails to use "such skill, prudence and diligence as lawyers of ordinary skill and capacity commonly possess" (Burrell, 1982:259). Skill and diligence require that the tax practitioner be on the "margin" of the law, reducing tax liability by every legal means. But prudence requires that he or she not jeopardize the client or self by taking positions that may be disallowed.

In a competitive market, tax preparers compete to attract customers. This competition, combined with the tax preparer's duty to act in the interest of the client within the scope of the law, prevent him or her from taking entirely riskless tax positions, which he or she would otherwise take in order to avoid penalties. My interpretation below of how tax advisors balance legal duties and market forces is that they must be compensated by taxpayers for bearing risk of penalty, but if they are compensated, then they permit underreporting.

For completeness, I summarize here some empirical information on the profile of tax advisors. Preparers may be classified in the following five broad categories:[18] self-prepared (about half); unpaid assistance (10 percent; this includes IRS-sponsored services as well as friends and relatives);

CPAs, lawyers, and public accountants (17 percent); tax services (21 percent) (includes large firms such as H&R Block, whose preparers work under the supervision of professionals, but who are mainly not lawyers or CPAs); other paid assistance (7 percent) (largely part-year preparers who do not work under the supervision of professionals). The parenthetical percentages of returns are reported by Klepper and Nagin (1987), based on their study of 1979 TCMP data.

Klepper and Nagin document how the choice of preparer varies systematically with income and complexity of the return. Most self-prepared returns are prepared by nonbusiness taxpayers, and, among those, mostly by low-income taxpayers. High-income nonbusiness taxpayers mostly use lawyers, CPAs, or public accountants, although self-preparation is the next most likely method. Proprietors and farmers use lawyers, CPAs, and public accountants most frequently (about half), with tax services being the next most likely.

Klepper and Nagin (1987) and Mazur and Nagin (1987) hypothesize that tax preparers serve the function of enforcing unambiguous aspects of the law and exploiting ambiguous aspects. Klepper and Nagin construct measures of noncompliance and measures of ambiguity, and argue that the data support their hypothesis. One interpretation of this evidence is that taxpayers are uncertain which items have a reasonable basis for being deducted (are "ambiguous"), and the role of tax advisors is to clarify it for them. Consistently with the model above, taxpayers in these two models underreport to the optimal extent, but when they have uncertainties about what is deductible, sometimes they make mistakes.

Another strand of empirical research surveys taxpayers and preparers to discover their attitudes toward compliance. Jackson and Milliron (1987) summarize recent evidence on preparers' tax aggressiveness as it relates to attributes of the client, attributes of the preparer, and the decision context (e.g., penalties and probability of detection). Some of this evidence directly supports the hypothesis that resolving uncertainty is a primary motive to seek tax advice. For example, Yankelovich et al. (1984) report that 63 percent of the taxpayers they interviewed ranked accuracy of the return as the most important reason to seek advice.

The Three Roles of Preparer Penalties

"Penalty" can be understood in the broad sense that includes the possibility of disbarment or criminal conviction rather than pecuniary losses. Since violations of professional ethics jeopardize the tax advisor in these ways, one can think of tightening the ethics as increasing the preparer penalties, provided one also accounts for the probability of conviction.

The previous section assumed that the tax advisor permits the taxpayer to underreport income as it suits the taxpayer, without changing the probability of audit or penalty. But if there are preparer penalties for underreporting, in addition to the taxpayer's penalties, then the f in expression (3), describing the optimal $r(i)$ when tax advice is sought, should be higher than in expression (1), describing the optimal R^*.

Milliron (1987) reports evidence that the client's attitude toward risk is the single most important determinant of how aggressive a tax position the advisor takes. But if the taxpayer asks the preparer to permit underreporting because he or she considers it a good gamble, then the preparer will presumably demand a large fee to compensate for the possible preparer penalties. Thus, even though the taxpayer does not pay the preparer's penalty directly, the combined incentives of taxpayer and preparer to underreport income must reflect the combined fine.

If preparers operate in a competitive market, so that their profits are restricted to zero in equilibrium, a taxpayer who wants to cheat must provide a preparer who permits him or her to do so an additional fee equal to $pf''(i - r(i))$, where f'' is the advisor's penalty. Here I assume the preparer is risk neutral with respect to an individual taxpayer's return, and the additional fee is just the expected fine incurred by underreporting. Thus, the first role of preparer penalties is to increase the compounded penalty rate a dishonest taxpayer faces, which discourages underreporting. The second role of penalties is to dissuade taxpayers from seeking tax advice, since tax advice is more costly or less valuable when there are preparer penalties.

A third and more subtle role for preparer penalties concerns quality assurance.[19] Two asymmetries of information arise between tax preparers and taxpayers. First, since taxpayers are poorly informed about true tax liabilities, they have no ability to distinguish high-quality tax advisors with accurate knowledge of the law from low-quality, badly informed tax advisors who misrepresent themselves as especially clever (and thereby get more clients) by falsely claiming there are many legal tax deductions that the taxpayer did not think of. The problem of discerning quality is worse in tax preparation than in other professional services because certification by a professional body is not required. Essentially anyone can enter the market and try to find a clientele. Without some mechanism to distinguish high-quality tax preparers from low-quality tax preparers who wish to "hit and run" and make a profit, tax advising would break down.

The second asymmetry of information between tax advisor and taxpayer is that the tax advisor cannot entirely verify the financial information provided by the taxpayer. This applies more to non-W2 earnings such as honoraria, which the taxpayer may simply not mention, than to deductions, which the taxpayer can be required to document.

That quality assurance is a real problem emerged recently in a General Accounting Office study of IRS taxpayer assistance advice, in which 39 percent of the GAO's queries were answered incorrectly.[20] One explanation for this poor showing is simply that IRS tax advisors have no incentive to be correct. Their advice is anonymous and nonbinding on the IRS.

One might hope there are market mechanisms that eliminate ill-trained tax advisors from the private sector, if not from the public sector. For example, willingness to offer insurance might allow high-quality advisors to distinguish themselves from low-quality advisors. If the tax advisor or tax preparer insures the taxpayer against wrong advice by a commitment to represent the taxpayer costlessly in a legal proceeding (or better yet, to pay all the taxpayer's possible fines),[21] he or she makes credible the allegation that the suggested deductions or tax shelters are legal and not merely a way to entice the unwary taxpayer into buying bad advice that looks attractive because it lowers the tax bill.

Although limited insurance is observed,[22] the second asymmetry of information, that the tax advisor observes only what the taxpayer reveals, prevents this mechanism from working perfectly. If the tax advisor insured the taxpayer against losses due to audit and fine, the taxpayer would withhold from the tax advisor (and from the IRS, at least before audit) information about true taxable income, since, once the advisor becomes liable for fines, the taxpayer is better off underreporting income. This problem is typically called "moral hazard." The moral hazard problem can be solved by contract only if there is some way for the tax advisor to prove what information the taxpayer provided. To be enforceable, such an insurance contract could cover only ambiguous tax items for which the aggressive tax position had a "reasonable basis in law." But since taxpayers often want to take tax positions with no such basis, an insurance contract would be evidence of a conspiracy to defraud the IRS and therefore be unenforceable. Hence the moral hazard problem.

Preparer penalties substitute for insurance as a mechanism to force low-quality tax advisors out of the market. A preparer who takes many untenable positions (possibly by mistake) will be frequently penalized, just as if he or she had issued insurance, and will therefore leave the market. With preparer penalties, rather than insurance, the taxpayer has reduced incentive to withhold information from the tax advisor, since the taxpayer can be penalized for underreporting.

Third Parties in Tax Enforcement: Policy Implications

Returning to the question of whether policy should encourage use of third parties, we have discovered that the criteria may conflict. While resolving uncertainty through tax advice enhances taxpayer well-being by reducing risk, it may also reduce the Treasury Department's revenue (when other enforcement parameters are fixed). Risk bearing is an "invisible" cost, while losses in revenue are all too visible.

One way to maintain revenue while encouraging taxpayers to resolve their uncertainties is to raise the probabilities of audit but to revoke the additional fines imposed on third parties.[23] This would encourage taxpayers to resolve their uncertainties and thus not bear involuntary risk, but it requires additional resources for auditing. There is a tradeoff between bearing resource costs for more audits and bearing "utility costs" for increased risk.

On the other hand, while preparer penalties discourage taxpayers from seeking advice, and this may be contrary to the public interest, they serve the beneficial purpose identified above of forcing low-quality tax advisors out of the market. Revoking preparer penalties might have the deleterious effect of making tax advice less reliable. Since taxpayers would not discover this until too late (audit), tax advisors' function of resolving uncertainty would be undermined.

Jackson and Milliron (1987) refer to the fact that in the past decade the Congress has progressively tightened preparer penalties, and the IRS has recently proposed to interpret the preparers' duties in light of Circular 230 more stringently. They report that this has been seen by the professional tax community as an attempt to convert advocates for taxpayers into an arm of the government. Indeed, it can hardly be seen otherwise and is probably effective. It is not surprising that Milliron and Toy found in their (1986) survey of CPA attitudes toward compliance that CPAs favor reduction of tax rates over increased penalties as a way to increase compliance. Increasing preparer penalties will increase the Treasury's revenue without increasing the audit budget through increased compliance of taxpayers who seek advice and increased revenue from taxpayers who are dissuaded from seeking advice.[24] But, as I have discussed above, this may not serve the public interest.

So far I have assumed that the amount of complexity and cause for taxpayer confusion is inherent in the tax code, and I have addressed the narrow question of whether tax advice to resolve uncertainty should be encouraged. But the amount of ambiguity and complexity in the tax code is itself subject to choice, partly by the Congress, since they set the tax code, and partly by the IRS, since the IRS can issue rulings and take other action to inform preparers and taxpayers of how the tax code will be enforced. Some perspectives on complexity are provided by Slemrod (this volume, Chapter 5), Scotchmer and Slemrod (1988), and Beck and Jung (1987a,b). With some caveats, the latter three papers support the idea that "fuzzing" up taxpayer's information, without giving him or her the opportunity to seek tax advice, increases reported income and revenue.

In the context where confused taxpayers have no opportunity to resolve their uncertainty, as when the randomness is due to auditors' judgments rather than ignorance about well-defined details of the law, Scotchmer and Slemrod (1988) showed it is not optimal to remove all randomness from assessed tax liabilities. Removing the last bit of ambiguity is costly and does not increase expected ability. Since the cost of seeking advice will deter taxpayers from resolving a small amount of uncertainty, we can probably infer from this that, while risk bearing is costly, it is not necessarily optimal to remove *all* ambiguity from the tax code. Further, some of the ambiguity is an inevitable consequence of special tax provisions introduced to remedy equity or incentive problems, and it is therefore inappropriate to think of removing complexity only in terms of enhancing revenue collections or reducing risk bearing.

To summarize the policy lessons in this essay, they are that (1) resolving taxpayer uncertainty increases utility by reducing risk but may also reduce net revenue, and (2) this does not imply that taxpayer confusion (complexity in the tax code) is a good way to raise revenue. Raising revenue by inducing risk-averse taxpayers to take conservative tax positions may have the advantage of saving real enforcement costs, such as auditors' time, but substitutes a different cost paid by taxpayers—either the bearing of risk or costly tax advice. In a social sense, forcing taxpayers to bear risk or seek advice may be more costly than enforcing an unambiguous tax code with a high audit budget, even though taxpayers' costs are "invisible" to the IRS, while audit costs add to the deficit.

Notes

1. Jackson and Milliron (1987) quote this number from IRS data, and Klepper and Nagin (1987) compute it from 1982 Tax Compliance Measurement Program data.
2. Klepper and Nagin (1987) and Jackson and Milliron (1987) quote IRS summary statistics from 1979 TCMP data as revealing that, although only 45 percent of returns were prepared by third parties, these accounted for 74 percent of identified noncompliance. We cannot conclude that preparers encourage non-compliance, however, since preparers disproportionately handle complex, high-income returns for which noncompliance is possible (Klepper and Nagin).
3. These functions are generally agreed upon by academic authors on the subject, except that (ii) is generally not called "resolving uncertainty."
4. This is not precisely true, since costs of tax preparation are deductible, and the IRS therefore shares the cost. The taxpayer will seek advice whenever his or her share of the cost is less than the private cost of tax preparation.
5. Scotchmer and Slemrod (1988) show a similar result, that if the taxpayer's uncertainty about taxable income increases, his or her expected payments to the government will typically also increase. See also Beck and Jung (1987a,b). In those discussions, there is no question of resolving uncertainty. Here I show that, in an *ex ante* sense, a taxpayer's expected payments to the government will often be larger if uncertainty is not resolved than if it is. But the policy tradeoff is the same in both cases; a reduction in revenue versus a reduction in taxpayers' expected utility, due to risk bearing.
6. Allingham and Sandmo (1972) introduced the idea that cheating on taxes is a "portfolio choice," with the risk established by the audit probability and fine rate. The view that only fines are persuasive is extreme. Eugene Bardach (1987) has taken a broader perspective and discusses moral arguments that might have force. Other chapters in this book focus on determinants of taxpayer behavior other than maximizing expected utility.
7. Another alternative to seeking tax advice would be to go to the library. I assume tax advice is cheaper, since the tax advisor spreads the cost of his or her trip to the library among many advisees.
8. Where does this leave the "honest" but confused taxpayer? The well-meaning honest taxpayer who makes a "best guess" will presumably "guess" in the manner that maximizes expected utility. That is, he or she becomes indistinguishable from the strategically dishonest taxpayer who makes a portfolio choice about how much risk to bear by underreporting income. Giving the honest taxpayer an excuse for assuming such a mind-set might reduce compliance considerably if honest taxpayers become "strategic" taxpayers.
9. But civil penalties are not optimally low. Suppose penalties were "infinite" and

the probability of audit were trivially small. A risk-averse taxpayer could avoid all risk by reporting the maximum conceivable tax liability and essentially never get audited. As a consequence of avoiding all risk, the "effective" tax rate is higher than stipulated, but this may not concern us if all taxpayers overpay tax in the same amount.

10. The June 1987 survey of the IRS reveals that only 8 percent of preparers have paid penalties, and presumably on only a small proportion of the returns they handled. Of course this is not evidence that the IRS is reluctant to impose such penalties. The frequency of imposing penalties could be low because the threat of penalties effectively discourages aggressive tax positions.

11. For example, the Congress changed the allowable fines in the Tax Reform Act of 1986.

12. This assumes R^* is interior to the support of F, as it will be if $pf < (1 - p)$.

13. This is provided $r(i)$ is less than i, as it will be if $p \leq 1/(1+f)$, so that underreporting is a "fair bet." The optimal report $r(i)$ is equal to i if the derivative (4) has positive value for all $r \leq i$.

14. In the definition of Mazur and Nagin, "ambiguous" income could credibly be thought nontaxable and therefore falls within the "reasonable basis in law" stipulation of legal ethics.

15. If $p \geq 1/(1+f)$, then $r(i)=i$ for each i, and R^* would be the maximum income in the support of F. By assuming that $p \leq 1/(1+f)$, I assume that some tax evasion is in the taxpayer's utility-maximizing interest. At current enforcement levels, this assumption certainly holds.

16. When the probability of audit does not depend on reported income, then an increase in revenue is also an increase in net revenue (net of audit costs). This is why I have assumed here that the probability of audit is constant. The risk-neutral case is easier to analyze, and I thus found it of interest (1987) to examine whether the IRS's net revenue is still enhanced when the probability of audit depends on r and can depend on whether advice was sought.

17. Much of the information in this section reflects the useful writings of Burrell (1982) and Klepper and Nagin (1987), as well as useful discussion with B. Wolfman and my own reading of the relevant codes.

18. The IRS (1987) survey of tax practitioners uses this more aggregated taxonomy, as do Klepper and Nagin (1987) in their empirical analysis of 1979 and 1982 TCMP data.

19. This analysis has benefited from helpful discussion with Eddie Dekel.

20. This was reported by the *New York Times* (February 23, 1988). The 39 percent figure was disputed by the IRS, which claimed 25 percent was closer to accurate.

21. Such insurance would be socially valuable in a way beyond signaling quality. Since the taxpayer is risk averse and the tax advisor is risk neutral with respect to any client's tax return (because many returns are handled), it is efficient for the tax advisor to hold the risk.

22. For example, H&R Block represents all clients without charge before the IRS in an audit. The insurance is partial in that it is for legal fees but not for fines. Such guarantees are not typically given by attorneys and accountants, since the magnitude and costliness of possible legal proceedings are unpredictable in

complicated tax matters. But since clients have ongoing, often multifaceted relationships with these professionals, the problem of discerning quality is not so important.

23. I assume here that Congress reserves the right to set maximum fines, so the IRS cannot increase fines. If it could, then fines could be made sufficiently high that all taxpayers would resolve their uncertainty and report honestly. Since the probability of audit could be reduced to near zero, this would save enforcement costs and possibly risk-bearing costs. But as mentioned above, there are other reasons, such as equity principles of law, why fines could not be extreme.

24. But when the preparer penalty rate goes up, revenue from penalties may decrease as the number of taxpayers paying such penalties decreases.

References

American Bar Association Standing Committee on Ethics and
    n.d.   Professional Responsibilities, Opinions 314 and 85-352
American Institute of Certified Public Accountants
    1977   Statement on Responsibilities in Tax Practice No. 10, April 1977.
Allingham, M.G., and Sandmo, A.
    1972   Income tax evasion: a theoretical analysis. *Journal of Public Economics* 1: 323–338
Bardach, E.
    1987   Persuasion and Tax Code Enforcement. Unpublished paper, Graduate School of Public Policy, University of California, Berkeley.
Beck, P.J., and Jung, W.-O.
    1987a   Taxpayer Compliance Under Complexity and Uncertainty. Revised. Unpublished paper, College of Commerce, University of Illinois
    1987b   Taxpayer Compliance Under Uncertainty. Revised. Unpublished paper, College of Commerce, University of Illinois
Burrell, S.
    1982   Legal Malpractice of the Tax Attorney. *The Tax Executive* (July): 259–277
Internal Revenue Service.
    1987   Survey of Tax Practitioners and Advisers: Summary of Results by Occupation. Research Division, Internal Revenue Service, U.S. Department of the Treasury, Washington, D.C.
Jackson, B., and Milliron, V.C.
    1987   Research on the Practitioner's Role in the Compliance Process: State of the Art. Unpublished paper, University of Colorado at Boulder and The Pennsylvania State University
Klepper, S., and Nagin, D.
    1987   The Role of Tax Practitioners in Tax Compliance. Unpublished paper, Department of Statistics and School of Urban and Public Affairs, Carnegie-Mellon University.

Long, J., and Caudill, S.
    1987   The usage and benefits of tax return preparation. *National Tax Journal* 40: 37–45.
Mazur, M., and Nagin, D.
    1987   Tax Preparers and Tax Compliance: A Theoretical and Empirical Analysis, Unpublished paper, School of Urban and Public Affairs, Carnegie-Mellon University.
Milliron, V. C.
    1987   A Conceptual Model of Factors Influencing Tax Preparers' Aggressiveness. Unpublished paper, Department of Accounting, The Pennsylvania State University.
Milliron, V.C., and Toy, D. R.
    1986   Tax Compliance: An Investigation of Key Features. Unpublished paper, Departments of Accounting and Marketing, The Pennsylvania State University.
Scotchmer, S.
    1987   Who Profits from Taxpayer Confusion? Graduate School of Public Policy Working Paper No. 136. University of California, Berkeley.
Scotchmer, S. and Slemrod, J.
    1988   Randomness in Tax Enforcement, Unpublished Paper, University of Michigan. Previously titled Optimal Obfuscation in Tax Enforcement. Graduate School of Public Policy Working Paper No. 126. University of California, Berkeley.
Slemrod, J.
    1985   The Return to Tax Simplification: An Econometric Analysis. National Bureau of Economic Research. Working Paper No. 1756. Cambridge, Mass.
    1989   Complexity, compliance costs, and tax evasion. Chapter 5 in this volume.
Yankelovich, Skelly, and White, Inc.
    1984   Taxpayer Attitudes Study: Final Report. Public opinion survey prepared for the Public Affairs Division, Internal Revenue Service, December 1984, by Yankelovich, Skelly, and White, Inc., New York.

Robert B. Cialdini

7. Social Motivations to Comply: Norms, Values, and Principles

For well over a half century, social psychologists have been investigating the process of social influence, wherein one individual's attitudes, beliefs, or behaviors are changed through the action of another. For the past twenty years, I have been a fascinated participant in the endeavor. Although the accumulated social influence data base of my discipline has been frequently brought to bear on a variety of other domains, to date no systematic attempt to do so has been made with respect to tax compliance. The purpose of the present article, then, is to apply the perspective and developed evidence of social psychology to this issue.

In the process, my treatment will focus on a set of six principles that my own research perspective suggests most powerfully and regularly influence compliance decisions. Briefly, these principles involve pressures to comply because of tendencies to: (1) be consistent with prior commitments, (2) return an earlier gift, favor, or service, (3) follow the lead of similar others, (4) conform to the directives of legitimate authority, (5) seize opportunities that are scarce or dwindling in availability, and (6) accede to the requests of those we like.

Social Motivations to Comply
FOCUSING ON POWERFUL EFFECTS

Within the discipline of academic social psychology, research into the compliance process has concerned itself mostly with two questions: "Which principles and techniques reliably affect compliance?" and "How do these principles and techniques work to affect compliance as they do?" The first of these questions is concerned, of course, with the identification

Department of Psychology, Arizona State University

of real effects, while the second is concerned with their theoretical/ conceptual mediation. Almost without exception, the vehicle that has been employed to answer these two questions has been the controlled experiment. And this is altogether appropriate, as controlled experimentation provides an excellent context for addressing such issues as whether an effect is real (i.e., reliable) and which theoretical/conceptual account best explains its occurrence.

It is my argument, however, that when one's concern with the compliance process is more than purely academic, as is the case for taxpayer noncompliance, a different investigatory approach is called for. That is, when the question of primary interest involves determining the *power* of possible influences upon naturally occurring compliance, the controlled experiment becomes ill suited to the job. By the "power" of such influences, I am referring to their ability to change compliance decisions meaningfully over a wide range of situations and circumstances.

Those factors that increase the rigor and precision of experimental procedures simultaneously decrease their utility for assessing the power of the effects they uncover. Because the best-designed experiments (1) eliminate or control away all sources of influence except the one under study and (2) possess highly sensitive measurement techniques, they may register whisperlike effects that may be so small as to never make a difference when other (extraneous) factors are allowed to vary naturally. What's more, such ecologically trivial effects can be replicated repeatedly in the antiseptic environment of the controlled experiment, giving the mistaken impression of power when, in reality, all that has been demonstrated are the reliability and (in the best of instances) the conceptual mediators of the effects. Regrettably, knowing that an effect is genuine and how to explain it will not tell us whether its impact on the course of natural compliance behavior is large enough to warrant our nonacademic attention.

This is not to say that sound experimental procedure is without import in any concern about the pragmatics of compliance. I hardly mean to suggest that, as the practical value of recognizing which effects are real and how they work is immeasurable. Rather, it appears that rigorous experimentation should not be used as the device for deciding which compliance-related influences are powerful enough to be submitted to rigorous experimentation. Some other way must be found to identify the potent influences on the compliance process. Only these selected influences, then, would be considered worthy candidates for subsequent experimental analysis and eventual implementation. Otherwise, valuable time could well be spent seeking to investigate and to apply effects that are merely epiphenomena of the experimental setting.

THE DEVELOPMENT OF POWERFUL COMPLIANCE INDUCERS

If it is granted that a program to identify the most powerful influences upon naturally occurring compliance should precede experimental examination of how to best understand and implement such influences, the critical question soon becomes "How does one determine which are the most powerful compliance principles and tactics?" One possible answer involves the systematic observation of the behaviors of commercial compliance professionals.

Who are the commercial compliance professionals and why should their actions be especially informative as to the identification of powerful influences upon everyday compliance decisions? They can be defined as those individuals whose business or financial well-being is dependent on their ability to induce compliance (e.g., salespeople, fundraisers, advertisers, political lobbyists, cult recruiters, con artists). With this definition in place, one can begin to recognize why the regular and widespread practices of these professionals would be noteworthy indicators of the powerful influences on the compliance process: because the livelihoods of commercial compliance professionals depend on the effectiveness of their procedures, those professionals who use procedures that work well to elicit compliance responses will survive and flourish. Further, they will pass these successful procedures on to succeeding generations (for example, trainees). However, those practitioners who use unsuccessful compliance procedures either will drop them or will quickly go out of business; in either case, the procedures themselves will not be passed on to newer generations.

The upshot of this process is that, over time and over the range of naturally occurring compliance contexts, the strongest and most adaptable procedures for generating compliance will rise, persist, and accumulate. Further, these procedures will point a careful observer toward the major principles that people use to decide when to comply. The observer must resist the temptation to find these generally effective procedures at any single time or in a particular compliance setting, profession, or practitioner. In any one of these specialized instances, the observer may find regular, idiosyncratic practices that are only effective there or then. The key for an observer wishing to identify the major principles governing the compliance process is the ubiquitousness of the compliance practices that tap into those principles for their power. That observer might well be advised, then, to begin the entire investigative process with an assessment of the cross-situational prevalence of compliance tactics over a range of diverse compliance professionals.

TRANSCENDENCY

Several years ago I resolved to become a careful observer of compliance issues. This decision meant that I should orient myself initially to the study of compliance professionals and that I should conduct this study in the natural environment. Accordingly, I embarked on an extended program of observation in which I took training or employment in a host of compliance professions wherein my true identity and purposes were unknown to those around me.[1] In this fashion, it was possible to learn which compliance procedures were being used and taught across an array of merchandising, advertising, direct sales, promotion, and fundraising concerns. These first-hand experiences were supplemented with information from other sources such as instructional materials (e.g., salesmanship texts, handbooks on lobbying techniques) and personal interviews with especially successful practitioners.

In the process, I sought to register overarching compliance principles. Consequently, an informal "transcendency index" was developed to rate the principles in regular use. The index consisted of ratings derived from four test questions:

Does the principle transcend forms? A truly general influence on the compliance process is likely to appear in a multitude of versions and variations. Therefore, principles that appeared in numerous tactical forms were given high marks by this criterion. For example, one principle scoring well in this regard was commitment/consistency, which serves as the basis for a variety of frequently employed compliance techniques (bait and switch, foot-in-the-door, four walls, low-ball, building agreements, among others), each of which works by generating an initial commitment in the target person that is logically consistent with compliance with a subsequent, related request.

Does the principle transcend professions? By the earlier described logic, the fundamental principles governing the influence process will have risen to prominence in all long-standing influence professions. What's more, the practices that activate those principles will have been carried by practitioners migrating from one influence profession to another. Consequently, the principles in use across the widest range of the professions I sampled were assigned "star" character here. The principle of social validation scored highest in this category.

Does the principle transcend practitioners? Principles that can be engaged effectively by most practitioners are sufficiently powerful and general to sustain their effects through the many differences in style, appearance, and experience of practitioners. So, if within a given profession (e.g., public relations) a certain principle (e.g., reciprocity) was employed almost universally by members of the profession, it was graded higher in my scoring system.

Does the principle transcend eras? Some practices have a history of success; they are traditional (e.g., appeals to scarcity). Those principles that have stood the test of time, that have survived the vagaries of fads, trends, zeitgeists, and changing economic conditions are to be considered noteworthy by my system. These are the principles that seem to engage persisting features of the human condition.

Which are the transcendent principles of influence by virtue of this analysis? Six stood out from the rest: commitment/consistency, reciprocity, social validation, authority, scarcity, and friendship/liking.[2] A full account of the origins, workings, and prevalence of the six principles is available elsewhere (Cialdini, 1988). However, for the purpose of this chapter, the first of these principles was selected for detailed treatment, as it appeared to hold the most promise for issues of taxpayer compliance. The remainder of the chapter is devoted to an extended examination of the principle of commitment/consistency, on the one hand, and to smaller treatments of the remaining five principles, on the other. Along with the description of a principle is presented a sample of common practitioner tactics that make use of the principle. In addition, the treatment of the principles includes an attempt to offer research findings relevant to the hows and whys of the compliance process. Finally, the discussion of each principle ends with a section designed to explore possible research directions or applications for taxpayer compliance, or both.

Before proceeding, two caveats are in order. First, my survey of compliance practices and settings was far from exhaustive. Therefore, the judgments of tactic prevalence from that survey must be seen as those of one investigator, made in a moderately large but not necessarily representative set of compliance contexts. More work by independent researchers in additional settings is needed to bolster confidence in my findings. Second, it is important to note that, although I describe below various tactics of commercial compliance professionals, I do not mean to imply the advisability of using many of these tactics to enhance taxpayer compliance. Rather, the tactics are presented mainly to document the relevance of a related psychological principle to naturally occurring compliance. It is the principles, engaged only by ethical and policy-consistent practices, that I wish to suggest can be applied with benefit to the problem of taxpayer noncompliance.

Commitment/Consistency

THE MOST APPLICABLE PRINCIPLE

Social psychological theorists have repeatedly noted that most people possess a strong desire to be consistent within their attitudes, beliefs, words, and deeds. Several of the most prominent of these theorists have incorporated the "strain" for consistency into their perspectives on important areas of human behavior, assigning it the role of prime motivator (e.g., Festinger, 1957; Heider, 1958; Newcomb, 1953). Recently, recognition has grown concerning a somewhat different type of consistency drive than the private, intrapersonal variety that concerned the early theorists. The desire to *appear* consistent is currently seen as having substantial influence over much human action as well (Baumeister, 1982; Tedeschi, 1981). According to this view, the appearance of personal consistency is a socially desirable thing, and individuals will be consistent with their prior pronouncements and actions (i.e., commitments) to project a positive public image.

It is not difficult to understand why the tendency to look and be consistent is so strong. First, good personal consistency is highly valued by other members of the society, whereas poor consistency is negatively valued. The former is commonly associated with such positive traits as stability, honesty, and intellectual strength. The latter, on the other hand, is often seen as indicative of such undesirable traits as indecisiveness, confusion, weakness of will, deceitfulness, or even mental illness. Second, aside from its effect on public image, generally consistent conduct provides a reasonable and gainful orientation to the world. Most of the time, we will be better off if our approach to the world is well laced with consistency. Without it our lives would be difficult, erratic, and disjointed. Finally, good personal consistency provides a valuable shortcut through the density of modern life. Once we have made up our minds about an issue or have decided how to act in a given situation, we no longer have to process all of the relevant information when subsequently confronted with the same (or highly similar) issue or situation. All we need do is recall the earlier decision and respond consistently with it. The advantage of such a shortcut should not be minimized. It allows us a convenient, relatively effortless method of dealing with our complex environments that make severe demands on our mental energies and capacities. In this sense, the commitment/consistency principle takes on rule of thumb or heuristic status and, as such, is especially likely to influence decisions made under conditions of uncertainty (Kahneman, Slovic, and Tversky, 1982) or cognitive overload (Cohen, 1978).

An implication of the commitment/consistency principle for compliance can be worded as follows: *After committing oneself to a position, one should be more willing to comply with requests for behaviors that are consistent with that position.* Thus, the pressure for consistency is engaged through the act of commitment. A variety of strategies may be used to produce the instigating commitment. Certain of these do so by asking for initial agreements that are quite small but nonetheless effective in stimulating later agreement with related, larger requests. One such start-small-and-build strategy is called the "four walls" technique. As far as I know it has never been experimentally investigated. Yet, it is a frequent practice of door-to-door salespeople, who use it primarily to gain permission to enter a customer's home. I first encountered it while training as an encyclopedia salesman. The technique consists of asking four questions to which the customer will be very likely to answer yes. To be consistent with the previous answers, the customer must then say yes to the crucial final question. In the encyclopedia sales situation I infiltrated, the technique proceeded as follows: *First wall,* "Do you feel that a good education is important to your children?" *Second wall,* "Do you think that a child who does his or her homework well will get a better education?" *Third wall,* "Don't you agree that a good set of reference books will help a child do well on homework assignments?" *Fourth wall,* "Well, then, it sounds like you'll want to hear about this fine set of encyclopedias I have to offer at an excellent price. May I come in?"

A similar start-small procedure is embodied in the much more re-searched foot-in-the-door technique. A solicitor using this technique will first ask for a small favor that is virtually certain to be granted. The initial compliance is then followed by a request for a larger, *related* favor. It has been found repeatedly that people who have agreed to the initial, small favor are more willing to do the larger one (see Beaman et al., 1983, for a review), seemingly to be consistent with the implication of the initial action.

Other, more unsavory techniques induce a commitment to an item and then remove the inducements that generated the commitment. Remarkably, the commitment frequently remains. For example, the bait and switch procedure is used by some retailers who may advertise certain merchandise (e.g., a room of furniture) at a special low price. When the customer arrives to take advantage of the special, he or she finds the merchandise to be of low quality or sold out. However, because customers have by now made an active commitment to getting new furniture at that particular store, they are more willing to agree to examine and, consequently, to buy higher-priced merchandise there. A similar strategy employed by car dealers is the low-ball technique, which proceeds by obtaining a commitment to an action and *then* increasing the costs of performing the action. The automobile salesperson who "throws the low ball" induces the customer to decide to buy a particular model car by offering a low price on the car or an inflated one on the customer's trade-in. After the decision has been made (and, at times, after the commitment is enhanced by allowing the customer to arrange financing or take the car home overnight, for example), something happens to remove the reason why the customer decided to buy. Perhaps a price calculation error is found, or the used-car assessor disallows the inflated trade-in figure. By this time, though, many customers have experienced an internal commitment to that specific automobile and proceed with the purchase. Experimental research (Cialdini et al., 1978; Burger and Petty, 1981) has documented the effectiveness of this tactic in settings beyond automobile sales. On the conceptual level, this research indicates that the tactic is effective primarily when used by a single requester and when the initial commitment is freely made.

A unitary feature of these procedures (and others like them) is the induction of a proper commitment that is consistent with a later action desired by the compliance professional. The need for consistency then takes over to compel performance of the desired behavior. Of course, not all behaviors constitute "proper commitments." However, there is research evidence suggesting the types of commitments that lead to consistent future responding. The present context does not allow sufficient space for a thorough discussion of that evidence. Nonetheless, I would argue that a fair summary of the research literature is that a commitment is likely to be maximally effective in producing consistent future behavior to the extent that it is active (Bem, 1967), effortful (Aronson and Mills, 1959), public (Deutsch and Gerard, 1955), and viewed as internally motivated (i.e., uncoerced, Freedman, 1965).

Another approach to employing the commitment/consistency principle is also popular among commercial compliance professionals. Rather than inducing a new commitment to their product or service, many practitioners point out existing commitments within potential customers that are consistent with a purchase of the product or service offered. In this way, desirable existing commitments are made more salient to the customer and the strain for consistency is allowed to direct behavior accordingly. For example, insurance agents are frequently taught to stress to new homeowners that the purchase of a $100,000 home reflects an enormous personal commitment to one's home and the well-being of one's family. Consequently, they argue, it would only be consistent with such a commitment to home and family to purchase home and life insurance in amounts that befit the size of this commitment. Research of various sorts indicates that this sort of sensitization to commitments and to consequent inconsistencies can be effective in producing belief and attitude change (e.g., McGuire, 1960). But the most impressive work in this regard related to value and behavior change comes from Milton Rokeach (Rokeach, 1971, 1973, 1975). Recently, Ball-Rokeach, Rokeach, and Grube (1984) demonstrated long-term behavioral effects from a television program that focused viewers' attention on their personal commitments to certain values (e.g., freedom, equality) on the one hand, and their current beliefs and behaviors, on the other. Not only did uninterrupted viewers of this single program evidence enhanced commitment to these values, but they were also significantly more likely to donate money to support causes consistent with the values two to three months after the program had aired.

The Ball-Rokeach et al. (1984) results are reminiscent of an underappreciated study in the tax compliance literature. Schwartz and Orleans (1967) found that subjects who were interviewed one month prior to the tax-filing deadline were subsequently most tax compliant when the interview directed their attention to values related to tax compliance (social responsibility, citizen obligation to government, patriotism, and personal integrity). Schwartz and Orleans (1967) also found evidence of increased compliance among interviewees whose interview dealt with the legal sanctions associated with noncompliance; but this effect was systematically smaller than that of the values-focused subjects.

POSSIBLE TAX COMPLIANCE APPLICATIONS/RESEARCH DIRECTIONS

As regards the matter of applying the commitment/consistency principle to the problem of tax evasion, one major approach seems most promising. That is, rather than attempting to induce in citizens commitments consistent with full and proper payment of taxes, the IRS would be better advised to work from existing commitments that would serve this purpose. This might be accomplished via a three-step process: (a) identifying existing norms/values within the citizenry that can be conceptualized as related to issues of tax payment; (b) focusing attention on these norms/values as existing personal commitments; and (c) sensitizing the citizenry to the inconsistency between possessing such personal commitments and failing to be fully tax compliant.

The established norms/values most associated conceptually with taxpayer compliance could be identified experimentally through paired-comparison or multidimensional scaling techniques. One study (Harvey and Enzle, 1981) has shown that such methods can be effectively used to determine the norms that individuals group together cognitively. Although the work has not yet been done, it is not hard to speculate as to which norms/values might emerge as related to tax compliance. On the positive side would be such concepts as social responsibility, personal integrity, paying one's way, and patriotism; on the negative side would be such concepts as cheating, stealing, lying, criminal action, harming others, and weakening the nation.

Once these norms/values had been identified, a process would be needed for making them salient, throughout society, and emphasizing that tax noncompliance would be inconsistent with them. To do so, I would suggest that the IRS produce a television program along the lines of Ball-Rokeach et al.'s "Great American Values Test" program. The IRS show might be called something like the "National Tax Test."[3] It would be aired one month prior to April 15 and would be designed to provide the public with information about tax changes, liabilities, credits, forms, and so forth. This could be done in a "score yourself" test format wherein viewers tested themselves on their tax knowledge and simultaneously gained information. This format and a prime time network television audience would allow the IRS to direct the attention of a large segment of the taxpaying public on the connection between existing norms/values and tax compliance. It would be important not to use the program to propagandize but, instead, to draw attention to any inconsistencies (or consistencies) between what people are genuinely committed to and some unrecognized implications of tax behavior. For instance, Moore (1983) has pointed out that most people have strong values against harming other people and against weakening the nation, but they may not register that tax cheating does both. A new understanding of these relationships could be easily raised through information presented during the show. The results should be salutary; for example, Grasmick (1985) has evidence that taxpayers who have come to believe that other people are harmed by tax evasion report more tax compliance. Similarly, by demonstrating that tax evasion is a form of lying, cheating, and in some instances, crime, the television program information would help the public perceive tax noncompliance as wrong. And as a variety of studies have shown (see Kinsey, 1984:39, for a review), those individuals who regard tax evasion as wrong are likely to be more compliant.

A second kind of vehicle for focusing taxpayer attention on existing norms/values associated with full and proper compliance might be the tax form itself. That tax form has allowed individuals to check a box that would give a dollar to political campaigns. Perhaps the range of options could be widened to include the chance to donate an amount to a fund to be used to detect tax cheating. For those who donated to the fund, a strong pro-compliance commitment would be instilled that should direct their tax behavior accordingly. For others, just the presence of such a question on the form would be beneficial in (a) associating tax evasion with the moral norm against cheating, (b) reminding taxpayers of the legal sanctions against tax cheating, and (c) causing people to wonder how many Americans will contribute to the cause, thereby raising the issue of social disapproval for tax cheating. These three factors of moral commitment, legal sanctions, and social disapproval are precisely those that Grasmick and Green (1980) argue constitute "a concise and probably exhaustive set of factors" leading to the inhibition of illegal behavior.

Another type of existing personal commitment that might be employed to stimulate tax compliance is self-image. With self-image (as opposed to norms/values), one is less concerned about what one would like to be and more concerned with what one is. It could well be that a properly devised survey would uncover several traits that are both rated central to the self-images of many citizens and highly associated with tax compliance (e.g., honesty, integrity, helpfulness to the needy, fairness). Such a survey could also determine the extent to which these traits are possessed differentially by identifiable subgroups in the population—business people, working-class individuals, women, retired citizens, and others. With such information, tax compliance efforts could be tailored (through the slogans, channels, places, and times most likely to affect these subgroups) for specific audiences. For instance, if it were found that personal integrity plays an important role in the self-concepts of most business owners, then messages and slogans might emphasize the extent to which a person of high personal integrity pays the proper amount of tax "even when nobody is looking."

Further, such messages and slogans should be disseminated via the channels of government contact with business people. Alternatively, if it were found that personal integrity is primarily part of the self-concept of the retired individual rather than the business person, integrity-based communications might be presented in television announcements during daytime hours.

Reciprocity

THE PRINCIPLE

According to sociologist Alvin Gouldner (1960), who made an extensive review of the subject, every human society abides by a norm for reciprocation that directs us to provide to others the sort of behaviors they have provided us. By virtue of the norm of reciprocation, we are *obligated* to the future repayment of favors, gifts, invitations, and the like. A widely shared feeling of future obligation made an enormous difference in human social evolution because it meant that one person could give something (food, energy, care) to another with confidence that it was not being lost. For the first time in evolutionary history, one individual could give away any of a variety of resources without actually giving them away. Thus, a person could provide help, gifts, defense, or trade goods to others in a group knowing that, when the time came, repayment would be made. Sophisticated and coordinated systems of gift-giving, defense, and trade became possible, bringing immense benefit to the societies that possessed them. With such clearly adaptive consequences for the culture, it is not surprising that the norm for reciprocation is so deeply implanted in us by the process of socialization we all undergo.

An implication of the reciprocity principle for compliance can be worded as follows: *One should be more willing to comply with a request to the extent that the compliance constitutes a reciprocation of behavior.* Under this general rule, then, people will be willing to return a favor with a favor (e.g., Regan, 1971). A number of sales and fundraising tactics use this factor to advantage. The compliance professional initially gives something to the target person, thereby causing the target to be more likely to give something in return. Often, this "something in return" is the target person's compliance.

The unsolicited gift, accompanied by a request for a donation, is a commonly used technique that employs the norm for reciprocation. One example experienced by many people is the Hare Krishna solicitor who gives the unwary passerby a book or a flower and then asks for a donation. Other organizations send free gifts through the mail; legitimate and less-than-legitimate missionary and disabled veterans' organizations often employ this highly effective device. These organizations count on the fact that most people will not go to the trouble of returning the gift and will feel uncomfortable about keeping it without reciprocating in some way. The organizations also count on the willingness of people to send a contribution that is larger than the cost of the gift they received.

Retail stores and services also make use of the powerful social pressure for reciprocation in their sales techniques. It is not uncommon to find exterminating companies that offer free home inspections. These companies bargain on the fact that, once confronted with the knowledge that a home is infested with termites, the customer who feels indebted to a particular company will buy its services to repay the favor of a free examination. Certain companies, knowing that the customer is unlikely to comparison shop, have been known to raise the quoted price of extermination above normal for those who have requested a "free" inspection.

A variation of the norm for reciprocation of favors is that for reciprocation of concessions. A reciprocal concessions procedure (or door-in-the-face technique) for inducing compliance has been documented by Cialdini et al. (1975). When one bargaining party retreats from an initial demand to a second, smaller one, social conventions require the other party to reciprocate that concession. This reciprocal concessions strategy has been successfully used for charitable solicitations. Cialdini and Ascani (1976) used this technique in soliciting blood donors. They first requested a person's involvement in a long-term donor program. When that request was refused, the solicitor made a smaller request for a one-time donation. This pattern of a large request followed by a concession significantly increased compliance with the smaller request, as compared to a control condition of people who were asked only to perform the smaller, one-time favor (50 percent versus 32 percent compliance rate).

Possible Tax Compliance Applications/Research Directions
In an attempt to engage the principle of reciprocity to inhibit tax cheating, the IRS may wish to publicize to a much greater extent the degree to which it provides free tax education and aid programs to the public: the Volunteer Income Tax Assistance Program, the Tax Counseling for the Elderly Program, the Disaster Assistance Program, the Outreach Program, the Small Business Tax Workshop Program, as well as general walk-in and

toll-free telephone tax assistance. The benefit character of these services could be emphasized by relating the amount of money the services would have cost if rendered privately and by informing the public that they are available "to you should you ever need them." To examine the public's awareness of and perceived importance of these services in their relation to tax compliance, an experiment might be conducted in the context of an anonymous tax information survey. The survey would describe the services and ask about awareness of them. These descriptions and questions would appear in the survey either before or after questions inquiring into estimated levels of future personal tax compliance. Support for the need to publicize the services to the public would come from a certain data pattern: respondents would estimate greater future tax compliance if the services were described before rather than after the compliance estimate. If this effect should occur, it would be instructive to note whether it appeared primarily in those respondents whose prior awareness of the services was low.

It might also be possible to employ the reciprocity rule via the process of reciprocal concessions. Rather than arranging the tax form so that taxable income is figured through a series of integrated income and deduction calculations, perhaps all income calculations could be treated first and totaled. Only then would credits, exemptions, and deductions be figured and subtracted from the income total.[4] In this fashion, the perception may accrue that credits, exemptions, and deductions are concessions made by the IRS. It might then occur that more scrupulous reporting of tax liabilities would result as a return concession. Such a possibility represents an interesting direction for research on tax form design.

Social Validation

THE PRINCIPLE

People frequently use the beliefs, attitudes, and actions of others, particularly similar others, as a standard of comparison against which to evaluate the correctness of their own beliefs, attitudes, and actions (see Festinger, 1954). Thus, it is common for individuals to decide on appropriate behaviors for themselves in a given situation by searching for information as to how similar others have behaved or are behaving. Powerful modeling effects of similar others have been found in both adults and children in such diverse activities as altruism (e.g., Hornstein, Fisch, and Holmes, 1968), phobia remission (e.g., Bandura and Menlove, 1968), and suicide (Phillips, 1974).

Normally, the tendency to see an action as appropriate when like others are doing it works quite well. As a rule, we make fewer mistakes by acting in accord with social evidence than contrary to it. As such, social validation allows us a convenient shortcut. By processing what similar people do, we can usually decide what we should do, with a minimum of effort.

As regards compliance, an implication of the social validation principle can be worded as follows: *People should be willing to comply with a request for specific behavior to the degree that similar others are or have been performing it.* Charitable and other nonprofit organizations frequently make use of social validation information to encourage people to donate. The master of ceremonies at a telethon typically reads incessantly from a handful of pledge cards. The cards are chosen to represent a cross section of the viewing public so that all may have evidence of the similarity of contributors to themselves. The message communicated to the holdouts is clear, "Look at all the people like you who have decided to give; it must be the correct thing to do." Church collection plates (as well as bartender's tip jars) are often "salted" beforehand with folding money to provide social validation for the donation of sizeable amounts. Evangelical preachers are known to seed their audiences with "ringers," who are rehearsed to come forward at a specified time to give witness and offerings. Research by Reingen (1982) has demonstrated that individuals shown lists of prior contributors are more likely to donate to charity; further, the longer the list the greater the effect.

Social validation techniques are also used extensively by profit-making organizations. Advertisers love to inform us that a product is the "largest selling" or "fastest growing." They do not have to convince us directly that the product is good; they need only imply that many others think so, and mass opinion seems proof enough. Salespeople are trained to spice their presentations with numerous accounts of individuals who have purchased the product. When individuals testify in writing to the product's effectiveness, these testimonials are collected and prominently displayed. As in nonprofit contexts, one's tendency to decide how to behave on the basis of others' behavior is most pronounced when the others are viewed as similar to oneself (Brock, 1965).

POSSIBLE TAX COMPLIANCE APPLICATIONS/RESEARCH DIRECTIONS

The relevance of the social validation principle to matters of tax compliance is suggested in a pair of survey findings: (a) admitted noncompliers are more likely to estimate high levels of noncompliance within the general public (Westat, Inc., 1980); and (b) there is a clear, positive relationship between self-reported evasion and the tax evasion of friends and relatives—that is, similar others (see Kinsey, 1984: 35–36 for a review). Although issues of causality are not unambiguous with regard to these findings, the results do suggest the importance of information concerning one's social milieu. Thus, it might be effective for the IRS to publicize more widely evidence suggesting that the great majority of Americans do not report cheating on their taxes (Yankelovich, Skelly, and White, 1984), even under conditions designed to guarantee anonymity (Aitken and Bonneville, 1980), and that the majority rate tax evasion as a serious crime (see Kinsey, 1984:39 for a review). Perhaps such information could be offered as part of the "National Tax Test" television program described earlier.

On the negative side, the social validation principle might frequently work against tax compliance. That is, if taxpayers believe there is even a significant minority of tax cheaters, they may be inclined to cheat as well because the act would have acquired some social validation. The best way for the IRS to deal with the perception that many others are cheating may not be to deny the fact but rather to try to neutralize it by presenting tax cheaters as dissimilar to most taxpayers. Theoretically (Festinger, 1954), such a view of cheaters as dissimilar to oneself would remove them as valid sources of information about the appropriateness of one's own actions.

Authority
THE PRINCIPLE
Authorities are extremely influential behavior models (see Aronson, Turner, and Carlsmith, 1963; Milgram, 1974). Whether they have acquired their positions through knowledge, talent, or fortune, those positions bespeak superior information and power. For each of us this has always been the case. Early on, these people (e.g., parents, teachers) knew more than we did, and we found that taking their advice proved beneficial—partly because of their greater wisdom and partly because they controlled our rewards and punishments. As adults, we have different authority figures—employers, judges, police officers, and the like—but the benefits associated with following them remain the same. For most people, then, conforming to the dictates of credible authority figures produces genuine practical advantages. Consequently, it makes great sense to comply with the wishes of credible authority.

An implication of the authority principle for compliance can be worded as follows: *One should be more willing to follow the directions of a credible authority.* Social psychological research into the question indicates that a credible authority possesses two major characteristics: expertise and trustworthiness (Myers, 1983). Demonstrating expertise can usually be accomplished by showing evidence of superior experience, training, or information; and advertisers frequently do so ("Babies are our business, our only business"; "Makers of award winning spirits since 1884"). Establishing trustworthiness is more difficult, as it involves convincing others that one is fair, straightforward, and unbiased. Nonetheless, generating trustworthiness is worth the effort; cross-cultural research has indicated that it is a more influential trait than expertise (McGuinnies and Ward, 1980).

POSSIBLE TAX COMPLIANCE APPLICATIONS/RESEARCH DIRECTIONS
Although the IRS clearly possesses the status of appointed authority, recent survey findings (Yankelovich et al., 1984) suggest that there may be a problem with its status as a credible authority. Only a small majority of the public agrees that the IRS and its staff are "expert/knowledgeable" (58 percent), while a distressingly large minority (37 percent) does not. The same is true for perceived trustworthiness (59 versus 38 percent). If nearly 40 percent of American citizens cannot ascribe such traits as expertise and trustworthiness to the IRS, there is a clear problem of credibility.[5]

It seems likely that this problem stems from the IRS's association with a tax system that the majority of the public considers complicated and unfair (Yankelovich et al., 1984). The complicated character of the system no doubt leads to errors and inconsistencies among IRS personnel in dealings with the public (or at least to the public's perception of such errors and inconsistencies), thereby undermining the perception of competence. The complexity of the system also allows for various "loopholes" that contribute to the view that the system is biased and unfair. In order to bring about a large-scale reduction in the credibility problem, it might be necessary to enact a sizeable simplification of the tax system, such as has been passed by Congress.

Short of such a wide-ranging change, IRS auditors might enhance their perceived credibility by beginning an interview with a point in the taxpayer's rather than the IRS's favor. This tactic of arguing initially against one's own interests has been shown to enhance persuasiveness (Walster, Aronson, and Abrahams, 1966), presumably by establishing an image of credibility that makes subsequent communications more impactful (Settle and Gorden, 1974). Perhaps an experimental simulation study could be conducted in which a point in the taxpayer's favor is made by the auditor at the outset instead of at the end of an interview. One would expect greater auditor credibility and success when this point is made first.

Scarcity

THE PRINCIPLE

As opportunities, and the items they present, become more scarce, they are perceived as more valuable. There seem to be two major reasons why, for the things we can have, scarcity increases attractiveness. First, it is normally the case that what is less available *is* more valuable. Precious metals and stones, for instance, are precious precisely because of their limited supply. The fundamental relationship between supply and assigned worth is so common that an item's availability can be taken as an indication of its value. Research by Worchel, Lee, and Adewole (1975) has provided data concerning how and when scarcity affects perceived value. They found that cookies were rated as more desirable, more attractive to consumers, and more costly when they were scarce rather than abundant. Furthermore, the effect was greater when the scarcity replaced previous abundance and when it was caused by social demand. Other research has suggested that in addition to commodities, information also becomes more desirable—and more influential—when access to it is limited (Brock, 1968; Fromkin and Brock, 1971). A recent test of Brock and Fromkin's thinking found good support in a business setting. Wholesale beef buyers who were told of an impending imported beef shortage purchased significantly more beef when they were told that information about the pending shortage came from certain "exclusive" contacts the importer had (Knishinsky, 1982). Apparently, the fact that the news itself was scarce made it more valued and persuasive.

A second reason why increased scarcity leads to increased attraction is that, as things become less available, free access to them decreases. According to Brehm's reactance theory (Brehm and Brehm, 1981), the loss of free access to an item increases the drive to have it. Thus, when increasing scarcity limits access to something, reactance is generated, causing people to want and to try to possess the thing more than before. Much laboratory evidence supports reactance theory predictions (Brehm and Brehm, 1981). In addition, some support has been found in naturally occurring settings.

For example, Mazis (1975) showed that newly limited access to a certain type of detergent enhanced its attractiveness for customers.

As regards compliance, an implication of the scarcity principle could be worded as follows: *One should want to try to secure those opportunities that are scarce.* With the scarcity principle operating powerfully on the worth assigned to things, it should not be surprising that compliance professionals have a variety of techniques designed to use this principle to enhance compliance. Probably the most frequently used such technique is the limited-number (or Standing Room Only) tactic in which the customer is informed that membership opportunities, products, or services exist in a limited supply that cannot be guaranteed to last for long. In some instances, the limited-number information is true; in others it is not. In each case, however, the intent is to convince prospects of an item's scarcity and thereby increase its immediate worth in their eyes.

Related to the limited-number tactic is the "deadline" technique in which an official time limit is placed on the customer's opportunity to get what is being offered. Newspaper ads abound with admonitions regarding the folly of delay: "last three days," "limited time offer," "one week only sale," and many more. The purest form of a decision deadline—right now—occurs in a variant of the deadline technique in which customers are told that, unless they make an immediate purchase decision, they will have to buy the item at a higher price or they will not be able to purchase it at all. This tactic is used in numerous compliance settings. A large child photography company urges parents to buy as many poses and copies as they can afford because "stocking limitations force us to burn the unsold pictures of your children within twenty-four hours." A prospective health club member or automobile buyer might learn that the deal offered by the salesperson is good for that one time only; should the customer leave the premises without buying, the deal is off.

Recall that in the Worchel et al. (1975) study scarcity was most effective when it was produced by social demand. This finding highlights the importance of competition in the pursuit of limited resources. We want a scarce item even more when we have to compete for it. Advertisers often try to commission this tendency in their behalf. In their ads, we see crowds pressing against the doors of a store before the start of a sale, or we watch a flock of hands quickly deplete a supermarket shelf of a product. There is much more to such images than the idea of ordinary social validation. The message is not just that the product is good because other people think so, but also that we are in direct competition with other people for it. Real estate agents are taught to convey a similar idea to hesitant customers. A realtor trying to sell a house to a fence-sitting prospect sometimes calls the prospect to say that another potential buyer (real or fabricated) has seen the house, likes it, and is scheduled to return the following day to talk about terms. The tactic, called in some circles "goosing them off the fence," works by turning a hesitant prospect into a competitor for a scarce resource.

POSSIBLE TAX COMPLIANCE APPLICATIONS/RESEARCH DIRECTIONS

One domain in which the application of the scarcity principle might be easy to implement is that of delinquencies. Many people are delinquent each year in providing various kinds of information (W-2/W-4 forms, taxpayer identification numbers, and so forth) and payments to the IRS. Rather than setting a single penalty fee or interest penalty percentage, the IRS might wish to establish a series of incremental penalty levels, each associated with a specific deadline. For example, instead of assessing interest penalties for delinquent payments at, say, 10 percent, such payments would be raised to 12 percent interest after a given period and to 15 percent after another deadline. Under this system, the time periods when lower penalty levels apply become limited and thereby more attractive for timely compliance. Reasoning from the Worchel et al. (1975) findings, a still more effective system would base a delinquent's penalty level on his or her speed of payment relative to other delinquents' speed. That is, a delinquent whose payment was received within the first third of payments received would pay a 10 percent interest penalty; should the payment be received before the next third of cases was resolved, the interest penalty would be 12 percent; and so on. Although such a system involving social competition might be theoretically more effective, it might prove too difficult to operate.

On a larger, less easy to implement plane, it might be that many individuals are noncompliant because they experience reactance, that is, the tendency to resist constraints on their freedom of action (Brehm and Brehm, 1981). Apparently, a change is being considered within IRS circles (Loftus, 1985) that could reduce some of this reactance. Conceivably, taxpayers could check on their tax forms areas of government to which amounts of their tax payments would go. The political reality of this suggestion aside, it would reduce reactance by providing the taxpayer more freedom and should, theoretically, enhance compliance.

Friendship/Liking

THE PRINCIPLE

A fact of social interaction that hardly needs belaboring is that people are favorably inclined toward those they know and like. A compliance implication of this tendency could be worded as follows: *One should be more willing to comply with the requests of friends or other liked individuals.* Compliance professionals make use of the tendency to comply with the requests of friends by enlisting the friends of prospects in the request presentation. The clearest illustration of this strategy that I know is the home party concept, made prominent by the Tupperware Corporation but now used to sell everything from cookware to lingerie.

But what do compliance professionals do when a friendship is not present for them to exploit? Here the professionals' strategy is quite direct: they induce their customers to like them. Tactics designed to generate liking occur in a variety of forms that cluster around certain factors that research has shown to increase liking: similarity (Byrne, 1971), praise (Byrne and Rhamey, 1965), and cooperation (Sherif et al., 1961).

The last of these factors, cooperation, has been shown to enhance positive feelings and behavior (see Aronson, Bridgeman, and Geffner, 1978; Cook, 1978) and seems most germane to issues of tax compliance. Those who cooperate toward the achievement of a common goal are more favorable and helpful to each other as a consequence. That is why compliance professionals often strive to be perceived as cooperating partners with a target person. Automobile sales managers frequently cast themselves as "villains" so that the salesperson can "do battle" in the customer's behalf. The cooperative, pulling-together kind of relationship that is consequently produced between the salesperson and the customer naturally leads to a form of liking that promotes sales. A related technique is employed by police interrogation officers to induce a suspect to confess to a crime. Called "good cop/bad cop," the tactic begins when a pair of interrogators confronts a suspect with vastly different styles. One officer (bad cop) takes a harsh, hard approach and pretends to try to bully the suspect into confessing. He then leaves the suspect alone with a second officer (good cop) who takes a soft, conciliatory approach. Good cop tries to convince the suspect that he does not approve of bad cop's style or methods and that he is allied with the suspect against bad cop. If he will only confess, good cop will work with the suspect to see that he gets fair treatment from the judicial system and that bad cop's threats of severe punishment will go unrealized. This cooperative orientation is often effective in winning trust and compliance from the suspect.

POSSIBLE TAX COMPLIANCE APPLICATIONS/RESEARCH DIRECTIONS

It might be possible to apply the cooperation component of the friendship/liking principle to matters of tax compliance. That is, there exists within the IRS system a program (the Problem Resolution Program) and certain people (Taxpayer Ombudsman and Problem Resolution Officers) charged with cooperating with and advocating for taxpayers toward the resolution of conflicts or difficulties. The functions of these individuals and the purpose of this program might well be more widely advertised to the taxpaying public, as they currently seem underrecognized. In addition, when an IRS advocate has intervened on behalf of a taxpayer's interests and some resolution of the problem has emerged, taxpayer compliance with that resolution would be increased if the advocate/cooperator had even a small role in any IRS request for taxpayer action; perhaps this could be accomplished, when appropriate, by having the advocate/cooperator write a cover letter or merely co-sign a letter asking for timely action. A test of this possibility could be provided through an experimental simulation study in which the likelihood of a taxpayer's full compliance with an IRS decision was assessed after a letter announcing the decision was either co-signed or not by an advocate for the taxpayer in the matter. It would also be instructive to vary in such a design the extent to which the advocate had been successful in creating certain IRS concessions to the taxpayer.

Conclusion

At the outset of this chapter, it was suggested that, because of the natural-selection-like pressures under which they work, much could be learned about the compliance process from an examination of the most pervasive practices of commercial compliance professionals. An analysis of the pervasiveness of such practices was argued to point a careful observer to the psychological principles that most powerfully influence naturally occurring compliance decisions. One such analysis, undertaken by the author, generated six major compliance principles: commitment/consistency, reciprocity, social validation, authority, scarcity, and friendship/liking.[6] The first of these principles, commitment/consistency, was given special attention, as it was judged most promising in its relation to tax compliance. But in all cases, attempts were made to find ways to apply the principles to tax compliance matters. It is perhaps instructive that in these attempts, the author had little difficulty in locating connections between each of the principles and tax compliance issues. The difficulty, instead, came in finding vehicles within the system for engaging the power of these principles. That is, there appears to be a dearth of appropriate channels for directly influencing taxpayers regarding compliance; and those that do exist tend to be oriented toward threats of sanctions (e.g., yearly information campaigns concerning tax prosecutions). For instance, in the process of searching for a proper vehicle for engaging commitment/consistency pressures toward tax compliance, it seemed necessary to invent one (the "National Tax Test" TV program).

If there is one overall recommendation that seems warranted in this regard, it is that a special program, staff, and budget be created (perhaps within the Office of Public Affairs) to seek out and create channels within the system for communicating directly with large segments of the public concerning the personal and social responsibilities (and benefits) of timely tax compliance.

Notes

1. In certain cases, a highly placed individual within an organization was informed of my research aims and cooperated both to conceal my identity and to arrange for a proper placement. In most instances, however, I remained incognito to all in an organization throughout my association with it. On leaving an organization, I gave a full revelation of my intent and identity, along with a promise that I would protect the organization's anonymity.
2. It should be noted that evidence for the pervasiveness of a seventh principle, material self-interest, was also abundant. Practitioners of all sorts frequently appealed to the desire to maximize one's material benefits and minimize one's material costs in their campaigns for compliance. However, I did not treat this principle in separate detail, as I considered it a motivational given and less interesting as a consequence. In this regard, and with special relevance to taxpayer compliance, I concur with Alfred Blumstein (1983:171) that, although material sanctions are important, "primary attention must be directed at maintaining the integrity of the social contract under which compliance is motivated internally rather than by external coercion." Nonetheless, the important impact of material sanctions cannot be dismissed (Grasmick and Green, 1980).
3. Several programs of this sort have been produced in the past, some of which, the "National Drivers Test," for example, proved very successful in drawing top ratings.
4. John T. Scholz of the National Research Council's Panel on Compliance Research is to be credited with this suggestion.
5. This is especially so when one recognizes that there are no data collected on the percentage of Americans who view the IRS as *both* expert and trustworthy—the

combination of traits that constitutes credibility—but that this percentage is likely to be lower than that for either trait considered alone.

6. See Note 2.

References

Aitken, S. S., and Bonneville, L.
  1980 A General Taxpayer Opinion Survey. Prepared for the Office of Planning and Research, Internal Revenue Service, March 1980, by CSR Incorporated, Washington, D.C. (Contract No. TIR-79-2)

Aronson, E., Bridgeman, D. L., and Geffner, R.
  1978 The effects of a cooperative classroom structure on students' behavior and attitudes. In D. Bar-Tal and L. Saxe, eds., *Social Psychology of Education: Theory and Research.* Washington, D.C.: Hemisphere.

Aronson, E., and Mills, J.
  1959 The effect of severity of initiation on liking for a group. *Journal of Abnormal and Social Psychology* 59: 177–181.

Aronson, E., Turner, J. A., and Carlsmith, J. M.
  1963 Communication credibility and communication discrepancy as a determinant of opinion change. *Journal of Abnormal and Social Psychology* 67:31–36.

Ball-Rokeach, S., Rokeach, M., and Grube, J. W.
  1984 *The Great American Values Test.* New York: Free Press.

Bandura, A., and Menlove, F. L.
  1968 Factors determining vicarious extinction of avoidance behavior through symbolic modeling. *Journal of Personality and Social Psychology* 8:99–108.

Beaman, A. L., Cole, C. M., Preston, M., Klentz, B., and Sleblay, N. H.
  1983 A meta-analysis of fifteen years of foot-in-the-door research. *Personality and Social Psychology Bulletin* 9:181–196.

Baumeister, R. F.
  1982 A self-presentational view of social phenomena. *Psychological Bulletin* 91: 3–26.

Bem, D. J.
  1967 Self-perception: An alternative interpretation of cognitive dissonance phenomena. *Psychological Review* 74:183–200.

Blumstein, A.
  1983 Models for structuring taxpayer compliance. Pp. 159–172 in P. Sawicki, ed., *Income Tax Compliance: A report of the ABA Section on Taxation, Invitational Conference on Income Tax Compliance.* Washington, D. C.: American Bar Association.

Brehm, S. S., and Brehm, J.
  1981 *Psychological Reactance.* New York: Academic Press.

Brock, T. C.
  1965 Communicator-recipient similarity and decision change. *Journal of Personality and Social Psychology* 1:650–654.
  1968 Implications of commodity theory for value change. Pp. 243–273 in A. G. Greenwald, T. C. Brock, and T. M. Ostrom, eds., *Psychological Foundations of Attitudes*. New York: Academic Press.
Burger, J. M., and Petty, R. E.
  1981 The low-ball technique: task or person commitment. *Journal of Personality and Social Psychology* 40:492–500.
Byrne, D.
  1971 *The Attraction Paradigm*. New York: Academic Press.
Byrne, D., and Rhamey
  1965 Magnitude of positive and negative reinforcements as a determinant of attraction. *Journal of Personality and Social Psychology* 2:884–889.

Cialdini, R. B.
  1988 *Influence: Science and Practice*. Second edition. Chicago: Scott, Foresman and Company
Cialdini, R. B., and Ascani, K.
  1976 Test of a concession procedure for inducing verbal, behavioral, and further compliance with a request to give blood. *Journal of Applied Psychology* 61(3):295–300.
Cialdini, R. B., Cacioppo, J. T., Bassett, R., and Miller, J. A.
  1978 Low-ball procedure for producing compliance: Commitment then cost. *Journal of Personality and Social Psychology* 36:463–476.
Cialdini, R. B., Vincent, J. E., Lewis, S. K., Catalan, J., Wheeler, D., and Darby, B. L.
  1975 Reciprocal concessions procedure for inducing compliance: the door-in-the-face technique. *Journal of Personality and Social Psychology* 31:206–215.
Cohen, S.
  1978 Environmental load and allocation of attention. In A. Baum, J. E. Singer, and S. Valins, eds., *Advances in Environmental Psychology* Vol. 1. Hillsdale, N.J.: Lawrence Erlbaum Associates
Cook, S. W.
  1978 Interpersonal and attitudinal outcomes in cooperating interracial groups. *Journal of Research and Development in Education* 12:28–38.

Deutsch, M., and Gerard, J. H.
  1955 A study of normative and individual judgments. *Journal of Abnormal and Social Psychology* 51:629–636.

Festinger, L.
  1954 A theory of social comparison processes. *Human Relations* 2:117–140.
  1957 *A Theory of Cognitive Dissonance*. Stanford, Calif.: Stanford University Press.
Freedman, J.
  1965 Long-term behavioral effects of cognitive dissonance. *Journal of Experimental Social Psychology* 1:145–155.

Fromkin, H. L., and Brock, T. C.
  1971   A commodity theory analysis of persuasion. *Representative Research in Social Psychology* 2:47–57.
Gouldner, A.
  1960   The norm of reciprocity. *American Sociological Review* 25:161–178.
Grasmick, H. G.
  1985   Personal correspondence to Frank Malanga, Internal Revenue Service, with memo on Oklahoma City Survey. Dated February 13.
Grasmick, H. G., and Green, D. E.
  1980   Legal punishment, social disapproval and internalization of inhibitors of illegal behavior. *Journal of Criminal Law and Criminology* 71(3):325–335.
Harvey, M. D., and Enzle, M. E.
  1981   A cognitive model of social norms for understanding the transgression-helping effect. *Journal of Personality and Social Psychology* 41:866–875.
Heider, F.
  1958   *The Psychology of Interpersonal Relations*. New York: John Wiley & Sons.
Hornstein, H. A., Fisch, E., and Holmes, M.
  1968   Influence of model's feeling about his behavior and his relevance as a comparison other on observers' helping behavior. *Journal of Personality and Social Psychology* 10:222–226.
Kahneman, D., Slovic, P., and Tversky, A. eds.
  1982   *Judgment Under Uncertainty: Heuristics and Biases*. Cambridge: Cambridge University Press.
Kinsey, K. A.
  1984   Survey Data on Tax Compliance: A Compendium and Review. American Bar Foundation Tax Compliance Working Paper 84-1, December 1984. American Bar Foundation, Chicago.
Knishinsky, A.
  1982   The Effects of Scarcity of Material and Exclusivity of Information on Industrial Buyer Perceived Risk in Provoking Purchase Decisions. Unpublished Ph.D. dissertation, Department of Marketing, Arizona State University.
Loftus, E. F.
  1985   To file, perchance to cheat. *Psychology Today* (April): 35–39.
Mazis, M. B.
  1975   Antipollution measures and psychological reactance theory: A field experiment. *Journal of Personality and Social Psychology* 31:654–666.
McGuinnies, E., and Ward, C. D.
  1980   Better liked than right: trustworthiness and expertise as factors in credibility. *Personality and Social Psychology Bulletin* 6:467–472.
McGuire, W.
  1960   Cognitive consistency and attitude change. *Journal of Abnormal and Social Psychology* 60:345–353.
Milgram, S.
  1974   *Obedience to Authority*. New York: Harper & Row.
Moore, M. H.
  1983   On the office of taxpayer and the social process of taxpaying. Pp. 275–292

in P. Sawicki, ed., *Income Tax Compliance: A Report of the ABA Section on Taxation, Invitational Conference on Income Tax Compliance*. Washington, D.C.: American Bar Association.

Myers, D. G.
  1983   *Social Psychology*. Glenview, Ill.: Scott, Foresman and Co.

Newcomb, T. M.
  1953   An approach to the study of communicative acts. *Psychological Bulletin* 60:393–404.

Phillips, D. P.
  1974   The influence of suggestion on suicide: substantive and theoretical implications of the Werther effect. *American Sociological Review* 39:340–354.

Regan, D. T.
  1971   Effects of a favor and liking on compliance. *Journal of Experimental Social Psychology* 7:627–639.

Reingen, P. H.
  1982   Test of a list procedure for inducing compliance. *Journal of Applied Psychology* 67:110–118.

Rokeach, M.
  1971   Long-range experimental modification of values, attitudes, and behavior. *American Psychologist* 26:453–459.
  1973   *The Nature of Human Values*. New York: Free Press.
  1975   Long-term value change initiated by computer feedback. *Journal of Personality and Social Psychology* 32:467–476

Schwartz, R. D., and Orleans, S.
  1967   On legal sanctions. *University of Chicago Law Review* 34:274–300.

Settle, R. B., and Gorden, L. L.
  1974   Attribution theory and advertiser credibility. *Journal of Marketing Research* 11:181–185.

Sherif, M., Harvey, O. J., White, B. J., Hood, W. R., and Sherif, C. W.
  1961   Intergroup Conflict and Cooperation. University of Oklahoma Institute of Intergroup Relations. Unpublished paper, Norman, Okla.

Tedeschi, J. T., ed.
  1981   *Impression Management Theory and Social Psychological Research*. New York: Academic Press.

Walster, E., Aronson, E., and Abrahams, D.
  1966   On increasing the persuasiveness of a low prestige communicator. *Journal of Experimental Social Psychology* 2:325–342.

Westat, Inc.
  1980   Self-Reported Tax Compliance: A Pilot Survey Report. Prepared for the Internal Revenue Service, March 21, 1980, by Westat, Inc., Rockville, Md.

Worchel, S., Lee, J., and Adewole, A.
  1975   Effects of supply and demand on ratings of object value. *Journal of Personality and Social Psychology* 32:906–914.

Yankelovich, Skelly, and White, Inc.
   1984   Taxpayer Attitudes Study: Final Report. Public opinion survey prepared
           for the Public Affairs Division, Internal Revenue Service, December,
           1984, by Yankelovich, Skelly, and White, Inc., New York.

John S. Carroll

8. A Cognitive-Process Analysis of Taxpayer Compliance

The purpose of this chapter is to explore the usefulness of a cognitive approach to taxpayer compliance. The assumption is made that taxpayers make compliance-relevant *decisions* about reporting, filing, listing income, claiming deductions, and so forth, and that this decision-making metaphor can be useful as a general mode of taxpayer behavior.

The federal government is supported by income taxes. About 53 percent of federal tax revenues comes from individual income taxes and another 11 percent from corporate income taxes (IRS, 1985:21). Noncompliance arises in several basic ways: failure to file a return, underreporting of (legal or illegal) income, overstating deductions, and refusing to pay what is owed. For 1981, the IRS estimated that noncompliance with the tax code created lost revenues of $81.5 billion, enough to pay the national deficit for that year (IRS, 1983). Both IRS estimates and survey results of self-reported tax cheating show that noncompliance increased substantially in the late 1970s (Kinsey, 1984). There is no question that noncompliance is a serious problem that creates financial costs and furthers a climate of disrespect, antagonism, and selfishness in the relationships between citizen and polity. Recognition of this problem led to the creation of the taxpayer compliance panel at the National Research Council.

If we consider taxpaying behaviors to be the result of purposive decision-like cognitive processes, then theories of decision making become relevant to explaining why taxpayers comply or fail to comply with the tax requirements. The basic premise of decision models is that people have preferences and choose alternatives so as to achieve preferred outcomes. I will first describe decision models based on utility maximization, beginning with concepts of economic rationality. Economists consider utility theory

Sloan School of Management, Massachusetts Institute of Technology.

to be a description of individual behavior, an equilibrium toward which behavior tends in the long run. Psychologists treat utility models as a standard or prescription of rational behavior against which actual behavior is compared (e.g., papers in Kahneman, Slovic, and Tversky, 1982). Considerable research has been devoted to testing utility models against actual behavior, compiling characteristic "errors" or "biases" defined in terms of the utility model, and seeking refinements of the utility model that would better describe the strategic and heuristic aspects of actual decision making. In the second section of this chapter, I depart from positivist testing and modification of utility models and explore, with a finer-grained cognitive approach based on an understanding of the operation and limitations of the human mind, what goes on in the minds of taxpayers. Decision heuristics uncovered by this approach are discussed, including some new thoughts about hierarchical and intertemporal decision making. Research directions are suggested that use the cognitive approach to pose policy-relevant questions about taxpayer decisions and behaviors.

Utility-Maximizing Models of Decision Making

EXPECTED UTILITY

The standard economic model of decision making specifies that decisions maximize expected utility. The expected utility of any decision alternative is assessed by identifying the possible consequences or outcomes, assigning a desirability or utility to each outcome, and attaching likelihoods to uncertain outcomes. Each outcome is multiplied by its likelihood and the weighted or discounted outcomes are summed to create the expected utility of that alternative. The alternative with the most favorable expected utility is then selected and implemented.

For example, a taxpayer may be considering an illegal deduction of an amount that reduces his tax by $100 and judges the probability of audit to be 5 percent. If audited, the taxpayer would have to pay the $100 plus a penalty of 50 percent of the taxes owed ($50). If we ignore interest rates and treat the taxpayer as risk-neutral, then the expected utility analysis would involve two alternatives: (1) not taking the deduction, in which case the result is some current wealth state, W, and (2) taking the deduction, which can result in two outcomes—W plus $100 if the taxpayer is not audited, and W minus $50 if the taxpayer is audited. The expected utility of being honest is simply $U(W)$, and the expected utility of cheating is $.95[U(W+100)]+.05[U(W-50)]$. For the risk-neutral taxpayer, we can assume that $U(W)=0$ and $U(W+X)=X$ for convenience, and the result is that the expected utility of being honest is 0, compared to 92.5 for cheating. The taxpayer therefore cheats.

The expected utility formulation allows for risk attitudes to be represented in the shape of the utility function. A concave shape implies risk aversion (actually, the concave shape confounds risk aversion and diminishing marginal return for money [Schoemaker, 1982]). A risk-averse person would refuse a fair bet such as a coin toss for $1, because the added utility of the extra dollar is smaller in magnitude than the subtracted utility of losing. A convex shape represents risk seeking, and such a person would take the bet because the possible added utility is greater than the equally possible subtracted utility. It is possible to generate an extremely risk-averse utility function that would lead the potential tax cheat above to comply, even though he or she has only a 5 percent chance of being audited and faces a relatively small loss.

The same kind of analysis has applied the normative economic model to criminal behavior (e.g., Becker, 1968). Failure to comply with the tax laws can be considered a form of criminal behavior. Criminal behavior, and property crimes in particular, have been viewed by many social scientists as rational acts resulting when individuals evaluate the expected utility of both criminal and noncriminal activities, and then choose the alternative with the highest net payoff. Thus, if the gains of tax cheating or any form of criminal behavior outweigh the risks, then people will cheat on their taxes or commit the appropriate crime. This viewpoint suggests that tax cheating could be deterred by increasing the risks involved (e.g., more surveillance, harsher penalties [e.g., Blumstein, 1983]).

EXTENDING THE UTILITY MODEL

The same analysis is able to accommodate other, nonmonetary consequences associated with each alternative. For example, being honest may carry positive self-evaluations (pride) or negative self-evaluations (feeling like a sap, regret), whereas cheating may make people feel competent and stimulated if they succeed, or guilty and anxious if they are caught. Other consequences such as the regard of friends, reputation, going to jail, losing one's job, and becoming a tax consultant can be accommodated by assigning them a utility (either a monetary equivalent or a satisfaction score). The consequences do not even have to involve self-interest: positive utility could be assigned to the use of one's money by the government to provide services, or to the moral impact of a "tax revolt" on wasteful government spending (see Sears and Citrin, 1982). In such a way all consequences are made measurable and commensurable, without changing the underlying logic of calculating expected utility. A more complicated analysis considers that these outcomes may be different in kind, requiring a multiattribute utility (Keeney and Raiffa, 1976). Instead of a single utility dimension, there is instead a utility space permitting more complex trade-offs and interactions among types of utility.

Utility analyses can also be extended like a decision tree to consider sequences of probabilistic outcomes. For example, a sophisticated taxpayer might consider the likelihood of being audited, and the consequences of an audit might be partially certain (e.g., having to gather records and write letters) and partially risky (will the IRS disallow a particular deduction?). If the IRS disallows a deduction, several outcomes are possible (pay the tax on it, pay the tax plus fine, pay the tax plus large fine, pay and go to jail). If more severe penalties are experienced, additional consequences are possible, such as public disapproval, loss of friends, loss of business income or job. Additional choices may reside on branches of this tree, such as the options available if one is audited and fined (pay the fine, appeal, conceal it from friends, leave town, among others). The complete assessment of these complex scenarios would be quite difficult, and it is not surprising that such analyses are often the province of professionals called decision analysts who aid decision makers to structure decision problems and work them through to a conclusion. It is interesting to note that decision analysts consider their contribution to be the process of structuring and restructuring a problem rather than the computational aspects of calculating an "answer" (Keeney and Raiffa, 1976).

UTILITY-LIKE MODELS

Formal utility theories offer axiomatic mathematical justification for their structure. However, many other models have been developed that have some of the same components or structure as the formal models, but lack the axiomatic basis. These are considered useful descriptive models of decision making. We will discuss two families of these utility-like theories: expectancy theories and policy-capturing threories.

Expectancy theories propose, as does utility theory, that people seek desired outcomes and weight these outcomes by their likelihood. For example, the theory of reasoned action (Ajzen and Fishbein, 1980) proposes that behavior is determined by intentions to enact that behavior which arise from two components: attitude and norms. Attitude toward the behavior is computed in utility-like fashion as the product of the likelihood that the behavior will produce a consequence multiplied by the favorability of the consequence, summed over all relevant consequences. Norms are also computed in utility-like fashion as the product of the likelihood that salient referent others or groups think a person should enact the behavior multiplied by the motivation to comply with their wishes, summed over all relevant referent others. Relevant consequences and salient referent others are elicited from groups of respondents using consensus and common sense as criteria for identification. Although the particular mechanics of the questions and formulae are different from formal utility theory, the net result is to propose that people choose behaviors that maximize a combination of expected personal and interpersonal consequences.

There are many varieties of expectancy theories (see Feather, 1982; Porter and Lawler, 1968; Vroom, 1964) that direct attention to many of the same variables and have similar multiplicative form. They propose that people are motivated to perform behaviors that are expected to lead to desirable consequences. There is no doubt that such theories are good predictors of behavior or that people generally seek favorable consequences.

Policy-capturing models of decision making predict decisions from linear combinations of input cues or judgmental dimensions, often using multiple regression as an analytic procedure for revealing the functional relationships between cues and decisions (Hammond et al., 1975; Slovic and Lichtenstein, 1971). The weights associated with dimensions, whether empirically derived or directly elicited, are considered to represent the relative importances of the dimensions, or the decision maker's "policy." The "dimensions" of policy-capturing models are abstractions or correlates of the "consequences" of utility theories. For example, in choosing a tax preparer, policy-capturing models could include cues such as quality of firm, reputation, and training, which serve as proxies for the consequences of amount of tax to pay and risk of various penalties.

Whereas formal utility theories begin with the multiplicative model specified by theory, policy-capturing studies usually begin with a simpler linear model and typically find that more complex terms (configural judgments) offer little extra explanatory power. Thus, returning to our example of a person considering cheating on his tax return, the policy-capturing approach might first try a model treating penalty and likelihood of audit as separate dimensions that are weighted and added. An additional cross-product term would be tested to see if it helped explain judgments or decisions. In this fashion, studies of the evaluation of crime opportunities in terms of dimensions of probability and consequences find additive relationships rather than the multiplicative terms required in utility theory (Carroll, 1978, 1982).

In considering these various models, the real issue is the extent to which a particular model is correct in its details and whether any discrepancies matter. This depends on what the model is being used for: is it meant to predict aggregate behavior or individual behavior, or to correspond to the *process* by which individuals make decisions? Paramorphic models (Hoffman, 1960) are good predictors but do not reproduce the process or mechanisms by which the behavior came about. Various combinations of so many intuitively reasonable predictors are bound to correlate with behavior, particularly when cues are positively correlated with each other (see Dawes and Corrigan, 1974, on strength of linear models). Rather specific and data-intensive tests may be necessary to distinguish among models (e.g., experiments and functional measurement [Anderson, 1981]). For example, determining whether the combination of probabilities and consequences is additive or multiplicative might require either lots of well-controlled data or careful study of the domain where the probability of a consequence reached zero. A model that predicts everyone cheats a little more when the economy is worse may predict aggregate tax revenues as well as does a model that explains the outcomes as an increase in specific categories of tax cheaters, but these models have different policy implications.

Policy Implications

If taxpayers are maximizing utility, then the way to ensure compliance is to make the expected utility of reporting and paying appropriate taxes higher than the expected utility of various forms of noncompliance. The deterrence hypothesis does this by increasing the costs of noncompliance through surveillance and penalties. For example, Blumstein (1983) argues that the penalties for overstating deductions or failing to report income are far too low. If taxpayers perceive a 5 percent chance of discovery, then discovery should carry a penalty twenty times the taxes saved to deter a risk-neutral tax cheat. Other unpleasant consequences could be added on to the discovery process, such as public disclosure, seizure of property, nasty audit examiners, or whatever. Of course, the risk is a full-blown war between tax cheats, sympathizers, and the government (U.S. Congress,

1983: 47). More audits, withholding, and reporting requirements, and "Big Brother" data files that cross-check taxpayers with reports of income sources, charities, utility companies, and so forth seem necessary to increase the risk of detection. However, such tactics may only create a larger underground economy and less visible ways to cheat (Kagan, this volume, Chapter 3). There are extreme structural changes that would greatly curtail the opportunity for tax cheating: making tips or barter nontaxable, eliminating deductions, going to an all plastic economy (no cash) with central reporting of all transactions, and so forth.

It is also possible to make tax cheating less beneficial (lower the tax rates) or to make compliance less costly (simpler forms) and more beneficial (increase the value of services received for tax money [Kinsey, 1984:4]).

If we turn our attention to multiattribute utility theories that identify nonmonetary outcomes (e.g., Ajzen and Fishbein, 1980), the question becomes, "What outcomes are taxpayers seeking or avoiding by complying or not complying?" It appears, for example, that concepts of fairness are important to taxpayers and that the tax laws do not jibe with common ideas of fairness. The same failure to list a cash transaction could be motivated by greed, a belief that one's taxes are too high, a comparison with others who do not report such transactions, a desire for redress for the imposition of the tax laws, or simple laziness.

BEHAVIORAL DECISION THEORY

Utility theory posits a high degree of rationality. Taxpayers and tax cheaters are expected to gather information relevant to risks and benefits, and combine this information in a systematic way (e.g., weight the desirability of outcomes by their probabilities of occurrence and add).

This view of rationality and human behavior has been challenged in the past several decades by researchers who believe human rationality is severely limited. Beginning with Simon (1945, 1955, 1957), a field of study has developed primarily within psychology that examines human behavior as intendedly rational but limited in attention, memory, and computational capability. This information-processing or cognitive school examines the ways in which human cognitive functions are limited, the mechanisms for achieving adequate performance within these limits, and the consequences for behavior.

March and Simon (1958), March (1978), Fischhoff, Goitein, and Shapira (1983) and others have identified assumptions underlying economic utility theories that seem to require overly rational behavior. First, economists assume that preferences change slowly relative to incentives. However, decision researchers have suggested that preferences may be very unstable (Fischhoff et al., 1980), may be the *result* of decisions rather than their cause (Festinger, 1957; Weick, 1977), or may stabilize only after considerable experience (Schein, 1978). Second, utility theory assumes that *all* alternatives are considered, evaluated, and compared so that the best can be chosen. However, beginning with the satisficing rule proposed by Simon (1955), behavioral decision theorists have suggested that only a limited set of alternatives is considered, that search may stop when a satisfactory alternative is found, and that information about each alternative may be evaluated by rules other than expected utility, such as comparison against criteria or some other noncompensatory strategy (Einhorn, 1970; Montgomery, 1983; Tversky, 1969). Third, numerous researchers have remarked on the difficulty people have in dealing with probabilities (Tversky and Kahneman, 1974). Although the concept of weighting outcomes by probabilities seems clear in utility theory, the way people actually respond to probability does not seem to follow the calculus of probability (Kahneman and Tversky, 1979; Einhorn and Hogarth, 1985).

The rapidly developing literature known as behavioral decision theory is replete with empirical demonstrations that people violate the asssumptions of economic utility theory (for reviews see, e.g., Slovic, Fischoff, and Lichtenstein, 1977; Kahneman et al., 1982; Hogarth, 1980). For example, simple gamble pairs can be constructed in which one gamble offers a high probability of winning a small amount and the other offers a low probability of winning a large amount. When asked to bid to play each gamble once, people typically bid more for the one with a large potential gain. However, when asked to choose which they would play if they could only play one, they choose the one where they are most likely to win. Such a discontinuity between choices and bids is inconsistent with any normative rationality. These errors persist when people are rewarded with money for good performance (Grether and Plott, 1979) or when actual gamblers in Las Vegas casinos play the same gambles on roulette wheels for real money (Lichtenstein and Slovic, 1973).

A particularly detailed and applicable use of behavioral decision theory was a study of the failure to buy federally subsidized flood insurance (Kunreuther et al., 1978). According to utility principles, this insurance was offered at highly favorable rates, asuming that residents had accurate risk and cost data and combined them to maximize utility. However, a national survey of flood-prone areas revealed that residents assessed their risks and costs differently from the experts. Some of these differences arose from judgmental biases discussed later. However, even considering residents' *own* assessments, those who bought insurance and those who did not exhibited similar distributions of expected utility. Instead, it appeared that residents' purchasing decisions depended on informal decision rules such as whether neighbors and relatives bought insurance, what their insurance agent said, and whether they could tolerate another thing to worry over.

Rather than summarize the behavioral decision theory literature, I will review research on a specifically relevant domain showing that criminal behavior is governed by mental processes somewhat different from utility models.

BEHAVIORAL RESEARCH ON CRIMINAL DECISION MAKING

Conceptually, we may divide the decision process of a potential criminal into intelligence (information gathering) and choice (use of rules to turn information into a decision). Several studies have given potential criminals the information presumed necessary for evaluating a crime opportunity and have examined the choice rule that was followed. Research that manipulated the amount of gain, likelihood of gain, severity of punishment, and likelihood of punishment in hypothetical crime situations found that subjects are sensitive to these variables but do not combine them into the interaction terms (representing the expected risks and payoffs) necessary for computing expected utility (reviewed in Carroll, 1982). Carroll (1978) conducted individual-level analyses and found that responses to the information were essentially additive. Many subjects focused on only one dimension and either ignored the others or made minor adjustments based on one or two other dimensions. Only 41 percent of subjects were responsive to the likelihood of capture; 60 percent to the likelihood of success; 67 percent to the penalty; and 84 percent to the available money. These data suggest very strong "dimensional preferences" (Slovic and Lichtenstein, 1968) *and* a tremendous difficulty combining multiple pieces of relevant information into a single judgment. These results are quite consistent with decision behavior in other domains such as clinical psychology and medicine, where experienced decision makers exhibit considerable inconsistency, dissensus, and use of simple additive rules rather than the complex configural rules they claim to use (e.g., Camerer, 1980; Goldberg, 1970; Johnson et al., 1982).

Other research suggests that potential criminals not only fail to use a rational choice rule, but also fail to gather appropriate information. The

Assembly Committee on Criminal Procedure (1975) studied knowledge of criminal penalties and concluded, "It appears that knowledge of penalties can not act as deterrents since these are unknown until after a person has committed a crime or become a prisoner" (p. 78). Paternoster et al. (1982) report a panel study showing that behavior more strongly determines perceptions of risk than perceptions influence behavior. Research on tax-payers also shows various misconceptions, including overassessments of the likelihood of audit and misconceptions about the role of the IRS in tax law creation (Aitken and Bonneville, 1980; ICF, 1985).

The above studies suggest that potential criminals (and people in general) are deficient in their ability to evaluate alternative courses of action. However, other criminological research suggests that experienced criminals have a great deal of technical and interpersonal skill and knowledge relevant to specific crime opportunities. Interviews with experienced criminals suggest that certainty and severity of punishment are not static properties of crime, but rather are under partial control of the criminal. Criminals are expert at controlling or minimizing risk. Thus, it makes little sense to ask the abstract question; "What is the probability that a burglar will get caught on a particular attempt?" although statistics exist to compute such a probability by estimating number of burglaries and burglars caught. It makes more sense to ask, "How do you keep from getting caught?" The criminal's skill in leaving no evidence that will stand up in court, in manipulating the legal system through bargains and bribes, in setting up and carrying out crimes and disposing of the gains is indicative that an experienced criminal faces different opportunities and sanctions than does an amateur (Inciardi, 1975; Letkemann, 1973). This research is consistent with studies showing that people will accept risks they consider controllable, such as driving a car, far in excess of risks they consider uncontrollable, such as environmental carcinogens (Slovic et al., 1980; Starr, 1969).

This viewpoint is, in fact, consistent with the research on expert decision making. Experts are viewed as *knowing* a great deal, but being unable to apply or combine that knowledge in a sufficiently systematic way. Thus, "bootstrapping" techniques have arisen for creating decision aids that utilize expert knowledge but do the combination rule in a mechanical way (Camerer, 1980; Dawes, 1971; Sawyer, 1966). Johnson (in press) has called attention to the knowledge experts have of rare events, what are called "broken leg cues." Broken leg cues are valid but appear very infrequently, and therefore are difficult to elicit from experts or to detect in a regression study with samples of decisions. However, they are an advantage experts have over models of more typical cases.

Carroll (1982) has suggested that research showing that people consider only one or a few pieces of information at a time and research showing that criminal behavior seems responsive to complex and multiple factors can be reconciled by allowing the decision process to be extended over time in such a way that features are sequentially incorporated into decisions and behavior. Thus, the criminal uses considerable judgment and knowledge in evaluating a particular opportunity, but at any one moment is only making limited use of simple information.

For example, one of Letkemann's (1973) interviewees remarked: "When I was down to a certain level I would go out" (p. 22). Lack of money was one factor initiating a search for a good opportunity. Another interviewee provided a sequential ordering of decision factors:

> Usually, the assessment of economic value precedes the assessment of risk. A safecracker may, while on legitimate business, spot a particularly "easy" safe. He may then assess the probable economic value of the safe's contents. Whether the value is high or low, if the risks are low, he may "make" the safe. On the other hand, if both are high, he may also attempt the job. (p. 151)

This simple contingent process model (Payne, 1973) can be interpreted as:
(1) assess money in pocket (if high, no crime; if low, go to step 2);
(2) assess certainty of success (if low, no crime; if high, go to step 3);
(3) assess amount of gain (if low, go to step 4; if high, go to step 5);
(4) assess risk (if high, no crime; if low, go to step 5);
(5) commit crime—a process with substeps involving the planning and execution of the crime.

In comparison with utility theories, the above decision process is not optimal because it lacks thorough consideration of alternatives and information, and formal combination of information into an assessment of each alternative. However, the process is certainly responsive to the environment and possibly highly effective. Johnson and Payne (1985) suggest that simple heuristic rules can approximate the decision quality of the utility rule at a lower "cost" in time and effort.

Clarke and Cornish (1985) and Weaver and Carroll (1985) have suggested that criminal decision making can further be separated into at least two kinds or levels of decisions: a decision to enter (or leave) the role of criminal, which is a decision to be open and aware of certain events and opportunities; and decisions about specific opportunities. This corresponds to strategic versus tactical, or career versus job choices. For example, in a study of expert and novice shoplifters, Weaver and Carroll found that experts make very rapid considerations of specific shoplifting opportunities, and focus on tactical choices for avoiding detection and acquiring an item, but do not consider distal consequences such as jail or social embarrassment. Novices take twice as long considering an item and seem to both reason out tactical choices from scratch and consider more fundamental issues of the moral, legal, and social consequences of shoplifting and getting caught. This suggests that experienced shoplifters not only know more about tactics, but also have made a prior "standing decision" (see Cook, 1981) or "standard operating procedure" (Cyert and March, 1963) that established their willingness to shoplift when suitable opportunities are found. Those opportunities are then assessed on different (partially overlapping) characteristics from the prior decision. An interesting question that we will discuss later is what shifts the decision process from tactical decisions back to reevaluating the standing decision.

PROSPECT THEORY

Prospect theory (Tversky and Kahneman, 1979) is intended to account for certain empirical phenomena in risky decision making typically involving simple gambles. These phenomena appear to violate the utility-maximizing model. Errors and biases have accumulated over the years such as the Allais paradox, certainty effects, a confusing empirical literature on risk prefernces, and preference reversals induced by trivial shifts in wording (Hershey, Kunruether, and Schoemaker, 1982; Hershey and Schoemaker, 1985; Hogarth, 1980). Prospect theory postulates mathematical choice processes that can account for many of these phenomena in a parsimonious way.

Prospect theory retains the structure of utility theory by including a utility-like valuing function, a probability-like weighting function, and the multiplicative computational rule. However, several changes are introduced into the evaluation phase of utility theory in order to account for the results of empirical research on decisions: (1) value is calculated relative to a reference point rather than total wealth position, allowing the separation of "gains" from "losses"; (2) the shape of the value function varies with each individual, but the "modal" value curve is concave in the region of gains and therefore risk averse, but convex for losses and therefore risk seeking, and the loss curve is steeper than the gain curve; and (3) probabilities are replaced by a decision weight curve that is discontinuous in shifting from certainty to risk (producing a "certainty effect") and shallow for low probabilities (resulting in the probability of an event and its complement summing to less than 1.0). Some of the phenomena utility theory associates with risk attitudes are explained in the value function, but others are explained in the decision weights.

The revised evaluation phase in prospect theory is only part of its contribution to the theory of decision making. Before prospects are evaluated, there is an earlier phase called editing or framing which defines the domain of alternatives, the outcomes of each alternative, and sets a reference point. It is in this editing phase that real-world decisions are transformed into prospects (gamble-like abstractions) and later evaluated prior to choice.

The implications of prospect theory for taxpayer compliance are many. The basic message is that changes in the objective costs and benefits of compliance may have erratic impact on taxpayers because of the editing and evaluation processes. For example, a discontinuity in the decision weight function between certainty and small probabilities implies a fuzzy point at which risk shifts from "no chance" to "risky" and then is weighted more heavily than objectively warranted. Once this point is reached, increases in probability have *less* impact than one would expect. However, changes in high probabilities have much larger impact on preferences than proportional changes in low probabilities. Since the exact location of the discontinuity is unspecified, it is difficult to base policy on its existence. If the probability of penalty were doubled, and taxpayers were made aware of this, it might have no impact if they believed the probability was very small anyway (twice nothing is nothing), might have some impact but not twice the effect if the probabilities were in the shallow part of the curve, might have moderate impact if the probabilities were in the steep part of the curve, and might have very large impact if the change shifted people from certainty (of no risk) to uncertainty.

This situation is made more complex by the editing operation. The same objective situation can be framed in many different ways. A person who takes an illegal deduction may face a 1 percent chance of being fined in a given year, but over a thirty-seven-year period the same person faces about a 50 percent chance of at least one fine. Slovic et al. (1978) found that reframing the probability of a serious auto accident from per trip to per lifetime increased favorability toward seatbelts and predictions of own use.

The editing operation also affects how probabilities are combined. The 1 percent chance of a fine may reflect a 2 percent chance of an audit and a 50 percent chance of a fine if audited. The evaluation of this two-stage probability is not equivalent to the evaluation of the product ($p = 1\%$).

Tversky and Kahneman (1981) found that people tend to respond to the second stage probability more strongly than the first stage, suggesting that it may be possible to get more impact for the same policy by advertising a highly probable conditional probability rather than a low-probability event. Or, the auditing sample itself could be reframed as an intensive audit of randomly selected *counties* such that the probability of being audited given that your county is selected is much higher. Similarly, Slovic et al. (1976) found that subjects evaluate the probability of a chain of events by the overall coherence of the chain, and the highly likely conditional events can compensate for the unlikely ones. This leads to the paradoxical result that longer conditional chains may be rated more likely than shorter ones (also Tversky and Kahneman, 1982b).

The proposition that outcomes are evaluated against a reference point, coupled with the changes in the value functions as outcomes change from gains to losses, has considerable power for explaining the impact of contextual information on preferences. For example, doctors confronted with a hypothetical epidemic that would kill 600 people if unchecked prefer a program that will "save" 400 lives to a program that has a one-third chance of saving no lives and a two-thirds chance of saving all 600 lives. However, they prefer a program with a one-third chance that 600 will die and a two-thirds chance that no one will die to a program where 200 will die. The difference in the choices is that in the "saving" lives version, the reference point is set as if the 600 had died and the saving of 400 lives is a gain from that reference point, but in the second version the reference point is set with no one dead yet and 200 deaths represent a loss.

Someone who has paid $7,000 in taxes and owes another $100 at the end of the year could frame his situation as a $100 loss, a $7,100 loss, a $500 gain over last year when he paid $7,600 in taxes, or almost any gain or loss if he takes as a reference point what his neighbor or his coworker or "people like him" are paying. Since people find losses aversive, we might expect that someone would strive harder to reduce a "loss" than to make an equivalent "gain," even though the distinction may depend on a reference point that seems arbitrary to us.

Loftus (1985) proposed that withholding has the effect of shifting the reference point and, therefore, increases in withholding will decrease the motivation to reduce the taxes owed at filing time (by legal or illegal means). This seems reasonable *if* the reference point is indeed zero taxes owed on April 15 *and* if the reference point on salaries and other withheld income sources also shifts to the new reduced levels (which may not be reduced but simply less increased from last year than otherwise). The theoretical principles for how people bundle gains and losses are (Thaler, 1983): (1) a series of small gains is preferred to one large gain, (2) one large loss is preferred to a series of small losses, (3) it is better to offset a small loss against a larger gain, and (4) it is better to keep separate a small gain and a larger loss. Although we know that people will try very hard to reduce losses, we do not know how they frame changes in tax requirements over time. Increased withholding on salaries or dividends or tips *could* be perceived as a series of small losses. In such a case, prospect theory proposes that it is better to bundle small losses together into one large loss to reduce the impact (as we do in using credit cards). However, increased withholding *could* be perceived as a small loss bundled together with a larger gain (salary or salary increases), which would make it preferred to the end-of-year large loss.

Although prospect theory has considered the importance of the editing phase and has studied several potent framing effects, there is as yet no theory of *how* the editing processes work. In a general way, "frames" can be thought of as viewpoints or metaphors that help structure ill-structured problems, thus separating figure from ground, highlighting some aspects of a situation and hiding others (Russo and Schoemaker, 1985). For example, do taxpayers frame their tax behavior as "compliance" or "avoidance" (Scholz, 1985)? If compliance, then the taxpayer may have strategies for identifying legal obligations and fulfilling them. If avoidance, then the taxpayer may have strategies for identifying loopholes and scams. These seem to imply fundamentally different behaviors. As a second example, Reaganomics seems to have framed taxes as an indication of government waste, a loss to the individual taxpayer and to the society (i.e., less spending). It has increased the sense of unfairness and failure to get value from tax money, as indexed by opinion polls about attitudes toward taxes (ICF, 1985). On the other hand, it is possible to frame taxes as a contribution and sharing. In this way, the "frame" serves both to make salient certain benefits or costs of taxpaying and to establish a reference point of what government services are worth, what "should" be paid, or what is "fair."

Prospect theory, as well as the utility theories previously discussed, requires people to judge the probabilities and outcomes attendant on various alternatives. Utility theory considers probabilities and dollar equivalents to be constituents, or primitives, of the decision process. Even studies attempting to disprove utility theory typically supply probabilities

and dollar outcomes. They thus turn uncertain decisions into risky decisions (Einhorn and Hogarth, 1985; Lopes, 1983) and shortcut the process
of assessing probabilities and outcomes. This simplification has been very
useful for disproving the economic utility model since, presumably, human
performance would deteriorate even further in more ambiguous and complex contexts. However, if our goal is to understand and model actual
decisions rather than to disprove the utility model, we must recognize that
such changes and simplifications in problems can have serious impacts on
results (Hershey et al., 1982; Payne, 1982). Changes in the way information is presented (e.g., graphs versus numbers), the order of presentation,
the context or wording of questions, all have been shown to affect decisions. In the next section we discuss the way people assess probability and
outcomes using judgmental heuristics.

JUDGMENTAL HEURISTICS

Judgments of probability have in some ways had a parallel history to the
study of decision making. In the beginning were formal mathematical
models, in this case Bayes's theorem for updating probabilities (Edwards,
1954) and the entire probability calculus. Evidence began accumulating
that people did not follow Bayes's theorem (Slovic and Lichtenstein,
1971). A major breakthrough occurred in a series of papers by Kahneman
and Tversky in the early 1970s, summarized in Tversky and Kahneman
(1974). They suggested that people have a fundamentally different understanding of probability than that reflected in the accepted mathematical
models.

Research shows the dominance of the particular, the personal, and the
comparative over the general, the impersonal, and the absolute. For example, in judging the likelihood of being penalized for cheating on taxes, most
people would not consider statistical information about the number of
people penalized in a given year to be as compelling as specific instances
(Kahneman and Tversky, 1972; Nisbett and Ross, 1980), especially events
that happened to the self or a known other (Tyler, 1980). Likelihood would
be evaluated by recalling or imagining (and sometimes seeking out) instances of the event. The ease with which such instances can be brought to
mind, known as availability (Tversky and Kahneman, 1973), determines
the subjective sense of likelihood or confidence in future occurrence. Although the availability heuristic is often useful for estimating likelihood,
and usually gives good results, it tends to favor events that are easily
imaginable or recallable. For example, a recent well-publicized plane crash

creates widespread concern for airline safety, which gradually abates as the salience of the event decreases over time. Similarly, a well-publicized conviction for tax fraud should make the perceived likelihood of punishment temporarily increase, and the same event can be made more salient with pictures and emphasis on connections to taxpayers living in the same city or having other similarities to the convicted person; the IRS seems to save some juicy fraud convictions for late March to take advantage of the availability heuristic just before taxes are due.

However, not all information that is available is considered relevant or even used in an expected way. The representativeness heuristic (Kahneman and Tversky, 1972) describes a process by which information is matched for similarity with proposed hypotheses or understandings of the causes of events. Thus, a coworker who relates that she never reports tips and has never been audited could outweigh, for her colleagues, a news story about IRS prosecutions of major tax cheats or a news story about stepped-up auditing activities. The reason is that the coworker is highly similar to the taxpayers in question and the one case is considered very compelling in comparison with stories about people whose lives and noncompliance activities are different, or with abstract information about probability in general. In fact, stories of the prosecution of major tax cheats may have paradoxical effects similar to the "gambler's fallacy"—the small tax cheat feels safer knowing the IRS is busy with other types of problems. Many items of information could be viewed as indications of danger from some perspectives and safety from others. Kunreuther (1976) found that many people in flood-prone areas *dropped* their flood insurance after a flood, apparently from the belief that since a "once-in-ten-years" flood had just happened, they were now "safe." If the person believes that auditing resources are fixed (like the supply of floods), then every revealed case *decreases* personal risk. If the person is assessing auditing probabilities, then every revealed case *increases* personal risk!

Thus, people seek an underlying structure to information, but the structure they want has commonsense meaning and causality rather than the acausal categorization of events in formal probability theory. This distinction is most clearly seen in the difference between causal and diagnostic information (Tversky and Kahneman, 1980, 1982a). Although the two types of data are equally informative in a statistical sense, people reason with causal information far more readily than with diagnostic information. For example, they understand that a tall father is very likely to have a tall son but are less willing to predict that a tall son is likely to have a tall father.

Statistical information that fits a causal hypothesis is readily used: a particular automobile accident is more likely to involve a Green cab than a Blue cab because Green cabs have a higher accident rate (interpretable as Green cabs having worse drivers). But statistical information that is equally informative yet lacks a causal interpretation is not used: the same accident is not judged more likely to involve a Green cab simply because Green cabs are more numerous.

The fact that information is interpreted in terms of prior understandings is well exemplified by the tendency to confirm or support hypotheses. People tend selectively to attend to, recall, and interpret information in such a way as to support their own views. For example, Lord, Ross, and Lepper (1979) found that people given one research study that supported their views on capital punishment and one that supported the opposite position became even more convinced of their own position and interpreted the contrary study as being methodologically weak. By giving credence to supporting evidence and disparaging opposing evidence, it is always possible to become more convinced of one's own correctness. Thus, people not only rationalize the morality of their own conduct (Sykes and Matza, 1967), but also the evidence about likely consequences and even about past consequences (dissonance reduction [Festinger, 1957]). A classic example in the domain of public risk is that the Three Mile Island nuclear reactor accident convinced anti-nuclear people that reactors were a terrible danger because so many unanticipated events could trigger a near-disaster; yet the same event convinced pro-nuclear people that reactors were safe because the safety systems really did work under a severe test (Slovic et al., 1980). This is not to imply that people cannot learn or revise their opinions, but only to say that people do not give up their supposed knowledge easily.

One of the most powerful and pervasive psychological tendencies is to reason comparatively rather than absolutely. Prospect theory draws upon this tendency, and so does the anchoring and adjustment heuristic. This heuristic suggests that we estimate unknown quantities, whether likelihood or outcome, by adopting an anchor and using our knowledge about the current situation to adjust the anchor. Unfortunately, we find that the revision process is usually incomplete and the adjustment is not sufficient—estimates remain too close to the anchor. The fact that confidence limits are usually too narrow is explicable as the provision of an estimate range by adjustment from the best guess (Lichtenstein, Fischhoff, and Phillips, 1982). The phenomenon that choices among gambles may be inconsistent with bids can be interpreted as anchoring and adjustment. Specifically, choice is based on overall evaluation and comparison of the gambles, but bids apparently create an anchor on the possible monetary winnings, which are then adjusted or discounted (insufficiently) for likelihood and risk (Lichtenstein and Slovic, 1971, 1973).

Einhorn and Hogarth (1985) proposed that the assessment of frequency evidence to estimate a probability is based on a combination of anchoring and adjustment and imagination or availability. They suggest that estimates of probability are anchored on the proportion of evidence and arguments supporting a hypothesis, and then adjusted for the amount of evidence, alternative hypotheses, and evidence that can be imagined. On the basis of a few simple assumptions, their evidence model predicts a relationship between strength of evidence and probability that, under certain conditions, is very similar to prospect theory's decision weight function. Their theory implies that attitudes toward uncertainty (or ambiguity in their terminology), in addition to risk attitudes, affect preferences. For example, hypothetical businessmen were more likely to insure against a low-probability loss when there was uncertainty about the probability of loss, but less likely to insure against a high-probability loss when there was uncertainty (Study 4). Thus, preferences among alternatives depended on risk and uncertainty in complex ways. In the context of tax compliance, an illegal deduction with a low probability of detection would be increasingly avoided if there were less certainty about the likelihood of detection; this model would perhaps counteract the risk-seeking tendencies in prospect theory. However, a deduction with a higher probability of detection might be more sought after under uncertainty; this instance would augment risk seeking. Without research directed at the specific parameters of the Einhorn and Hogarth model, such predictions can only be stated as if–then hypotheses.

Anchoring and adjustment principles can also be seen in decision making on the larger scale. Lindblom's (1959) statement of "incrementalism" and March and Simon's (1958) "problemistic search" both refer to the tendency to base decisions on past decisions with small revisions. Budget decisions are typically based on past budgets; Jimmy Carter's attempt to introduce "zero-based" budgeting points out the enormous effort involved in starting from scratch. Presumably, taxpayers follow routines and use as a model their previous year's tax forms or a friend's tax forms in order to avoid starting from scratch. The problem, of course, is that change is slow and responses to changes in the tax laws or one's personal situation may be absent or insufficient (see Scholz, 1985).

COMMENTS ON UTILITY MODELS

Utility models have taken us a long way toward understanding decision processes because they are simple, broadly applicable, mathematically tractable, and sensible for theory and application. They also fit human behavior and market behavior in useful ways. However, several decades of research demonstrate that utility models are wrong in almost every detail. Even Nobel Prize economists are willing to speak out against the model (Arrow, 1982). Research and theory has benefited by having a benchmark or comparison (or straw man), and new models drawing on the structure of utility theory but incorporating psychological principles are revolutionizing the field because they combine the scope and power of utility models with stronger empirical support (e.g., prospect theory). Considerable progress is also being made by assuming that deviations from utility models represent ways to optimize decision quality and decision costs, a metautility (Beach and Mitchell, 1978; Payne, 1982; Johnson and Payne, 1985).

However, there is a compelling alternative approach to the study of decision making that avoids starting from utility models. Essentially, the utility models postulate simple algebraic rules for evaluating or selecting alternatives given certain classes of information. They are basically input-output models that use utility models to predict whatever emerges from the "black box" of the human mind, and thus define away the necessity of studying mediating mental processes. The alternative is to put aside the axioms and optimizing rules and ask the more inductive psychological question, "How do people make decisions?" Considerable progress has been made addressing this question from a cognitive approach, and it is to this theory and research that we now turn.

The Cognitive Approach to Decision Making

The cognitive approach considers the human mind as an information-processing system. Interest centers on those mechanisms and processes by which the mind takes in information, transforms it, and constructs a response. In contrast to behaviorists who traditionally sought to interrelate responses directly to stimuli and preferred to summarize the entire mental apparatus in terms of "prior learning history," the cognitivists hypothesize a detailed set of mental mechanisms that, in principle, could reference detectable physiological events and structures.

The human mind is typically conceived as a set of sensory transducers that produce an initial input, an attention mechanism that serves as a gateway to further processing, a series of memories that store sensory input and transformed inputs for greater and lesser periods of time, and a central processing unit or working memory that operates on information. Many cognitive psychologists use the metaphor of the computer as a way to understand the mind and computer programs as a way to express theories of mental processes.

LIMITED RATIONALITY

The fundamental principle underlying this analysis of the mind is the concept of limited rationality, or physical limits on the various processes that comprise thinking (e.g., Newell and Simon, 1972). Thus, attention, memory, computational capacity, and so forth are all limited. In order to function in a complex world, people must create simplified views of that world and simple strategies for responding to our approximations or educated guesses. The resulting simplifications are usually quite adequate, but in particular circumstances they can be shown to be a very poor representation of reality.

Information-processing researchers sometimes adopt the same strategy as those following the "psychophysical paradigm" (Phillips, 1983) by assuming a correct answer and examining deviations from correctness. However, the goal is not a cataloguing of errors and biases but an identification of situations in which useful descriptive information can be found. Discrepancies suggest the presence of intuitive strategies and other limited processes. Descriptive models can then be developed that mimic the way people behave. In this way, researchers can identify fundamental and generalizable processes at an intensive level of detail. Suggestions can even be made for improving performance in real-world situations. However, the transition from demonstrations of errors and biases to real-world implications is tenuous because additional mechanisms may exist in natural settings (e.g., learning, [Hogarth, 1981]; organizations [Cyert and March, 1963]).

PROCESS-LEVEL DESCRIPTIONS

The hallmark of the cognitive approach is the attempt to describe in detail the characteristics of mental apparatus (e.g., the size of short-term memory) and the step-by-step processes by which tasks are performed. At the extreme, highly stylized laboratory tasks allow the study of elementary information processes (Posner and McLeod, 1982). For example, the task of scanning a list to find a particular character would enable the testing of models of attention, memory, and similarity judgments. More complex but well-structured tasks such as mental arithmetic and chess have successfully been analyzed into component acts (Simon, 1978). Detailed comparisons of human behavior with computer programs have allowed the development of basic knowledge about attention, memory, and problem-solving strategies.

The same goals and style are evident in the cognitive approach to more complex but ill-structured tasks (Simon, 1973). These are tasks for which there is no obvious way to break up and process the elements of the task. Instead, people essentially recreate their own version of the task and solve it in their own way. General principles can be adduced and theories can be built in considerable detail, but behavior cannot be reduced to the atomic level of elementary information processes.

In the past decade, the cognitive approach has become a major conceptual and methodological viewpoint in fields that are considerably less structured and bounded than the original domain of research. Cognitive approaches to social psychology, medicine, criminal justice, and so forth seem to offer rigor and precision for these fuzzier domains. The themes characterizing this approach include the selection or construction of bounded tasks with apparent cognitive content, careful research designs or controls on the tasks, observations intended to suggest process-level detail, and step-by-step mechanistic models.

The methods of the cognitive approach generally involve individuals engaged in a definable task, an extension of the laboratory origins of the field. The desired level of theoretical detail requires observations capable of revealing such detail. There are two basic strategies to make observations extremely informative: (1) to structure the task so carefully that performance implies specific mechanisms, and (2) to look for products and indicators of the separate processes under observation.

The cognitive approach has mostly been limited to brief repetitious tasks requiring an answer, and to subjects who are presumed to want to get the right answer. It has mostly ignored how people acquire the knowledge, skills, and motives they bring to the tasks, long-term effects of behavior, or social conventions and relationships. It has only begun to think about how the tasks chosen for study relate to the more complex and interwoven tasks in the "real world." In short, the approach presumes basic inherent processes of the human mind with interchangeable domain-specific content from a particular task. Accordingly, it should be evident that I am presenting the cognitive approach not as "the answer" to the study of decision making, but as a valuable and insightful line of theory and research that also has its limitations.

DECISION HEURISTICS

Schwab, Olian-Gottlieb, and Heneman (1979:146) conclude their review of studies of expectancy-value models with the comment that "there is a nagging suspicion that expectancy theory overintellectualizes the cognitive processes people go through when choosing alternative actions." Highly simplified decision rules, such as satisficing (choosing the first alternative that is good enough), habit, or modeling of others' behavior seem to be more frequent than the systematic intellectual activity assumed in utility theories. In this section, we will review studies emerging from the cognitive approach that seek to identify decision-making behaviors rather than presume or test the utility model.

Behavioral research has proposed or discovered a variety of decision rules or heuristics. The guiding assumption is that people have a repertoire (Kelley, 1973; Payne, 1976) of such procedures, some of them widely shared, some more specific to individuals or to particular tasks. A currently active area of research and theorizing is to study the conditions under which different decision strategies are used (Payne, 1982). Some of this research suggests that strategy choice is itself a utility-maximizing choice balancing effort and other decision costs against the quality of the decision outcomes (i.e., decision strategies differ in their likelihood of selecting the best alternative) (Beach and Mitchell, 1978). Other research seems to suggest that people learn through trial and error or select through a less sophisticated process a strategy that is easy enough and good enough in the particular situation (Payne, 1982; Johnson and Payne, 1985).

Rather than enumerate the variety of decision rules uncovered to date (see, e.g., Svenson, 1979), it seems more reasonable to discuss the dimensions on which these rules vary. First, some rules are organized around alternatives while others are organized around attributes. For example, utility-like models process the information about each alternative and produce a score for that alternative; the highest-scoring alternative is then chosen. In a contrasting example, the elimination-by-aspects rule (Tversky, 1969) sorts all alternatives on the most important attribute or dimension and holds for further consideration only those alternatives scoring highest. Ties are broken by considering the next most important attribute until only the best alternative (or alternatives if more than one are to be chosen) is left. A particular alternative never gets a summary "score" that can be generalized beyond the choice set. The addition of a new alternative affects the ordering in ways that depend on the particular alternatives in the choice set.

Second, some decision strategies are compensatory, in that unfavorable information can be counteracted by other highly favorable information, but other strategies are noncompensatory. Utility models and additive policy-capturing models allow attributes to compensate or average. A low probability of being penalized for cheating on taxes could be compensated by a huge penalty for the few people that are caught (see Blumstein, 1983). In contrast, a satisficing or conjunctive rule requires that certain key attributes be above criteria or thresholds. Any attribute that falls below criterion cannot be compensated by other attributes that are highly favorable. For example, those taxpayers with a strong code of honesty might not "trade off" honesty against monetary gain: it is enough to know that tax cheating is dishonest.

Third, strategies differ in the extent to which they are task specific or generalizable. Payne (1973) describes the task of choosing among risky gambles as a contingent process model in which the gambles are first classified as "good" or "bad" gambles based on the probability of winning compared to the probability of losing, and then the amount to win and lose are processed comparatively in different ways depending on the initial classification. It seems likely that people have an endless capacity to create task structures and task-specific decision procedures (Humphreys and Berkeley, 1983; Phillips, 1983)—to instantiate decision strategies in new ways, to combine familiar routines, and to create new procedures. It is therefore not surprising that individual differences in decision strategies are substantial and that strategies change in response to "seemingly minor changes in tasks" (Einhorn and Hogarth, 1981:61).

Research investigating these decision procedures has uncovered characteristics of tasks that shift decision makers from strategy to strategy. When faced with more alternatives, decision makers tend to use noncompensatory strategies that quickly reduce the magnitude of the task (Payne, 1976; Payne and Braunstein, 1978). Phased decision rules seem common; in these, multiple alternatives are screened by a noncompensatory rule until only two or three are left, which are then compared by a more effortful but more powerful compensatory strategy. Other features of the decision task such as number of attributes, time pressure, response mode, and information display format are reviewed in Payne (1982).

However, substantial individual differences in strategy use have been found. Weaver and Carroll (1985) studied the decision making of expert and novice shoplifters as they walked through retail stores. Novices seem to be deterred by any undesirable attribute, a conjunctive rule, whereas experts balanced deterrents with facilitators or discounted the deterrents in the face of additional information, a compensatory rule. Experts seem to develop appropriate task-specific rules (Johnson, 1988; many others) but may have difficulty stepping up a level to consider the usefulness of their rules, as in studies of creativity that show a failure to innovate by those with a great deal of experience in a domain (Hogarth, 1980).

It is important to realize that the cognitive approach has revealed these decision strategies not simply by measuring output judgments as a function of input task attributes and situations, but also by developing new methods for observing the hypothesized mental processes comprising these strategies (Carroll, 1980; Payne, Braunstein, and Carroll, 1978; Svenson, 1979). Process-tracing techniques such as the monitoring of information search, collection of verbal protocols, and measurement of response time offer new insight into mental mechanisms. For example, the difference between strategies organized by alternative and strategies organized by attribute can be physically revealed in information search studies where decision makers scan information in dramatically different ways depending on which strategy they are using. Verbal protocols, statements made during the task, and output judgments as a function of input conditions reinforce the information search data to make a strong case for the *process* by which people decide.

HIERARCHICAL DECISION MAKING

The fact that there are multiple ways to come to a decision suggests a hierarchical process: a strategy must be "chosen"; it then "chooses" the alternative to be enacted. This could create an infinite regress: how do we choose a strategy to choose a strategy to . . . ? Humphreys and Berkeley (1983) and Jaques (1976, 1978) suggest several levels of decision problem representations, each setting the conditions under which the next level operates. Expertise, abstract analytical ability, cognitive complexity, cognitive style (e.g., Kilmann and Mitroff, 1976) and other traits and experiences could be considered to reference both the extensiveness of options at any level and the number of levels that can be deliberately traversed (i.e., a "high level" person can deliberately question a fundamental assumption that alters the strategies for selecting decision procedures).

Such a hierarchical structure, in which prior decisions or acceptance of procedures or premises serves to structure further decision making, has the advantage of efficiency in that the full range of issues need not be confronted at once, but this very partitioning of decisions reduces the resultant decision quality, because higher-level structures tend not to change (March and Simon, 1958; Cyert and March, 1963; Lindblom, 1959). The concept of a "frame" in prospect theory (Tversky and Kahneman, 1981) similarly expresses the simplification of a problem by the selection (consciously or unconsciously) of a particular set of definitions and viewpoints. Our discussion of criminal behavior suggests that the decision to be a criminal precedes or sets the boundaries around decisions to commit specific crimes. In discussing decision strategies, we can talk about choosing not to decide (Corbin, 1980), deciding to experiment in order to learn how to decide (Einhorn, 1980; Hogarth, 1981), and so forth, which reflect this movement across levels. In organizations, standard operating procedures (March and Simon, 1958; Cyert and March, 1963) have the effect of efficiently handling common situations with the attendant cost of not recognizing or responding well to new situations.

Applying these ideas to income tax compliance requires that we consider compliance to involve a series of decisions and a set of strategies that may differ among taxpayers and across situations. The simple act of basing your tax return on your neighbor's could reflect either low-level or high-level processing. It would be very low level if the person copies the various elements of the neighbor's tax return, substituting only where amounts differ. It would be somewhat higher level if the taxpayer imitates the neighbor's rules and procedures rather than his products. It could be even higher level if the taxpayer imbeds the imitation routine in another routine, such as "follow his rules on those parts of the form that are similar to mine and follow other rules on different parts of the form, or under different circumstances."

Operating at a high level implies laying out a tax plan, including recording and reporting information, setting withholding, finding tax relief opportunities, remaining aware of changes in the tax laws, and so forth. Once the planning is accomplished, tax behavior consists mostly of following the plan—e.g., putting records safely away, opening an IRA, and so forth. Later behaviors, such as computing deductions, are constrained by all the earlier tax-relevant behavior. Of course, a tax plan, no matter how detailed, does not guarantee the diligence necessary to follow it (Scholz, 1985). Once the habit of not recording business expenses emerges, very different routines have to be engineered to create the tax-reporting figures out of a "shoebox" of receipts (or, worse yet, no shoebox of receipts).

Operating at a low level implies very little planfulness, or following the same plan every year, and a mad scurrying near April 15 to assemble and interpret tax materials. For simple situations this may be sufficient, but for others it may mean carrying scraps of paper to a tax preparer to be magically turned into a return, or estimating various figures to reach a "reasonable" or "fair" result.

Taxpayers undoubtedly differ in how "top-down" or rationalistic, planful, and proactive their tax compliance decisions are. They may switch back and forth between self-aware and deliberate decision making and the habitual, unthoughtful carrying out of procedures set down earlier in the process. For most people, "popping up" a level and considering premises as problematic is unusual. Most taxpayers simply hire a third-party preparer to operate for them at higher levels; I wonder how the client conceptualizes the acts of the preparer.

The above analysis presumes that at the highest level the taxpayer has established a frame or problem statement of "How do I pay my taxes?" or "How do I comply with the tax laws?" However, it is possible to reframe the entire problem as "How can I pay the least taxes"? or "Where can I cheat?" or even as "How can I pay my fair share?" These questions involve motivation or moral reasoning (Kohlberg, 1976), referring to the relationship between citizen and government as one based on fear, personal gain, norms, rationality, or morality (Kinsey, 1985; Vogel, 1974). We could view this as a problem of conformity (Cialdini, 1986) or organizational socialization (Van Maanen and Schein, 1979).

Surveys of taxpayers reveal several attitudinal types that could be interpreted in terms of a basic motive or frame: (1) honest taxpayers, (2) utility maximizers, (3) beaten taxpayers, (4) equity seekers, and (5) need mobilized (freely translated from terms used by Yankelovich et al., 1984). It is interesting to consider what might generate a transition from one type to another (see Scholz, 1985). For example, how many examples of unfairness and frustrating interactions with tax forms are necessary to turn honest taxpayers into equity seekers? How much need will mobilize a beaten taxpayer? How much rational debate on taxpaying does it take to turn everyone into utility maximizers?

Even when the taxpayer defines the appropriate behavior as cheating rather than compliance, this cheating can also be done in a planful, high-level way, or a reactive, low-level way. An auto mechanic could have made a "standing decision" to look for ways to avoid paying taxes owed. Reasons for making such a decision could include personal need, a sense of frustration with his economic progress, a sense of inequity when considering rich people or publicity about rich people who pay very little taxes, pronouncements of the government decrying waste of (his) tax money, contact with friends or other mechanics who regularly cheat, a desire to get whatever he can, a need to feel superior, and so forth. Given such a decision to avoid paying taxes where possible, the more planful, top-down strategies call for assessing overall amounts or percentages to hide, types of transactions to avoid recording, and other goals and rules. A less planful mode is simply to look out for good opportunities, such as customers who pay in cash and have frequent transactions so they are known to be "safe" and are unlikely to keep track (see Kagan, Chapter 3). This "now-and-then" behavior may be guided by elaborate rules or by something closer to "impulse buying"— the occasion arises, the thought of cheating occurs, and the situation passes a few simple criteria of risk. An even less planful mode is to come to the end of the year with a few shoeboxes full of records and some bills to pay. Several "trial balances" may be attempted and a strategy constructed at that time for balancing safety and need, or for meeting a target tax amount.

The factors that produce a decision to be open to noncompliance may therefore differ from the factors that effect a particular decision to cheat or a particular tactical choice. Even if we consider tax behavior to occur only during tax season, it is possible that the decision to cheat is made once and that later actions are predicated on a currently unquestioned prior premise that the person is "open" to such opportunities.

I envision the context of taxpaying to be similar to the "garbage can" model (Cohen, March, and Olsen, 1972) in that there are taxpayers looking for relief, IRS publications providing information, third-party preparers offering advice, tax shelters and other "solutions" looking for "problems" they can solve, media reporting a broad variety of tax-relevant information, tax consultants trying to design new strategies, and many different kinds of taxpayers circulating in the "garbage can"—all affecting one another in various ways. Although the "garbage can" may seem like just a visual metaphor, it has been found useful in analyzing organizational decisions (March and Olsen, 1976) and presents a description of preferences as emerging from a discovery process that includes acting and experiencing outcomes (March, 1978; Weick, 1977). My personal garbage can of mail in the past few months includes a solicitation to buy a book called *How to Beat the IRS* (secrets of a former IRS agent), the opportunity to subscribe to the

Tax Avoidance Digest and get free gifts such as "Tax Secrets Worth a Fortune" and "27 Major Loopholes in the Tax Laws," and a request for a contribution to the National Taxpayers Union promising to fight for changes in the federal pension plan supported by our taxes!

The concept of hierarchical strategies suggests that change occurs at lower levels more readily than at higher levels, and that change typically involves modifications or additions to existing behavior rather than major shifts. Change occurs because of the continual press of events and opportunities in the "garbage can," but the taxpayer has to be prepared to change and capable of exercising the new behaviors. The stimuli to change are manifold: changes in the tax laws that force changes in tax strategies, acute financial need that makes the year-end "bottom line" unacceptable, the financial gymnastics of a tax preparer, accidents and errors that bring no negative consequences, friends' revelations of their own tax strategies and outcomes, repeated media disclosure of legal and illegal tax avoidance tactics, growing feelings of inequity, frustration with tax forms, or simply the propensity to explore when some slack is available.

It seems clear that we have created a societal climate that prevents stability for many taxpayers. Frequent changes in the tax laws, the economic incentives to innovators who create legal tax avoidance strategies, the publicity given to corporations and the wealthy who strive to reduce their taxes, the public debate over the fairness and effectiveness of taxes, negative feelings toward government encouraged by the Reagan administration, the societal emphasis on personal well-being and deemphasis of communal motives, and so forth—all push in the direction of thinking about taxpaying more, making the taxpaying process more costly and frustrating, and defining one's behavior as "tax avoidance."

COMPETENCE OF TAXPAYERS

Any analysis of taxpayer compliance and noncompliance would have to consider decisions as the confluence of three factors: opportunity, skills, and motivation. Opportunity and skill combine in two ways. First, deliberate tax cheating occurs when skill is sufficiently *high* to take advantage of opportunities to cheat. The taxpayer has to become aware of an opportunity and then select or develop a strategy to use the opportunity. Naturally, such actions require a certain motivation to carry out these behaviors in the face of costs such as time, effort, and anxiety over risks. Second, accidental tax cheating occurs when skill is sufficiently *low* that errors are made.

The IRS analysis of audit research presumes that noncompliance has two components: tax cheating that produces undercompliance, and errors that result in random under- and overcompliance. Thus, results showing 38 percent of taxpayers with underpayment errors and 8 percent with overpayment errors is interpreted as 30 percent net undercompliance (i.e., 30 percent cheat, and 16 percent make errors that cancel out) (IRS, 1983; Kinsey, 1984). However, errors are likely to be omissions, and omissions of income that produce undercompliance are likely to far outweigh omissions of deductions that produce overcompliance. Intensive IRS audits find that 17 percent of taxpayers fail to list income sources of $50 or less (Kinsey, 1984).

Opportunity, skills, and motivation are all influenced by the complexity of the behaviors required to comply with the tax codes. For example, the Form 1040 instructions are written at an average tenth-grade readability, beyond the capabilities of at least 25 percent of adults (U.S. Comptroller General, 1978). I recently attempted to complete a Series 5500 form for Keogh accounts that was new for 1984. I was unable to figure it out without help from an accountant and further discovered an error in the form that would have produced a nonsensical final result had I followed the instructions word for word.

Such complexity has a direct effect on accidental tax cheating, by making the forms too difficult to fill out accurately. It also makes tax compliance a *social* situation, by forcing large numbers of taxpayers to seek some sort of assistance from the IRS, family and friends, or tax preparers. Further, it creates more opportunities for tax cheating because there are so many different "niches" and so many gray areas where the laws are vague or the only accessible traces of transactions are by personal report. More of these "niches" are available to more skilled taxpayers or those who have access to such skills through knowledgeable friends or paid tax advisors.

Further, and possibly most important, the complexity of tax forms has major motivational impact. First, it creates frustration and thereby generates efforts to get around the requirements or get back at the IRS. Second, it creates feelings of inequity as those experiencing more difficulty realize that others can pay for arcane expertise and profit from the complexity. Third, it offers a challenge to some taxpayers who would like to beat the system. Finally, the complexity changes the perceived risks associated with noncompliance. Taxpayers may believe the system is so cumbersome that they are less likely to be caught, or recognize that it is so complex that everyone will make errors. Long (1981) emphasizes that "it is difficult to speak of a 'correct' return" and that an instructor at an IRS school for training revenue agents told her that "agents could find 'errors' in 99.9 percent of all tax returns, if they wanted to" (p. 205). But this complexity blurs the line between legitimate (albeit aggressive) tax avoidance and tax evasion, making the IRS hesitate to label anyone a deliberate tax cheat and to apply heavy penalties. Presumably, many tax evaders realize that they can claim to have made an error or to have been confused, and merely have to pay the taxes they would have paid in any case.

Steps to simplify tax forms and tax requirements would thus have many benefits. More people could do their own returns and feel better about the process. The sense of equity would be enhanced. The opportunities for cheating would be reduced, particularly those available to the more wealthy. The risks associated with noncompliance might be seen more clearly and administered more closely. The costs of administering the tax code would greatly decrease. However, there are constitutencies that bene-fit from complexity (the IRS [Long, 1981]; paid tax preparers) and reasons to believe that complexity increases uncertainty and therefore reduces non-compliance (Popkin, 1985)—at least sometimes (Einhorn and Hogarth, 1985).

The simplification and clarification of tax forms requires an understand-ing of how people think about and process their taxes. It is more than just a question of reading level. Instructions should follow the natural categories and the temporal and hierarchical organization of taxpayers' behavior. There may need to be several forms for different levels of sophistication.

Research Directions

The history of deterrence efforts is not highly encouraging. Many appar-ently successful deterrence strategies had only temorary effects. People adapt; they revise probabilities with experience, reframe for themselves, adopt new avoidance strategies, and so forth. This is the history of attempts to deter shoplifting (Bickman et al., 1979), drunk driving (Ross, 1982), and family violence (Tauchen and Witte, 1985). Before large-scale changes or influence attempts are recommended, we need a better model of taxpayer behavior that can predict long-term as well as short-term effects and that is general enough to be informative across changes in the tax laws.

The current research efforts using intensive audits and public opinion polls are helpful but incomplete. Besides the possibility of bias, these strategies have not provided much detail about taxpaying behavior. I believe issues of "How much?" have dominated over issues of "What?" and "How?" and "Why?" We need a much better understanding of the many varieties of taxpaying behavior. Once we understand how competence, motivation, and opportunities play out over time into strategies and changes in behavior, we will be better able to deal with issues of prevalence and the effectiveness of possible interventions. I have organized the discussion of research directions around methods: surveys, tests, process tracing, longitudinal studies, and field quasi-experiments.

SURVEYS

Survey research and focus groups, the sort of research that has already been done (ICF, 1985; Yankelovich et al., 1984), can reveal considerable information about taxpayer behavior and strategies if the right questions are asked. Questions about noncompliance have generally lumped together many kinds of noncompliance. They have not been addressed at overall strategies or at what generates reevaluation of strategies. Careful and intensive survey work should be done on the following questions:

1. What series of events occurs during the year relevant to taxes?
2. What strategies do you use to collect information, keep records, report information, reduce your taxes, and prepare to pay your taxes?
3. When is the last time you changed the way you report, pay, or compute your taxes? What did you change and why?
4. Can you think of other ways to do your taxes? Can you think of ways to avoid paying taxes, including ways that are illegal and sure to get you in trouble? For each of these tax-avoiding strategies, explain how you heard of it or thought it up, how much you think you could save, what the risks are and how likely they are, and why you aren't doing them.
5. What are you doing now to reduce your taxes? Continue as in Question 4.
6. Suppose I could guarantee you that you would not be audited next year no matter what you put on your tax forms. What would you do differently?
7. This year the IRS is going to audit some income tax forms on a random basis. However, in exchange for agreeing to be audited, you can have a $50 tax rebate. Would you be willing to do this? What is the smallest rebate you would accept in exchange for being audited? Suppose your return was to be placed in a pool with a 50 percent

chance of being audited. What is the smallest rebate you would accept in exchange for being placed in that pool?

8. What exactly happens when you are audited? What is the worst thing that could happen, and the best? How would your family, friends, and employers feel if they knew you were audited? How would they feel if they knew you had to pay a penalty for failure to report all your income?

The first use of such surveys should be to identify concepts and issues such as types of strategies and types of taxpayers. It would be entirely appropriate to focus attention on groups that are considered "high risk" such as part-time contractors, owners of cash businesses, and so forth (Witte, 1985). However, given the danger that previous methods may not have revealed all the market niches for noncompliance, it may be desirable at an early stage to do some sampling for heterogeneity. The second use of surveys is to identify the prevalence (and therefore the impact and potential savings) of various tax strategies, noncompliance activites, and taxpayer types. This is a critical policy step, but it should not be pushed ahead of our understanding of taxpaying itself.

COMPETENCY TEST

A second mode of data collection would be a tax competency test, aimed not at motivation but at ability. Some of the above questions address what people know about tax strategies. The tax competency test would begin with some factual questions about the law, what taxes are used for, the penalties for noncompliance, and the likelihood of these penalties. A second part would ask respondents to interpret tax instructions and fill out a sample form on the basis of given input information. The third part would be most important. Given a complex set of information, including income sources and expenses and record availability about a hypothetical person, respondents would be asked to fill out tax forms and to design a tax strategy for that person. Instructions could vary in terms of avoiding an audit, paying the minimum taxes, showing available cash at tax time to be very small or very large, and so forth. The complex cases should be designed around known problem areas, such as people with a lot of cash income.

Such a test could be administered to samples of taxpayers of various types and to tax preparers. Although people are unlikely to admit that they use illegal or questionable tax strategies, the purpose of this test is to distinguish two issues: what people believe they *should* do in the sense of preparing a tax return in the manner desired by the IRS (and their competency to know what to do and carry it out), and what people *know how* to do but are afraid to imply that they actually do. In order to elicit the latter knowledge, the test has to be presented under some conditions as a challenge and a hypothetical instance (e.g., what would an unscrupulous tax preparer do?) with no implications for the respondent's own tax behavior.

PROCESS TRACING

The aim of the process-tracing approach is to focus as closely as possible on cognitive processes involved in tax behavior. Although survey research can also address these questions, it is thought that people have limited ability to report retrospectively on their cognitive processes. Process-tracing methods are designed to supplement self-reports by getting "closer" to the mental events. Process-tracing studies would be a labor-intensive but detailed way to identify taxpaying behaviors. This hopefully would give better information about issues such as the following:

1. What is the temporal patterning of tax-relevant behaviors and decisions among various types of taxpayers?
2. Why do people decide to cheat on their taxes? When does the decision occur?
3. What causes people to "pop up" a level and reconsider their standing decision to be honest or to cheat? How frequent or rare is this?
4. What sort of strategies and plans do people use? What distinguishes more planful people from more impulsive decision makers?
5. What causes people to shift from more planful to more impulsive strategies or the reverse?
6. What are the sources of innovation in taxpaying and tax-avoiding strategies? What circumstances produce innovation, and at what level does it tend to occur? What sort of people tend to be "lead users," and how are these innovations transmitted?

One good possibility is to collect verbal protocols from taxpayers. This would involve asking taxpayers to do their tax work under the watchful eye of a researcher and to "think aloud" while doing their taxes (Payne et al., 1978). If sufficient cooperation could be obtained (money and guarantees of anonymity), the study could involve subjects' own tax returns. Ideally, it would include not only the few hours when they fill out the forms, but also other times during the year when substantial tax planning or tax work occurs. This would require either training to self-administer the protocol procedure (perhaps backed up by tape-recorded instructions), or the continual availability of a researcher to show up on short notice and observe some taxpaying activities, or agreements with the taxpayer to structure such activities within negotiated time periods. Otherwise, the task could be hypothetical but realistic, and completed during one or more scheduled sessions.

The key to this research is the ability to get people to reveal noncompliance as well as compliance. Researchers would have to be adept at achieving rapport, and some ironclad guarantees would have to be worked out (immunity from audit?). Survey researchers have successfully elicited reports of tax cheating and other illegal behaviors (although presumably both are underreported). Weaver and Carroll (1985) used verbal protocols with self-reported experienced shoplifters during shopping trips in retail stores, but their "experts" were really talented amateurs rather than criminals who make a living by theft. However, even a process-tracing study of law-abiding taxpayers would be useful for better structuring our understanding of tax compliance decisions. Instructional sets could be overlaid to promote or inhibit noncompliance (Weaver and Carroll, 1985).

A second useful process-tracing approach would be the monitoring of information search behavior (Payne et al., 1978). What sort of information do people actively seek, what scanning strategies do they adopt, and how much of what they know comes casually from other people or is initiated from the outside (e.g., media, tax preparers, solicitations)? This could be done in a single time period by offering a large number of information pamphlets and observing what is actually read. In a field experiment, various types of information could be sent to people who would later be tested for their understanding and use of that information. Retrospective reports of search activity would be useful but probably incomplete, and diary reports (as suggested below) might be a reasonable way to track search behavior over extended time periods.

LONGITUDINAL STUDIES

Longitudinal studies are also needed, examining tax behavior across a year or several years (coupled with detailed cross-sectional surveys allowing comparison of new, early, middle, and late taxpayers). One relatively inexpensive procedure is a diary study, in which taxpayers are paid to keep a diary of all tax-relevant behaviors. Surveys utilizing a panel design would also be useful. The costs could be kept low by using some combination of mailed and telephone questionnaires after initial personal interviews.

FIELD TESTS OF INTERVENTIONS

Based on the conceptual work and results of surveys and other methods, it would be possible to field-test specific interventions. Manipulations of new tax forms, instructions, information on penalties and probabilities, information about fairness, and so forth could be tested in much the same way that marketers "test-market" their advertisements and new products. Even deterrence could be test-marketed by identifying a subgroup and convincing them that their returns had particular probabilities of being audited, and that they faced particular penalties. Quasi-experimental studies are also possible in the form of time-series data on various tax behaviors as changes occurred in the tax laws, audit practices, enforcement standards, and so forth. I was particularly struck by hints of a "bicentennial effect"—a drop in noncompliance in 1976—possibly caused by a (temporary) resurgence of collective consciousness (Kinsey, 1984). It may be that one-time quasi-experiments would be useful, especially if coupled with more carefully designed dependent measures such as the intensive surveys and process-tracing studies already mentioned.

CONCLUSION

The major thrust of the suggested research is to further our basic understanding of taxpayer behavior and to focus particularly on the way taxpayers think about decisions relevant to tax compliance. Underlying this approach is the assumption that attempts to deter noncompliance without understanding the sources and processes of noncompliance are unlikely to provide a satisfactory answer to the problem. Policy makers themselves tend to choose strategies that are readily at hand, such as increasing IRS audits and increasing penalties. However, we can choose from a much broader array of interventions, such as public information and education, new tax forms, tax simplification, various forms of contact with the IRS, and so on.

We must also recognize that the situation is dynamic: tax laws change, avoidance strategies arise from innovators, people adapt to fear-provoking communication, economic conditions change, monitoring technologies change, the economy changes from cash to electronic exchanges, people feel better or worse about government, and so forth. We need research that will enable us to understand taxpayers well enough to anticipate or incorporate some of these changes, and that probably means a research *process* that itself is adaptive.

The benefits to society include increased revenue, decreased costs of tax administration, and a shift in the numbers of people who "frame" their relationship to government in antagonistic versus communal terms. It is not desirable for a tax system to make criminals out of so many people that it must continually monitor, frighten, and punish them. It would be better if people saw value in paying their taxes, and if taxpaying behavior were simple and clear.

References

Aitken, S. S., and Bonneville, L.
  1980 A General Taxpayer Opinion Survey. Prepared for Office of Planning and Research, Internal Revenue Service, March 1980, by CSR, Incorporated, Washington, D.C. (Contract No. TIR-79-2)
Ajzen, I., and Fishbein, M.
  1980 *Understanding Attitudes and Predicting Social Behavior.* Englewood Cliffs, N.J.: Prentice-Hall.
Anderson, N. H.
  1981 *Foundations of Information Integration Theory.* New York: Academic Press.
Arrow, K.
  1982 Risk perception in psychology and economics. *Economic Inquiry* 20:1–9.
Assembly Committee on Criminal Procedure (California)
  1975 Public knowledge of criminal penalties. In R. L. Henshel and R. A. Silverman, eds., *Perception in Criminology.* New York: Columbia University Press.
Beach, L. R., and Mitchell, T. R.
  1978 A contingency model for the selection of decision strategies. *Academy of Management Review* 3:439–449.
Becker, G. S.
  1967 Crime and punishment: an economic approach. *Journal of Political Economy* 78(2):526–536.
Bickman, L., Rosenbaum, D., Baumer, T., Kudel, M., Christenholz, C., Knight, S., and Perkowitz, W.
  1979 Phase I Assessment of Shoplifting and Employee Theft Program: Final Report—Programs and Strategies. Report to the National Institute of Law Enforcement and Criminal Justice, Law Enforcement Assistance Administration, Department of Justice.
Blumstein, A.
  1983 Models for structuring taxpayer compliance. Pp. 159–172 in P. Sawicki, ed., *Income Tax Compliance: A Report of the ABA Section on Taxation, Invitational Conference on Income Tax Compliance.* Washington, D.C.: American Bar Association.
Camerer, C.
  1980 General conditions for the success of bootstrapping models. *Organizational Behavior and Human Performance* 27:411–422.

Carroll, J. S.
 1978   A psychological approach to deterrence: the evaluation of crime opportu-
        nities. *Journal of Personality and Social Psychology* 36:1512–1520.
 1980   Analyzing decision behavior: the Magician's audience. Pp. 69–76 in T. S.
        Walsten, ed., *Cognitive Processes in Choice and Decision Behavior*. Hillsdale,
        N.J.: Lawrence Erlbaum Associates
 1982   Committing a crime: The offender's decision. Pp. 49–67 in V. J.
        Konecni and E. B. Ebbesen, eds., *The Criminal Justice System: A Social-
        Psychological Analysis*. San Francisco: W. H. Freeman.
Cialdini, R. B.
 1989   Social motivations to comply: norms, values, and principles. Chapter 7 in
        this volume.
Clarke, R. V., and Cornish, D. B.
 1985   Modelling offenders' decisions: a framework for research and policy. In
        M. Tonry and N. Morris, eds., *Crime and Justice: An Annual Review of
        Research*. Vol. 6. Chicago: University of Chicago Press.
Cohen, M. D., March, J. G., and Olsen, J. P.
 1972   A garbage can model of organizational choice. *Administrative Science
        Quarterly* 17:1–25.
Cook, P. J.
 1981   Research in criminal deterrence: laying the groundwork for the second
        decade. In N. Morris and M. Tonry, eds., *Crime and Justice: An Annual
        Review of Research*. Vol. 2. Chicago: University of Chicago Press.
Corbin, R.
 1980   Decisions that might not get made. Pp. 47–68 in T. S. Walsten, ed.,
        Cognitive Processes in Choice and Decision Behavior. Hillsdale, N.J.:
        Lawrence Erlbaum Associates
Cyert, R. M., and March, J. G.
 1963   *A Behavioral Theory of the Firm*. Englewood Cliffs, N.J.: Prentice-Hall.

Dawes, R. M.
 1971   A case study of graduate admissions: Application of three principles of
        human decision making. *American Psychologist* 26:180–188.
Dawes, R. M., and Corrigan, B.
 1974   Linear models in decision making. *Psychological Bulletin* 81:95–106

Edwards, W.
 1954   The theory of decision making. *Psychological Bulletin* 51:380–417.
Einhorn, H. J.
 1970   The use of nonlinear, noncompensatory models in decision making.
        Psychological Bulletin 73:211–230.
 1980   Learning from experience. Pp. 1–20 in T. S. Walsten, ed., *Cognitive
        Processes in Choice and Decision Behavior*. Hillsdale, N.J.: Lawrence
        Erlbaum Associates
Einhorn, H. J., and Hogarth, R. M.
 1981   Behavioral decision theory: processes of judgment and choice. *Annual
        Review of Psychology* 32:53–88.

1985   Ambiguity and uncertainty in probabilistic inference. *Psychological Review* 92:433–461.

Feather, N. T., ed.

1982   *Expectations and Actions: Expectancy-Value Models in Psychology.* Hillsdale, N.J.: Lawrence Erlbaum Associates

Festinger, L.

1957   *A Theory of Cognitive Dissonance.* Stanford, Calif.: Stanford University Press.

Fischhoff, B., Goitein, B. and Shapira, Z.

1983   Subjective expected utility: a model of decision-making. Pp. 183–207 in R. W. Scholz, ed., *Decision Making Under Uncertainty.* New York: North-Holland.

Fischhoff, B., Slovic, P., and Lichtenstein, S.

1980   Knowing what you want: measuring labile values. In T. Walsten, ed., *Cognitive Processes in Choice and Decision Behavior.* Hillsdale, N.J.: Lawrence Erlbaum Associates.

Goldberg, L. R.

1970   Man vs. model of man: a rationale, plus some evidence, for a method of improving on clinical inferences. *Psychological Bulletin* 73:422–432.

Grether, D. M., and Plott, C.

1979   Economic theory of choice and the preference reversal phenomenon. *American Economic Review* 69:623–638.

Hammond, K. R., Stewart, T. R., Brehmer, B., and Steinmann, D. O.

1975   Social-judgment theory. Pp. 271–312 in M. F. Kaplan and S. Schwartz, eds., *Human Judgment and Decision Process.* New York: Academic Press

Hershey, J. C., Kunreuther, H., and Schoemaker, P. J. H.

1982   Sources of bias in assessment procedures for utility functions. *Management Science* 28:936–954.

Hershey, J. C., and Schoemaker, P. J. H.

1985   Probability vs. certainty equivalence methods in utility measurement: are they equivalent? *Management Science* 31:1213–1231.

Hoffman, P. J.

1960   The paramorphic representation of clinical judgment. *Psychological Bulletin* 57:116–131.

Hogarth, R.

1980   *Judgment and Choice.* New York: John Wiley & Sons.

1981   Beyond discrete biases: functional and dysfunctional aspects of judgmental heuristics. *Psychological Bulletin* 90:197–217.

Humphreys, P., and Berkeley, D.

1983   Problem structuring calculi and levels of knowledge representation in decision making. Pp. 121–158 in R. W. Scholz, ed., *Decision Making Under Uncertainty.* New York: North-Holland.

ICF Inc.

1985   Summary of Public Attitudes Survey Findings. Prepared for the Research Division, Internal Revenue Service, January 1985, by ICF Incorporated, Washington, D.C.

Inciardi, J. A.
  1975   *Careers in Crime.* Chicago: Rand McNally.
Internal Revenue Service.
  1983   *Conference on Tax Administration Research Strategies.* Office of Assistant
         Commissioner (Planning, Finance and Research), Vols. I and II. Wash-
         ington, D.C.: U.S. Department of the Treasury.
  1985   IRS Function Summaries: A Descriptive Summary of IRS Operations.
         Paper from the IRS Conference, Washington, D.C., January 1985. Internal
         Revenue Service, U.S. Department of the Treasury.

Jaques , E.
  1976   *A General Theory of Bureaucracy.* London: Heinemann.
  1978   Level of abstraction in mental activity. In E. Jaques, R. O. Gibson and D.
         J. Isaac, eds., *Levels of Abstraction in Logic and Human Action.* London:
         Heinemann.
Johnson, E. J.
  1988   Judgment under uncertainty: Process and performance. In M. Chi et al.,
         eds., *The Nature of Expertise.* Hillsdale, N.J.: Lawrence Erlbaum Asso-
         ciates
Johnson, F. J., and Payne, J. W.
  1985   Effort and accuracy in choice. *Management Sciences* 31:395–414.
Johnson, P. E., Hassebrock, F., Duran, A. S., and Moller, J. H.
  1982   Multimethod study of clinical judgment. *Organizational Behavior and
         Human Performance* 30:201–230.

Kagan, R. A.
  1989   On the visibility of income tax law violations. Chapter 3 in this volume.
Kahneman, D. A., Slovic, P., and Tversky, A., eds.
  1982   *Judgment Under Uncertainty: Heuristics and Biases.* Cambridge: Cam-
         bridge University Press.
Kahneman, D. A., and Tversky, A.
  1972   Subjective probability: a judgment of representativeness. *Cognitive Psy-
         chology* 3:430–454.
  1979   Prospect theory: an analysis of decision under risk. *Econometrica*
         47(2):263–291.
Keeney, R. L., and Raiffa, H.
  1976   *Decision With Multiple Objectives: Preferences and Value Tradeoffs.* New
         York: John Wiley & Sons.
Kelley, H. H.
  1973   The process of causal attribution. *American Psychologist* 28:107–128.
Kilmann, R., and Mitroff, I.
  1976   Qualitative versus quantitative analysis for management science: different
         forms for different psychological types. *Interfaces* 6:17–25.
Kinsey, K. A.
  1984   Survey Data on Tax Compliance: A Compendium and Review. American
         Bar Foundation Tax Compliance Working Paper 84-1, December 1984.
         American Bar Foundation, Chicago.
  1987   Theories and models of tax evasion. *Criminal Justice Abstracts* 18:403

(1987). Revision of American Bar Foundation Tax Compliance Working Paper 84-2, December 1984. American Bar Foundation, Chicago.

Kohlberg, L.
1976   Moral stages and moralization: the cognitive-developmental approach. In T. Lickons, ed., *Moral Development and Behavior.* New York: Holt, Rinehart, and Winston.

Kunreuther, H.
1976   Limited knowledge and insurance protection. *Public Policy* 24:227–261.

Kunreuther, H., Ginsberg, R., Miller, L., Sagi, P., Slovic, P., Borkan, B. and Katz, N.
1978   *Disaster Insurance Protection: Public Policy Lessons.* New York: John Wiley & Sons.

Letkemann, P.
1973   *Crime as Work.* Englewood Cliffs, N.J.: Prentice-Hall.

Lichtenstein, S., Fischhoff, B., and Phillips, L. D.
1982   Calibration of probabilities: the state of the art in 1980. In D. A. Kahneman, P. Slovic, and A. Tversky, eds., *Judgment Under Uncertainty: Heuristics and Biases.* Cambridge: Cambridge University Press.

Lichtenstein, S., and Slovic, P.
1971   Reversal of preferences between bids and choices in gambling decisions. *Journal of Experimental Psychology* 89:46–55.
1973   Response-induced reversals of preference in gambling: An extended replication in Las Vegas. *Journal of Experimental Psychology* 101:16–20.

Lindblom, C. E.
1959   The science of muddling through. *Public Administration Review* 19: 79–88.

Loftus, E. F.
1985   To file, perchance to cheat. *Psychology Today* (April): 35–39.

Long, S. B.
1981   Social control in the civil law: the case of income tax enforcement. Pp. 185–214 in H. L. Ross, ed., *Law and Deviance.* Beverly Hills, Calif.: Sage Publications.

Lopes, L.
1983   Some thoughts on the psychological concept of risk. *Journal of Experimental Psychology: Human Perception and Performance* 9:137–144.

Lord, C., Ross, L., and Lepper, M. R.
1979   Biased assimilation and attitude polarization: the effects of prior theories on subsequently considered evidence. *Journal of Personality and Social Psychology* 37:2098–2110.

March, J. G.
1978   Bounded rationality, ambiguity, and the engineering of choice. *Bell Journal of Economics* 9:587–608.

March, J. G., and Olsen, J. P., eds.
1976   *Ambiguity and Choice in Organizations.* Bergen, Norway: Universitetsforlaget.

March, J. G., and Simon, H. A.
1958   *Organizations.* New York: John Wiley & Sons.

Montgomery, H.
   1983   Decision rules and the search for a dominance structure: towards a process model of decision making. Pp. 343–369 in P. Humphreys, O. Svenson, and A. Vari, eds., *Analysing and Aiding Decision Processes.* New York: North-Holland.
Newell, A., and Simon, H. A.
   1972   *Human Problem Solving.* Englewood Cliffs, N.J.: Prentice-Hall.
Nisbett, R. E., and Ross, L.
   1980   *Human Inference: Strategies and Shortcomings of Social Judgment.* Englewood Cliffs, N.J.: Prentice-Hall.
Paternoster, R., Saltzman, L. E., Waldo, G. P., and Chiricos, T. G.
   1982   Causal ordering in deterrence research: an examination of the perceptions-behavior relationship. Pp. 55–70 in J. Hagan, ed., *Deterrence Reconsidered: Methodological Innovations.* Beverly Hills, Calif.: Sage Publications.
Payne, J. W.
   1973   Alternative approaches to decision making under risk: moments versus risk dimensions. *Psychological Bulletin* 80:439–453.
   1976   Task complexity and contingent processing in decision making: an information search and protocol analysis. *Organizational Behavior and Human Performance* 26:102–115.
   1982   Contingent decision behavior. *Psychological Bulletin* 92:382–402.
Payne, J. W., and Braunstein, M. L.
   1978   Risky choice: an examination of information acquisition behavior. *Memory and Cognition* 6:554–561.
Payne, J. W., Braunstein, M. L., and Carroll, J. S.
   1978   Exploring pre-decisional behavior: an alternative approach to decision research. *Organizational Behavior and Human Performance* 22:17–34.
Phillips, L. D.
   1983   A theoretical perspective on heuristics and biases in probabilistic thinking. Pp. 525–543 in P. Humphreys, O. Svenson, and A. Vari, eds., *Analysing and Aiding Decision Processes.* New York: North-Holland.
Popkin, W. D.
   1985   Statutes and Principles: The Case of the Internal Revenue Code. Talk delivered at the annual meeting of the Law and Society Association, San Diego.
Porter, L. W., and Lawler, E. E.
   1968   *Managerial Attitudes and Performance.* Homewood, Ill: Irwin-Dorsey.
Posner, M. I., and McLeod, P.
   1982   Information processing models—in search of elementary operations. *Annual Review of Psychology* 33:477–514.
Ross, H. L.
   1982   Interrupted time series studies of deterrence of drinking and driving. In J. Hagan, ed., *Deterrence Reconsidered: Methodological Innovations.* Beverly Hills, Calif. Sage Publications.
Russo, J. E., and Schoemaker, P. J. H.
   1985   Personal communication

Sawyer, J.
   1966   Measurement *and* prediction, clinical *and* statistical. *Psychological Bulletin* 66:178–200.
Schein, E. H.
   1978   *Career Dynamics: Matching Individual and Organizational Needs.* Reading, Mass.: Addison-Wesley.
Schoemaker, P. J. H.
   1982   The expected utility model: its variants, purposes, evidence, and limitations. *Journal of Economic Literature* 20:529–563.
Scholz, J. T.
   1985   Coping with complexity: a bounded rationality perspective on taxpayer compliance. *Proceedings of the Seventy-Eighth Annual Conference of the National Tax Association-Tax Institute of America.* Columbus, Oh.: National Tax Association.
Schwab, D. P., Olian-Gottlieb, J. D., and Heneman, H. G.
   1979   Between-subjects expectancy theory research: a statistical review of studies predicting effort and performance. *Psychological Bulletin* 86: 139–147.
Sears, D. O., and Citrin, J.
   1982   *Tax Revolt: Something for Nothing in California.* Cambridge, Mass.: Harvard University Press.
Simon, H. A.
   1945   *Administrative Behavior.* New York: Free Press.
   1955   A behavioral model of rational choice. *Quarterly Journal of Economics* 59:99–118.
   1957   *Models of Man: Social and Rational.* New York: John Wiley & Sons.
   1973   The structure of ill-structured problems. *Artificial Intelligence* 4:101–202.
   1978   Information-processing theory of human problem solving. In W. K. Estes, ed., *Handbook of Learning and Cognitive Processes,* Vol. 5. Hillsdale, N.J.: Lawrence Erlbaum Associates
Slovic, P., Fischhoff, B., and Lichtenstein, S.
   1976   Cognitive processes and societal risk taking. In J. S. Carroll and J. W. Payne, eds., *Cognition and Social Behavior.* Hillsdale, N. J.: Lawrence Erlbaum Associates.
   1977   Behavioral decision theory. *Annual Review of Psychology* 28:1–39.
   1978   Accident probabilities and seat belt usage: a psychological perspective. *Accident Analysis and Prevention* 10:281–285.
   1980   Facts vs. fears: understanding perceived risk. In R. Schwing and W. A. Albers, Jr., eds., *Societal Risk Assessment: How Safe is Safe Enough?* New York: Plenum.
Slovic, P., and Lichtenstein, S.
   1968   Relative importance of probabilities and payoffs in risk taking. *Journal of Experimental Psychology Monograph* 78 (3, Pt. 2).
   1971   Comparison of Bayesian and regression approaches to the study of information processing in judgment. *Organizational Behavior and Human Performance* 6:649–744.

Starr, C.
  1969   Social benefit vs. technological risk. *Science* 165:1232–1238.
Svenson, O.
  1979   Process descriptions of decision making. *Organizational Behavior and Human Performance* 23:86–112.
Sykes, G., and Matza, D.
  1957   Techniques of neutralization: a theory of delinquency. *American Sociological Review* 22:664–670.
Tauchen, H., and Witte, A. D.
  1985   Economic models of how audit policies affect voluntary tax compliance. In *Proceedings of the Seventy-Eighth Conference of the National Tax Association-Tax Institute of America.* Columbus, Oh.: National Tax Association.
Thaler, R.
  1983   Using Mental Accounting in a Theory of Consumer Behavior. Unpublished manuscript, Cornell University.
Tversky, A.
  1969   Intransitivity of preferences. *Psychological Review* 76: 31–48.
Tversky, A., and Kahneman, D.
  1973   Availability: a heuristic for judging frequency and probability. *Cognitive Psychology* 5:207–232.
  1974   Judgment under uncertainty: heuristics and biases. *Science* 185:1124–1131.
  1980   Causal schemas in judgments under uncertainty. In M. Fishbein, ed., *Progress in Social Psychology.* Hillsdale, N.J.: Lawrence Erlbaum Associates.
  1981   The framing of decisions and the rationality of choice. *Science* 211(30):453–458.
  1982a   Evidential impact of base rates. In D. Kahneman, P. Slovic, and A. Tversky, eds., *Judgment Under Uncertainty: Heuristics and Biases.* Cambridge: Cambridge University Press.
  1982b   Judgments of and by representativeness. In D. Kahneman, P. Slovic, and A. Tversky, eds., *Judgment Under Uncertainty: Heuristics and Biases.* Cambridge: Cambridge University Press.
Tyler, T. R.
  1980   The impact of directly and indirectly experienced events: the origin of crime-related judgments and behavior. *Journal of Personality and Social Psychology* 39:13–28.
U.S. Comptroller General
  1978   Further Simplification of Income Tax Forms and Instructions is Needed and Possible. Report to the Joint Committee on Taxation, U. S. Congress, July 5. Washington, D.C.: U.S. General Accounting Office.
U.S. Congress
  1983   *Background on Federal Income Tax Compliance.* Joint Committee on Taxation, U.S. Congress, June 21, 1983. Washington, D.C.: United States Government Printing Office.
Van Maanen, J., and Schein, E. H.
  1979   Toward a theory of organizational socialization. In B. M. Staw, ed.,

Research in Organizational Behavior, Vol. 1. Greenwich, Conn.: JAI Press.

Vogel, J.

1974   Taxation and public opinion in Sweden: an interpretation of recent survey data. *National Tax Journal* 27(December):499–513.

Vroom, V. H.

1964   *Work and Motivation.* New York: John Wiley & Sons.

Weaver, F. M., and Carroll, J. S.

1985   Crime perceptions in a natural setting by expert and novice shoplifters. *Social Psychology Quarterly.*

Weick, K. E.

1977   Enactment processes in organizations. In B. M. Staw and G. R. Salancik, eds., *New Directions in Organizational Behavior.* Chicago: St. Clair.

Witte, A. D.

1987   The nature and extent of unrecorded activity: a survey concentrating on recent U. S. Research. In Sergio Alessandrini and Bruno Dallago, eds., *The Unofficial Economy: Consequences and Perspectives in Different Economic Systems.* London: Gower Publishing.

Yankelovich, Skelly, and White, Inc.

1984   Taxpayer Attitudes Study: Final Report. Public opinion survey prepared for the Public Affairs Division, Internal Revenue Service, December, 1984, by Yankelovich, Skelly, and White, Inc., New York.

Panel and Committee Members

PANEL ON TAXPAYER COMPLIANCE RESEARCH

ANN DRYDEN WITTE (Chair), Department of Economics, Wellesley College, and National Bureau of Economic Research, Cambridge, Massachusetts

EUGENE S. BARDACH, Graduate School of Public Policy, University of California, Berkeley

WALTER J. BLUM, School of Law, University of Chicago

ALFRED BLUMSTEIN, School of Urban and Public Affairs, Carnegie-Mellon University

SIDNEY DAVIDSON, Graduate School of Business, University of Chicago

HARVEY GALPER, Peat Marwick Main & Co., Washington, D.C.

JERRY R. GREEN, Department of Economics, Harvard University

JAN KMENTA, Department of Economics, University of Michigan

JEROME KURTZ, Paul, Weiss, Rifkind, Wharton and Garrison, Washington, D.C.

RICHARD O. LEMPERT, School of Law, University of Michigan

DAVID F. LINOWES, Institute of Government and Public Affairs, School of Public Policy, University of Illinois

STEWART MACAULAY, School of Law, University of Wisconsin

RICHARD E. NISBETT, Institute for Social Research, University of Michigan

JOHN W. PAYNE, Fuqua School of Business, Duke University

RICHARD D. SCHWARTZ, School of Law, Syracuse University

BARBARA YNGVESSON, School of Social Science, Hampshire College

JEFFREY A. ROTH, *Study Director*
JOHN T. SCHOLZ, *Senior Research Associate*
GAYLENE J. DUMOUCHEL, *Administrative Secretary*

TERESA E. WILLIAMS, *Administrative Secretary*

COMMITTEE ON RESEARCH ON LAW ENFORCEMENT AND THE
ADMINISTRATION OF JUSTICE, 1987–1988

RICHARD LEMPERT (Chair), School of Law, University of Michigan

ALBERT J. REISS, JR. (Vice Chair), Department of Sociology, Yale University

ANTHONY V. BOUZA, Chief of Police, Minneapolis Police Department

JONATHAN D. CASPER, Department of Political Science, Northwestern University, and American Bar Foundation, Chicago, Illinois

JACQUELINE COHEN, School of Urban and Public Affairs, Carnegie-Mellon University

PHILIP COOK, Institute of Public Policy, Duke University

SHARI S. DIAMOND, Department of Psychology, University of Illinois at Chicago, and American Bar Foundation, Chicago, Illinois

DAVID P. FARRINGTON, Institute of Criminology, Cambridge University, England

ROBERT KAGAN, Department of Political Science, University of California, Berkeley

MARK H. MOORE, Kennedy School of Government, Harvard University

JOHN ROLPH, The Rand Corporation, Santa Monica, California

KURT L. SCHMOKE, Mayor, Baltimore, Maryland

JAMES F. SHORT, JR., Social Research Center, Washington State University

PATRICIA MCGOWAN WALD, U.S. Court of Appeals for the District of Columbia Circuit

STANTON WHEELER, Yale Law School, Yale University

BARBARA YNGVESSON, School of Social Science, Hampshire College

ANN DRYDEN WITTE (ex officio), Chair, Panel on Taxpayer Compliance Research; Department of Economics, Wellesley College, and National Bureau of Economic Research, Cambridge, Massachusetts

JEFFREY A. ROTH, *Study Director*
TERESA E. WILLIAMS, *Administrative Secretary*

Index

Net worth analysis, 130, 151 n. 2
Nixon, Richard M., 14
Noncompliance: defined, 2–3; typology,
    49, 56–62
Nonfilers, 178, 179; and complexity, 166,
    168–170
Nonprofit organizations, 58
Normative uncertainty/burden of
    compliance variable, 49
Nuclear reactors, 245

Observability. *See* Visibility of income
Occupational Safety and Health
    Administration, 112–113
Office of Management and Budget
    (OMB), 17, 25
Office of Public Affairs, 222
Opportunities, noncompliance, 136, 139,
    141, 142–143, 144, 146, 147. *See also*
    Natural invisibility; Visibility of
    income
Outreach Program, 212
Overreporting, 3, 173, 175, 187, 188, 257
Overtime pay, 60

Panel on Taxpayer Compliance Research, 1
Partnership income, 83, 116 n. 3, 172
Part-time workers, 100, 102, 115
Passive loss limitations, 16
Payers. *See* Third parties
Payne, John W., 238
Penalties, 145, 190, 219, 251; in criminal
    decision making, 236–237; as com-
    pliance function, 131; and deterrence,
    131–132, 133, 134–135, 143; estimated
    taxes, failure to pay, 57–58; exemplary,
    131, 146, 148; preparer, 185, 191–194;
    probability of, 138, 175, 176, 240, 243;
    and reporting, 145; in research, 263;
    severity of, 144; and utility, 233. *See
    also* Enforcement, tax law
Pennsylvania, steel industry, 61
Pensions payments, 81
Performance bonds, 94
Plastic economy, 234
Policy-capturing theories, 231, 232–233
Poor, 28, 34
Predictability, 157, 168, 177, 178–179; and
    complexity, 174–176. *See also*
    Complexity; Uncertainty

Privacy: enforcement and, 13–14, 29; and
    visibility, 78, 115
Privacy Protection Study Commission, 13
"Problemistic search," 246
Problem Resolution Program, 221
Procedural noncompliance, 49, 57–58
Process theory, 248–250; suggested
    research, 261–262
Proprietorship income, 141
Prospect theory, 9, 239–243, 245, 246, 247
Punishment. *See* Penalties

Reactance theory, 217–218, 219
Reagan, Ronald, 16, 17, 242, 256; and
    enforcement, 18; tax policy of, 14
Real estate industry, 20
Reasoned action theory, 231–232
Reciprocity: as social compliance
    technique, 204, 211–212; tax
    compliance applications, 212–213
Record keeping, 63, 173; as component of
    compliance costs, 161, 162; fraudulent,
    87, 105–108
Reference point, 240, 242
Regional variations in compliance, 57, 60,
    61–62, 68–69
Rent income: and compliance costs, 163,
    172; unreported, 83, 84, 100, 110
Representativeness heuristic, 244
Republican Party, 14
Research: on criminal decision making,
    236–239; data collection, 64–66;
    deterrence, 134–135, 147–151; and
    enforcement, 30–37, 41–42 n. 1; on
    information returns, 84; methodology,
    138–140, 144, 150; on tax compliance
    levels, 140–146; on taxpayer decision
    making, suggested, 258–263; under-
    ground economy, 31–32; using
    compliance typologies, 66–72
Restaurant industry: business lunch
    deductions and, 22; invisible income
    in, 105, 106; lobbies against tip income
    reporting, 19, 20, 22; TEFRA and, 119
    n. 23
Revenue Act (1978), 38
Risk aversion, 175, 187, 188, 195–196, 230,
    239
Risks, controllable, 237
Rokeach, Milton, 208